1918: Catastrophe to Victory
Volume 1

1918: Catastrophe to Victory
Volume 1
The German 'Ludendorff' Spring Offensive

John Buchan

ILLUSTRATED

LEONAUR

1918-Catastrophe to Victory
Volume 1
The German 'Ludendorff' Spring Offensive
by John Buchan

ILLUSTRATED

FIRST EDITION

Leonaur is an imprint of Oakpast Ltd

ISBN: 978-1-78282-704-7 (hardcover)
ISBN: 978-1-78282-705-4 (softcover)

http://www.leonaur.com

Publisher's Notes

Contents

CHAPTER 1

The Second Battle of the Somme

In the year 1809 Napoleon, having laid Austria prostrate, had the Continent of Europe at his mercy. Only Britain, outnumbered in fighting strength by five to one, maintained the contest. The great emperor, freed from other needs, was able to turn his superb armies against that southwestern angle of land which still defied him, and in 1810 Massena's veteran troops swept through Spain and Portugal. Wellington had little to comfort him except the conviction that the Napoleonic Empire was rotten at the heart, "sustained by fraud, bad faith, and immeasurable extortion." He could not foresee that the next five years would be the years of Borodino, Leipsic, and Waterloo. Similar in some degree was the case of the Allies towards the close of March 1918. They had to face the onslaught of a mighty engine of war whose strength could now be directed to a single front.

Inferior in numbers, inferior too in certain more vital elements of military power, they were doomed to see all their hard-won gains obliterated and to struggle desperately for time to recruit their strength. In 1810 Britain had been fighting for nearly two decades; in March 1918 the Allies had endured forty-three months of a far intenser strife. But as their need was the sharper, so was their relief the quicker. Wellington had to wait four years for salvation; in four months the Allies had repelled the peril and set their feet at long last on the road to victory.

At the end of February 1918, the Eastern front had gone out of existence. Russia, disjointed and anarchical, lay helpless in the grip of harsh treaties, and Germany was able to bring westward sufficient troops to abolish the small Allied numerical superiority. In March the opposing fronts were approximately equal in numbers, but Germany could at will call up a further reinforcement which would give her a margin of a quarter of a million men. On the Allied side there was no chance of such immediate increment. The American forces were slowly growing, but at the normal rate of increase several months must still elapse before they could add materially to the trained numbers in the field. France could make no new effort, and there had been as yet no adequate recruitment from Britain to fill the gaps left by Third Ypres and Cambrai.

The mind of the Allies was resigned to a defensive campaign for the spring, till America took her true place in the line, and it was assumed that the task would not be beyond their power. At the worst they believed that they would have to face a small numerical superiority; but they had faced greater odds at First Ypres and Verdun, and held their ground. Let the enemy attack and break his head against their iron barriers; he would only be the weaker when the time came for their final advance.

Far other was the mood of the German High Command. Sometime in February Ludendorff and Hindenburg met the *Reichstag* in secret session and explained their plan. They promised victory, complete and absolute victory in the field, before the autumn. The submarine campaign had not done all that had been expected of it, and it appeared that American troops could land in Europe. But they must come slowly, and during the next six months the Allies would have to fight their own battle. Now, if ever, was the hour to strike. German diplomacy and the German sword had brought peace in the East, and soon the same sword would lay prostrate the West.

America's armies, when they arrived, would find no Allies to stand by the side of, and that great nation, bowing to accomplished fact, would see the good sense of coming to terms; for clearly by herself she could not fight Germany across some thousand miles of sea. But a price must be paid for such a triumph. The Army chiefs put it at a million German losses; on reconsideration, they increased their estimate to a million and a half.

The *Reichstag* blessed the enterprise. The news of it spread among the German people, and a wave of wild confidence surged across Central Europe. German diplomats in neutral countries raised their drooping heads, and the speeches of German statesmen took on a new truculence. On 16th March, five days before the attack was launched, Helfferich delivered a lecture on "Germany and England." He told his hearers that the war would be decided not in distant parts of the globe, but on the battlefields of France. Where is Hindenburg? he asked:

GENERAL LUDENDORFF

He stands in the West with our whole German manhood for the first time united in a single theatre of war, ready to strike with the strongest army that the world has ever known.

To understand the mighty battle which followed it is necessary to examine in some detail the German plan. Let us consider first its general principles. Ludendorff's aim was to secure a decision in the field within four months. To achieve this, he proposed to isolate the British Army, by rolling it up from its right and pinning it to an entrenched camp between the Somme and the Channel—a Torres Vedras from which it would emerge only on the signature of peace. This done, he could hold it with few troops, swing round on the French, and put them out of action. His first step, therefore, must be to strike with all his might at the point of junction of Haig and Pétain. He assumed with some justice that it would be a weak point. The assumption is true only when two armies have divergent interests; for, as was to appear presently, the junction became the strongest point on the front.

But at the start Ludendorff was right in his judgment; for his plan would not at first be realised by his opponents, and, since there was no unified field command, there was likely to be some fumbling. Lastly, he saw that what he would do he must do quickly. "*Time's wingéd chariot*" would not wait for him. The German High Command did not at the time believe seriously in the Americans, for they reckoned that their arrival would be slow and their training imperfect; but it was the part of wisdom to take no risks.

Moreover, the happy anarchy of Russia might not continue for ever. Such being the general principles of his strategy, what advantages could he command in its execution? The first was his powerful army. He had withdrawn six German divisions from Italy and several from the Balkans; he had ready for use half of the 1920 class of new recruits; and he had brought some half-million men from the East.

What with captures from Italy and Russia, and those released from the Eastern front, he had an enormous concentration of guns, and he borrowed from Austria a quantity of batteries. At the beginning of the battle he was barely equal in total numbers to the Allies, though soon he was to have a considerable superiority. But from the outset, served by his admirable railways, he had the power of achieving a great local predominance, since the most intricate railway network of France was inside the German front.

In the second place, his position on interior lines gave him the possibility of strategic surprise. He could concentrate at some point in the angle of the huge salient running from the sea to La Fère, and from La Fère to Verdun. The Allies would, of course, be aware of this concentration; but till the actual attack they would not know on which side of the salient the blow was to fall. His dispositions would threaten the French in Champagne as much as the British at St. Quentin.

Finally, the nature of the ground behind the British lines seemed to have been devised for his purpose. His aim was to roll up the British right, and in the process, he would have the marshy valley of the Oise as a defence against French flank attacks, at any rate for the first stage. Wheeling northward, he would then drive Haig across the Somme, and thereby pin him to an enclosure, while his main effort turned against Pétain. In its essence it was the familiar plan of a break in a line sufficiently wide to allow the two halves to be driven in from the centre.

But the configuration of the battleground permitted the operation to be carried out in two stages. The rolling up of the British could be completed before the French came to their aid, and the British would be out of action before the attack developed on the French half. Only, it must be done speedily and completely; there was no great margin of time in such a programme.

The German habit, inherited from Moltke, was to decide upon a general strategic plan, towards which they marched undeviatingly, but to allow a wide latitude for the choice of particular objectives once they were in touch with the enemy. Ludendorff had therefore a single purpose—to split the Allied forces, hem in the British, and defeat the French; and this was to be effected by breaking the British right centre. But he was prepared to let circumstances decide for him the best methods of securing his aim as the battle developed. Hence it was an injustice to the German High Command to say that they struck for Amiens or Paris or the Channel Ports.

They struck for something far greater and more decisive than any geographical point. As the struggle went on, they seemed to be diverted towards minor objectives, but these were always subsidiary to their main purpose. Nor did they really relinquish that purpose till they were wholly outmanoeuvred and defeated.

We may now set down the detailed scheme of the first step. Out of 192 German divisions in the West, more than half were concentrated against the British. The actual front of attack was from Croisilles, on the Sensée, to Vendeuil, on the Oise, a distance of over fifty miles.

Against this line Ludendorff proposed to launch thirty-seven divisions—more than half a million men—as the first wave, to be followed by fresh troops in an endless wheel. It is clear from the way in which he disposed his forces that he believed he had detected certain weak sections on the British front.

One was the two re-entrants of the salient at Flesquières, which had been left by the Battle of Cambrai; another was just north of St. Quentin, where the low hill of Holnon dominates the little valley of the Omignon; a third was between St. Quentin and the Oise at the ridge of Essigny, east of the Crozat Canal. At such points a reasonable advance would mean the capture of important strategic positions. He hoped by the end of the first day to have driven the British behind the Upper Somme, and as a consequence, on the second day, to compel a general retreat of the whole line.

On the third day he had arranged for a great attack upon the British pivot at Arras. Success there would mean complete disaster to the British right wing, and a disorderly retirement westward towards Amiens and the sea. With the Oise to guard his flank, he was safe from serious danger for at least a week, and long before the French reserves, hastily brought from Champagne, could appear on the scene, he hoped to have cut all communication with the north and be facing southward to take order with Pétain.

The conception was bold and spacious, and based on sound principles of the military art. Apart from the strategic advantages we have referred to, Germany relied for success upon new tactics, which, as we have seen, von Hutier had first experimented with at Riga, and Otto von Below and von der Marwitz had proved at Caporetto and Cambrai. The history of the war was the history of new tactical methods devised to break the strength of an entrenched defence.

Neuve Chapelle saw the first attempt at the use of artillery to prepare the way for an infantry wedge, and Festubert and the French attack in the Artois saw the failure of the method. Three months later Loos and Champagne witnessed the device of the broad breach, which was defeated by the depth of the German defences. Then came the Somme and the doctrine of "limited objectives," combined with a creeping barrage, a method which was sure in its result but slow and laborious in its working, and which could only achieve a decision against an enemy whose power of recruitment was shrinking.

The defection of Russia altered the whole case, and the gradual pulverization of Germany's fighting strength became a futile aim in view of the fresh reserves of troops at her command. Cambrai had shown the dawn of a new tactics, the tactic of surprise, and the mind of the Allied Command was working towards its development. But Germany was beforehand. Her problem was to discover a tactics which would restore open warfare, and give a chance of an early decision. She deserves all credit for a brilliant departure from routine, a true intellectual effort to rethink the main problem of modern war. And her credit is the greater inasmuch as she contrived to keep it secret, and, in spite of Caporetto and Cambrai, the Allied Staffs, until the battle was joined, had no accurate knowledge of her plan.

What that plan was must be briefly sketched. It was based primarily upon the highly specialised training of certain units, and may be described as the system of *sturmtruppen* carried to its extreme conclusion. In practice it usually involved local superiority of numbers, even a crushing superiority, but such was not its essence, and it was meant to succeed even when the enemy was in stronger force. (For example, at the Third Battle of the Aisne the 1st Guard Division successfully engaged within three days seven French divisions, and another German division at the battle of 9th June defeated three French divisions).

The first point was the absence of any preliminary massing of troops near the front of attack. Troops were brought up by night marches only just before zero hour, and secrecy was thus obtained for the assembly. In the second place, there was no long artillery "preparation" to alarm the enemy. The attack was preceded by a short and intense bombardment, and the enemy's back areas and support lines were confused by a deluge of gas shells. The assault was made by picked troops, in open order, or rather in small clusters, carrying light trench mortars and many machine guns, with the field batteries close behind them in support.

The actual method of attack, which the French called "infiltration," may best be set forth by the analogy of a hand whose finger tips are shod with steel, pushing its way into a soft substance. The picked troops at the fingers' ends made gaps through which others poured, till each section of the defence found itself outflanked and encircled. A system of flares and rockets enabled the following troops to learn where the picked troops had made the breach, and the artillery came close behind the infantry. The troops had unlimited objectives, and carried iron rations for several days. When one division had reached the end of its strength another took its place, so that the advance resembled an endless wheel or a continuous game of leap-frog.

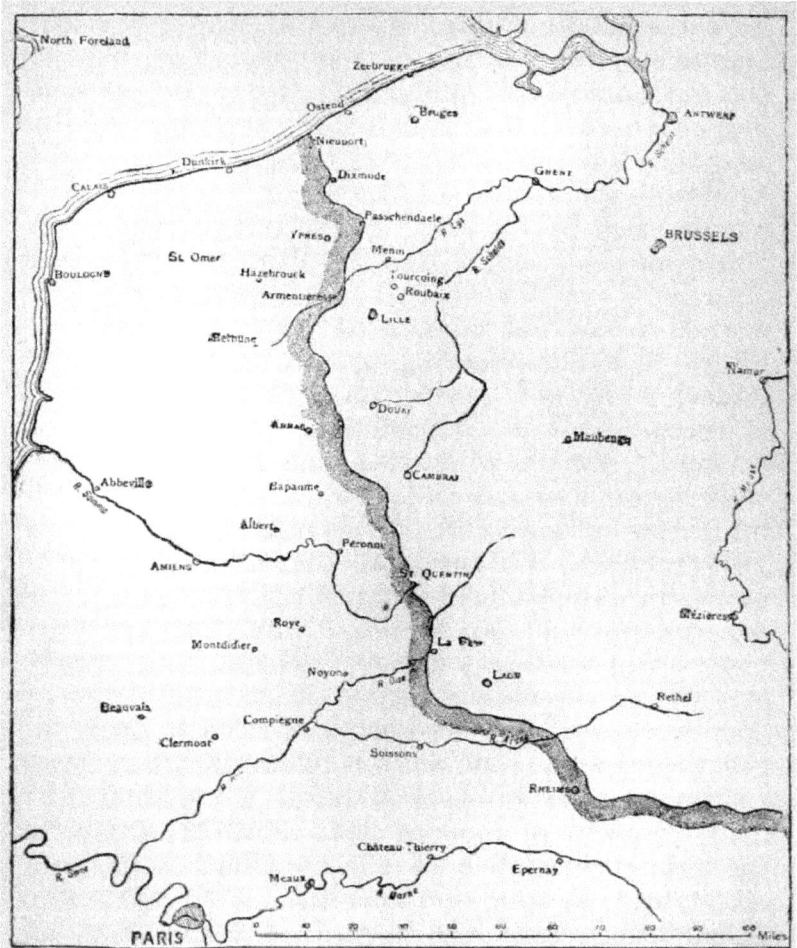

Sketch showing the Allied Front from the Sea to Champagne,
March 20, 1918.

This method, it will be seen, was the very opposite of the old German massed attack, or a series of hammer blows on the one section of front. It was strictly the filtering of a great army into a hostile position, so that each part was turned and the whole front was first dislocated and then crumbled. The crumbling might be achieved by inferior numbers; the value of the German numerical superiority was to ensure a complete victory by pushing far behind into unprotected areas. Advance was to be measured not by a few kilometres but by many miles, and in any case, was to proceed far enough to capture the enemy's artillery positions.

Obviously, the effect would be cumulative, the momentum of the attack would grow, and, if it was not stopped in the battle zone, it would be far harder to stop in the hinterland. It was no case of a sudden stroke, but of a creeping sickness which might demoralise a hundred miles of front. Ludendorff's confidence was not ill-founded, for to support his strategical plan he had tactics which must come with deadly effect upon an enemy prepared only to meet the old methods.

Their one drawback was that they involved the highest possible training and discipline. Every detail—the preliminary assembly, the attack, the supply and relief system during battle—presupposed the most perfect mechanism, and great initiative and resource in subordinate commanders. The German Army had now been definitely grouped into special troops of the best quality, and a rank and file of very little. Unless decisive success came at once, the tactics might remain, but the men to use them would have gone. A protracted battle would destroy the *corps d'élite*, and without that the tactics were futile.

The German High Command, as was its custom before a great offensive, had created new armies. Their dispositions on the 21st March in the battle area were as follows: From Arras southward lay the new XVII. Army under Otto von Below, the hero of Caporetto, with five corps, comprising twenty-three divisions. On his left, from Cambrai to just north of St. Quentin, with exactly the same strength, lay the II. Army of von der Marwitz, who had been in command during the battle of Cambrai. South of it, extending to the Oise, was the new XVIII. Army under Oskar von Hutier, with four corps, embracing twenty-three or twenty-four divisions. Beyond lay von Boehn's VII. Army, the right wing of which was to be drawn into the contest.

Of the corps commanders, some, like Fasbender and Conta, were old antagonists, but the majority were new men in the West, who had learned their trade in Eastern battles. Von Hutier himself was of this school. Before the war he had commanded the 1st Guard Division; but in the present campaign he had done all his work in Russia, and, at the head of the German VIII. Army, had taken Riga. It was fitting that one of the men chiefly responsible for the new tactics should be present to direct their final test. Otto von Below was also one of their begetters. He had first won fame at Tannenberg in August 1914, and had thereafter commanded for two years the German VIII. Army on the left flank in the East.

In November 1916 he took over the German forces in Macedonia, and distinguished himself greatly in the fighting at Monastic. In April 1917 he replaced von Falkenhausen in command of the German VI. Army after the loss of Vimy Ridge, and in September of the same year was put in charge of the new XIV. Army for the attack on Italy. There he remained until January 1918, when he joined the XVII. Army in France. (The von Below family is confusing. From Otto must be distinguished Fritz, who now commanded the I. Army in Champagne, and Eduard who commanded the 5th Corps.)

A new feature was to be noted in the German dispositions. The great stroke was designed not only to give Germany victory, but to revive the waning prestige of the royal house. So soon as the battle began it was announced that the emperor himself was in command. The armies of Otto von Below and von der Marwitz were included in the group of Prince Rupprecht of Bavaria, but von Hutier's army, which was meant to be the spearpoint of the thrust, was in the group of the Imperial Crown Prince. It was a *Kaiserschlacht*, this blow which was to open the path to a "German peace."

The position of the Allies in the face of such a threat was full of embarrassment. They were aware of what was coming, and in view of their past record they were confident that they could beat off any German assault, even though it were made with a slight superiority of numbers. But the enemy concentration in the angle of the great salient made it impossible for them to decide till the last moment against which section the attack would be delivered. The Germans took some pains to threaten the Champagne front and the Ypres area.

Pétain, not unnaturally, was anxious about his position on the Aisne—which was, after all, for the enemy the shortest cut to victory—and, since he held the exterior lines, any reinforcement of one part from another would be a matter of days. The difficulties of the British Command were still greater. Sir Douglas Haig had not received from home the numbers for which he had so often pleaded,

Field Marshal Sir Douglas Haig

and he had been compelled greatly to extend the length of his front. Up to January 1918 the right wing of the British had been Sir Julian Byng's Third Army. Before the middle of the month, however, the Third Army was moved a little farther north, and the post on its right taken by Sir Hubert Gough's Fifth Army from the Ypres area, which replaced the French in front of St. Quentin. (This decision had been arrived at by the British and French Governments as early as September 1917.) About the 20th of January the Fifth Army extended its right as far south as the village of Barisis, on the left bank of the Oise, thus making itself responsible for a line of 72,000 yards, or over forty-one miles.

Clearly this was a wildly dangerous extension for a weak force in an area which was one of the two possible objects of the coming enemy attack. The problem made Versailles uneasy, the more so as the British general reserves were scanty. It was provisionally arranged between Haig and Pétain that, in the event of the western side of the salient becoming the main battle-ground, the British reserves would be held mainly at the disposal of Byng's Third Army, while the French Third Army under Fayolle south of the Oise would extend its left to assist Gough. Such a plan had obviously many drawbacks, but it was difficult to make a better, since the French General Staff looked for the danger-point in Champagne.

To add to Haig's difficulties, he had to train his troops for the new defensive warfare, and the transition from offence to defence is one of the most critical tasks which a general can face. He had to adapt his army to the new grouping of units under which divisions were changed from a thirteen-battalion to a ten-battalion basis. (This was done in order to allow of the eventual brigading of American troops with British divisions.)

He had to prepare defences and communications in the areas recently won from the enemy. His strategical problem, too, was intricate. He had to face an attack anywhere on a front of 125 miles, and from Arras northward his hinterland was so narrow and so vital that he could not afford to lose much ground. It was different between Arras and the Oise, where twenty miles could be relinquished without strategic disaster. He was, therefore, compelled to keep the northern and central sections of his front well manned and their reserves not far off, and he did not dare to weaken them for the sake of the Somme area, even though the omens pointed to that as the probable German objective.

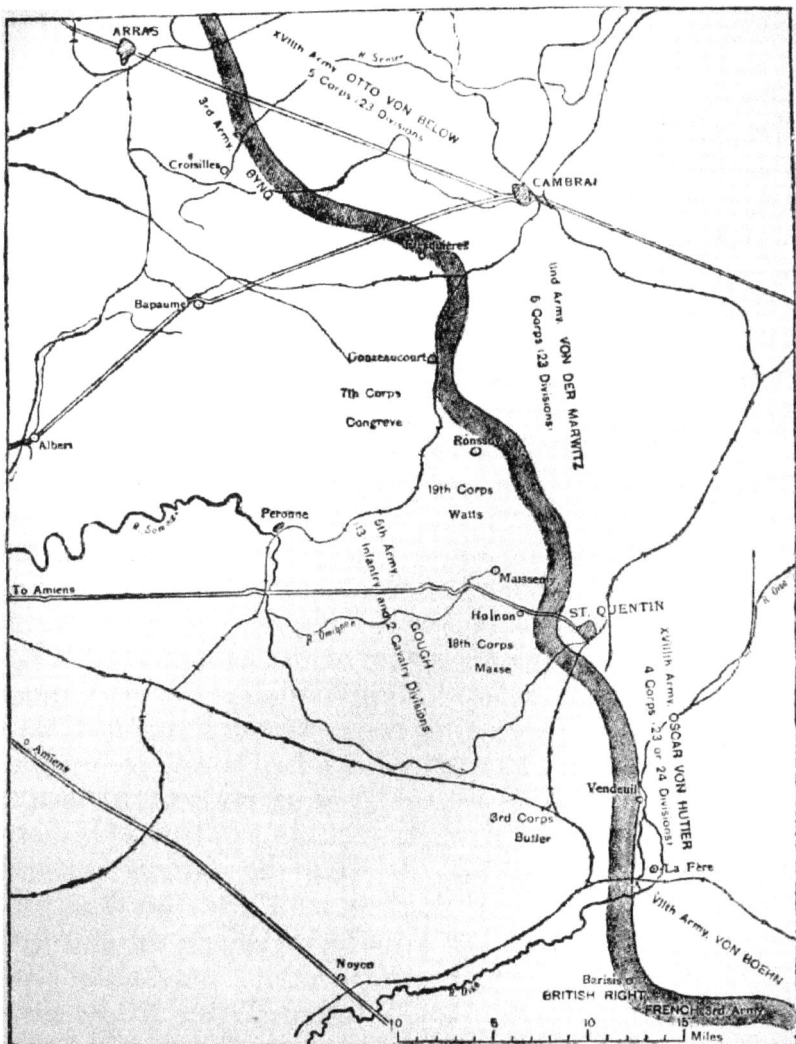

The Opposing Armies on the Front between Arras and the Oise.

In the middle of March, the British Third Army lay from just north of the Arras-Douai road to near Gouzeaucourt in the south. Byng had four corps—from left to right the 17th, under Lieutenant-General Sir Charles Fergusson; the 6th, under Lieutenant-General Sir Aylmer Haldane; the 4th, under Lieutenant-General Sir G. M. Harper; and the 5th, under Lieutenant-General Sir E. A. Fanshawe. He had in line ten divisions—from left to right the Guards, the 15th, the 3rd, the 34th, the 59th, the 6th, the 51st, the 17th, the 63rd, and the 2nd; and in reserve the 4th, the 56th, the 47th, the 40th, and the 19th. His total front was something over 40,000 yards. Gough on his 72,000 yards from Gouzeaucourt to the Oise had eleven divisions in line—in order, the 9th, the 21st, the 16th, the 66th, the 24th, the 61st, the 30th, the 36th, the 14th, the 18th, and the 58th. In reserve he had the 39th, the 50th, and the 20th Infantry Divisions, and two cavalry divisions, the 1st and 2nd.

His front was so extraordinary that it deserves a fuller exposition. From Gouzeaucourt to Ronssoy, along the ridge which represented the limit reached by the German counter-attack at Cambrai, lay the 7th Corps under Lieutenant-General Sir Walter Congreve, holding a front of 14,000 yards with three divisions and one in reserve. From Ronssoy to Maissemy, covering the valley of the Omignon, was the 19th Corps under Lieutenant-General Sir H. E. Watts, holding a front of 10,000 yards with two divisions and one in reserve. In front of St. Quentin, from the Omignon to the canalized Somme, was the 18th Corps under Lieutenant-General Sir Ivor Maxse, with three divisions in line, and one infantry and one cavalry division in reserve. Its front was approximately 18,000 yards.

On its right to the Oise lay Lieutenant-General Sir R. H. Butler's 3rd Corps, with three divisions in line and a cavalry division in reserve. It covered no less than 30,000 yards—an average of less than one bayonet to the yard. The reason of such a disposition was that eleven miles of this last front, between Moy and the Oise, were supposed to be protected by the river and its marshes.

The terrain of the sixty miles held by the British Third and Fifth Armies was in the main a series of bare plateaux, split into fingers by broad valleys running east and west. In the north were the east-flowing streams of the Scarpe, the Sensée, and the Cojeul, and, farther south, the Cologne and the Omignon running west to the Somme, and the canalized upper stream of the Somme itself. There were few woods save in the neighbourhood of Gouzeaucourt, and at Holnon, west of St. Quentin. Our front had no natural defences except on its right, where it ran along the Oise. But the early months of the year had been dry and the Oise marshes made only a feeble barrier.

Behind our centre lay the Somme in its big bend towards Péronne, with a channel some sixty feet broad and four deep; but in the event of retreat the Somme was not a line to rally on, for its tortuous course made it easy to turn on the north. On the south the Crozat Canal joined it with the Oise and provided a good reserve position. The key-points on the Fifth Army front were the high ground at Essigny, Holnon, and Ronssoy, commanding respectively the Crozat Canal, the valley of the Omignon, and the valley of the Cologne. For the Third Army the danger points were the re-entrants of the Flesquières salient and the vital hinge of Arras.

The British Command attempted to atone for its weakness in numbers by devising defences of exceptional strength. In front lay a "forward zone," organised in two sections—a line of outposts to give the alarm and fall back, and a well-wired line of resistance. In the latter were a number of skilfully-placed redoubts, armed with machine guns, and so arranged that any enemy advance would be drawn on between them so as to come under crossfire. The redoubts were set 2,000 yards apart, and the spaces between were to be protected by a barrage from field guns and corps heavy guns. The line of resistance and the redoubts were intended to hold out to the last, and to receive no support from the rear except for such counter-attacks as might be necessary.

The purpose of the "forward zone" was to break up the advancing enemy, and the principle of its organisation was "blobs" rather than a continuous line. Behind the "forward zone," at a distance of from half a mile to three miles, (in the Flesquières salient the battle zone was five miles behind the forward zone), came the "battle zone," arranged on the same plan except that it had no outposts. It was a defence in depth, elaborately wired, and studded with redoubts and strong points. A mile or two in its rear lay the final defensive zone, less elaborately fortified, and by no means completed when the battle began. The British Command had confidence in its arrangements, believing that the "forward zone" would break up the cohesion of any assault, and that the "battle zone" would be impregnable against an attack thus weakened.

Consequently, there were no serious alternative positions prepared in the rear; indeed, considering the small number of men available, it is hard to see how the army commanders could in the time have

STURMTRUPPEN

provided such safeguards. But a strong bridgehead position was in process of construction covering Péronne and the Somme crossings to the south. Certain arrangements also had been made in case of a comprehensive retreat, and orders had been issued well in advance as to the destruction of the Somme bridges. The two army commanders on the threatened front had each in his way a high reputation. Both were cavalrymen, and both had done brilliant work in the campaign.

Sir Julian Byng, as commander of the Canadian Corps, had taken Vimy Ridge in April 1917, and it was he who had instituted the new tactics of surprise at Cambrai. Sir Hubert Gough, after a meteoric rise to fame in the first year of war, had commanded the Fifth Army at the Somme and throughout the long struggle around Bullecourt during the Battle of Arras. At Third Ypres he had been given the chief part, and his army had borne the brunt of the heavy fighting in the first month of that action. But there he had somewhat failed in resource, and had squandered fine divisions against the enemy's defences without attaining his object. Hence his old reputation had become a little dimmed, and among his soldiers he had acquired the name of a general who tried his troops too high and used them blindly as battering-rams against the stoutest part of the wall.

The criticism was not wholly just, but it was widely made, and as a result the Fifth Army had lost something of its confidence in its leader. So, when misfortune overtook it, Sir Hubert Gough was naturally blamed, though, as will be made clear in this narrative, he did all that man could do in an impossible situation. It was the failure at Third Ypres which, as is the fashion of such things, clouded his record in an action from which otherwise he must have emerged with a new credit.

The first weeks of March saw the dry, bright weather of a Picardy spring. As early as the 14th our airplanes had reported a big concentration well back in the enemy's hinterland, and the Third and Fifth Armies were warned of an approaching battle. Many raids undertaken during these weeks established the arrival of fresh enemy divisions in line, though no idea could be got of the real German strength; and from the evidence of prisoners it appeared that Thursday, the 21st March, was the day appointed for the attack. On Tuesday, the 19th, the weather broke in drizzling rain, but it cleared on the Wednesday, with the result that a thick mist was drawn out of the ground and muffled all the folds of the downs. The night of the 20th-21st was heavy with this fog, which was destined to continue for several days.

At about 2 a.m. on the 21st the British front was warned to expect an assault. The forward zone was always fully manned, and at 4.30 a.m. the order was sent out to man the battle zone. All through the night the Germans under cover of the mist had been pushing up troops into line, till by dawn on the fifty odd miles of front between Croisilles and the Oise they had thirty-seven divisions within 3,000 yards of our outposts. Precisely at a quarter to five the whole weight of their many thousand guns was released against the British forward and battle zones, headquarters, communications, and artillery positions, the back areas especially being drenched with gas which hung like a pall in the moist and heavy air. Twenty miles and more behind the line, even as far back as the quiet streets of St. Pol, shells were dropped from high velocity guns.

Nor was the shelling confined to the battle-front. The French felt it in wide sections east and north-east of Rheims; it was violent north of Arras and on the line between La Bassée and the Lys; Messines and the Ypres area were heavily attacked, and Dunkirk was bombarded from the sea. So widespread and so severe an artillery "preparation" had not yet been seen in the campaign. The batteries of the Third and Fifth Armies replied as best they could, but no gunner or machine gunner or artillery observer could see fifty yards before him. Communication by visual signalling, airplanes, or pigeons was impossible, and the only method was wireless, which was slow and uncertain. And under the same cloak of mist little parties of the enemy were everywhere cutting the wire and filtering between our outposts.

It was a perfect occasion for the new German tactics. The infantry advance was timed differently along the front. In one place it began as early as eight o'clock, and by ten o'clock it was general. The men on the outpost line, beaten to the ground by the bombardment, and struggling amid clouds of gas, were in desperate case. In the thick weather the enemy was beyond the places where the cross fire of machine guns might have checked him long before the redoubts were aware of his presence.

The first thing which most of the outposts knew was that the Germans were well in their rear, and they were overwhelmed before they could send back warning. The S.O.S. signals sent up were everywhere blanketed by the fog. Presently the outposts were gone, and the Germans were battling in our forward zone. There the line of resistance did all that was expected of it. There garrisons and redoubts, till far on in the day, resisted gallantly; messages continued to be received from many up to a late hour, until that silence came which meant destruction.

The battle zone had been early manned, but the destruction of our communications kept it in the dark as to what was happening in front. Too often, too, in those mad hours of fog our batteries received their first news of the attack from the appearance of German infantry on their flank and rear. They fought heroically to the end, mowing down the enemy with open sights at point-blank ranges. About one o'clock the fog lifted, and then the German airplanes, flying low, attacked with machine guns our troops and batteries. The men in the battle zone could only wait with anxious hearts till the shock of the assault should reach them.

Before eleven o'clock the army commands had tidings that the enemy was through our forward zone on the extreme right opposite La Fère, where it had been vainly hoped that the Oise marshes gave security. Then came news that the same thing had happened north of the Bapaume-Cambrai road and at Lagnicourt and Bullecourt. At noon came a graver message. The Germans were in Ronssoy, *inside the battle zone*. They had taken Templeux le Guerard, and Hargicourt and Villeret, and were now in contact with the rear defences of the battle zone, and threatening to break through down the valley of the Omignon.

On the flanks of this area they were still held. The 24th Division, under Major-General Daly, was still defending Le Verguier, which was in the forward zone, and the 21st Division under Major-General David Campbell had not yielded a yard at Epéhy. At the Flesquières salient, too, where the attack had not been pressed, the forward zone was intact. But the grave fact remained that by noon, with these exceptions, the German infantry had everywhere reached our battle zone, and at Ronssoy had bitten deeply into it. Presently they were into it at the supposed impregnable section on the south between Essigny and Benay, and at Maissemy, above the valley of the Omignon.

At the last point, however, they were held by the 24th Division and the 61st (South Midland) Division under Major-General Colin Mackenzie, with the aid of troops from Major-General Mullens's 1st Cavalry Division. On the Third Army front the enemy had reached the battle zone at various points between the Canal du Nord and the Sensée. He had taken Doignies and Louverval, was on the edge of Lagnicourt, and farther north was in Noreuil, Longatte, and Ecoust St. Mein. The gallant 9th (Scottish) Division, under Major-General

25

FIELD MARSHAL JULIAN BYNG
COMMANDER OF THE CANADIAN CORPS

Tudor, on the left of the Fifth Army, was still maintaining its ground; the 17th Division, under Major-General Robertson, was in position astride the Canal du Nord; and at Lagnicourt the 6th Division, under Major-General Marden, was holding the first line of the battle zone.

In the afternoon the situation developed most gravely south of St. Quentin. The enemy was in Fargnier by four o'clock, and in the evening pressed in the 58th Division under Major-General Cator, and captured Quessy, at the south end of the Crozat Canal. Farther north the 18th Division, under Major-General Lee, assisted by troops of Major-General Pitman's 2nd Cavalry Division, held their ground in the battle zone, and even in the forward zone, till about midnight the stand of the latter was broken. Between Benay and the Somme Canal the 14th Division was forced back to the last line of the battle zone, though isolated detachments were still resisting east and north-east of Essigny. Around Roupy and Savy, where the Germans attacked with tanks—huge things mounting the equivalent of a field gun, but unwieldy across country—the 30th Division, under Major-General W. de L. Williams, stood firm in the battle zone and took heavy toll of the advancing enemy.

On the rest of the Fifth Army front the battle zone was intact, though hard pressed at Ronssoy, and the 9th Division still held their forward positions. In the Third Army area the heaviest fighting during the afternoon took place around Demicourt and Doignies and north of Beaumetz, where the famous 51st (Highland Territorial) Division under Major-General Carter-Campbell was engaged, assisted by battalions of the 19th Division, under Major-General Jeffreys. Lagnicourt fell, and for a moment it was believed that the enemy would break through between Noreuil and Croisilles. He reached St. Leger, and attempted to outflank the 34th Division, under Major-General Nicholson, at Croisilles. By the evening this attack had failed, as had the attack against the 3rd Division, under Major-General Deverell, on the left bank of the Sensée.

As the night fell the pressure still continued. It had been an amazing day. Against nineteen British divisions in line the enemy had hurled thirty-seven divisions as a first wave, and, before the dark came, not less than sixty-four German divisions had taken part in the battle—a number considerably exceeding the total strength of the British Army in France. Adding the reserves of the Third and Fifth Armies, we get a total of thirty-two divisions against sixty-four; and, as a matter of fact, many British divisions engaged during the day three or four German.

The forward zone had gone, except in the area of the 9th Division, but the battle zone remained, though at Essigny and Ronssoy and Noreuil it had worn perilously thin.

The greatest total advance of the enemy was some 8,000 yards on our extreme right. Counter-attacks to recover key points were out of the question owing to our lack of reserves, and the most we could do was to maintain our thin lines intact and prevent a break through. Our airplanes had warned us that the enemy was concentrating huge masses for the second day of the battle. It behoved us, therefore, to re-arrange our front. On the right of the Third Army the 5th Corps was retired from the Flesquières salient, and this involved a withdrawal by the 9th Division, which so far had yielded nothing.

Byng's line now ran in that area along the upland known as Highland Ridge, and then westward along the old Siegfried Line to Havrincourt and Hermies. On the right of the Fifth Army the 3rd Corps was withdrawn behind the Crozat Canal, and this meant that the right division of the 18th Corps, the 36th (Ulster), had to be withdrawn to the Somme Canal. With the dark the fog thickened, and all night long the work of destroying the canal bridges went on. The enemy was close up, and in some cases the destruction parties were annihilated before they could perform their work, so a few bridges were left practicable for the German infantry.

It had been a day of sustained and marvellous heroism—outposts standing out to the last; batteries fighting with only a man or two in the gun teams; handfuls desperately counter-attacking and snatching safety for others with their own lives. But it had taken heavy toll of our troops in dead and prisoners, and the remnant were very weary. Our front was now freed from any marked salient, and the barrier of the Somme and Crozat Canals had strengthened the critical section in the south. But the Fifth Army was still outnumbered by four to one, and there was no prospect of help yet awhile. The fog grew thicker in the night, and at the dawn of Friday, the 22nd, it was as dense as on the previous morning. Hence we could not use our artillery with effect on the German masses, who at the first light began to press heavily on the whole battle-ground.

It soon became clear that the enemy's main effort was against the Fifth Army, especially at the three critical points of the Cologne and Omignon valleys and the Crozat Canal. Early in the morning von Hutier had reached the Canal at Jussy, and by 1 p.m. he had crossed at Quessy and was pressing on to Vouel. The 58th Division made a great stand at Tergnier, but lost that village before the evening. In the afternoon the Germans crossed the canal also at La Montagne and Jussy, but were driven back by the 18th Division and the 2nd Cavalry Division. At the gate of the Cologne River von der Marwitz was as far west as Roisel, where the 66th Division, under Major-General Neill Malcolm, held their ground for a time.

South of the valley, however, Le Verguier had fallen by 10 a.m., and to the north Villers Faucon soon followed, so that both Roisel and Epéhy were threatened from the rear. Accordingly, the 66th Division was withdrawn to the third defensive zone between Bernes and Boucly, where they were supported by the 50th (Northumbrian) Division, under Brigadier-General Stockley. The 21st Division was also retired from Epéhy, and on their left the 9th Division was brought back with great difficulty to the third zone between Nurlu and Equancourt. By the afternoon almost the whole of the Fifth Army was in the third defensive position.

Throughout the day Byng held without serious trouble his new line in the Flesquières salient, but he had to face severe attacks between Havrincourt and the Sensée. The 17th Division made a gallant defence at Hermies, which was virtually outflanked; and the 51st Division and a brigade of the 25th stood firm in the Beaumetz area. In the late afternoon the 34th Division had at last to fall back from St. Leger; but on its left the 3rd Division retired its right flank to a front facing south-east, and held the enemy. Under enormous handicaps the Third Army contrived during the day to yield little ground, and to exact a high price for every yard.

But it was otherwise with the Fifth Army. By midday the German masses were forcing the gate of the Omignon, where the loss of Maissemy and Le Verguier had seriously weakened our line. Division after division pressed to the attack, and presently the whole of Gough's centre was out of the battle zone. We were driven from the ridge at Holnon, and in all that section the divisions in line were forced back behind the third zone of defence, where the two reserve divisions, the 20th and the 50th, took over the front to enable the others to reorganise behind them. In this most hazardous retreat the 36th Ulster Division, under Major-General Nugent, fought with especial brilliance.

By 5.30 p.m. the enemy was everywhere attacking the final zone. The 30th Division, on a front of over 10,000 yards, for some hours held up the assault between the Cologne and the Omignon, but in the evening they were pressed back from Poeuilly, and suddenly they

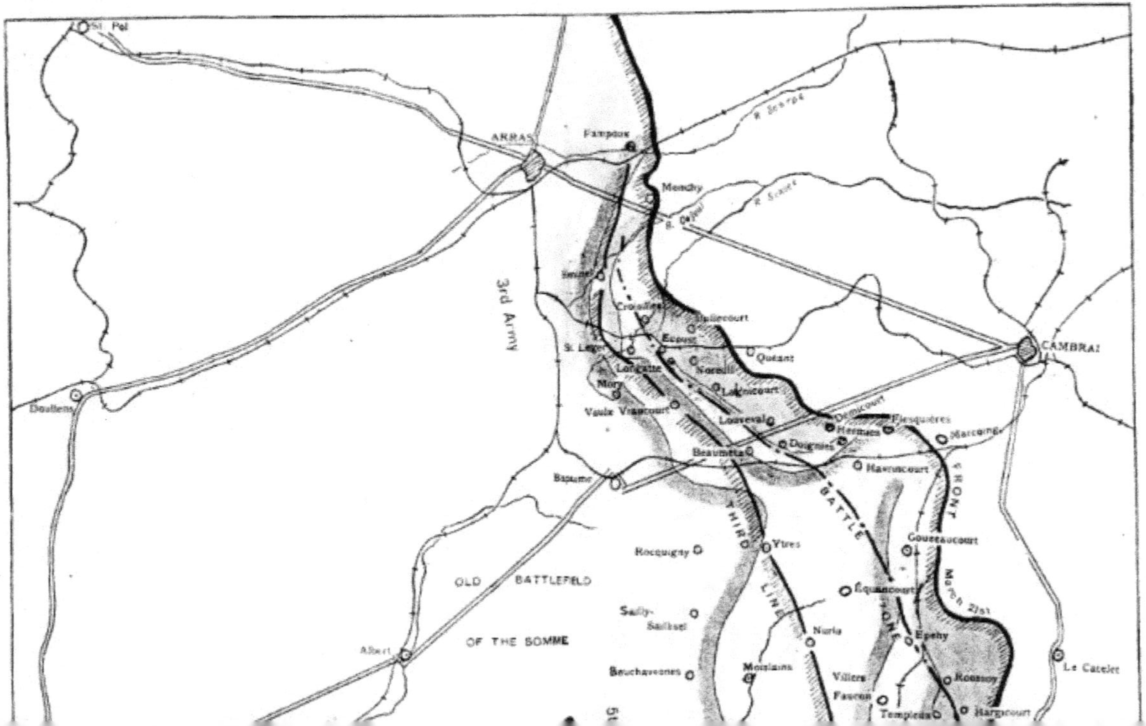

CAMBRAI

Le Catelet

FRONT

March 21st

Marcoing

Flesquières

LINE

Havrincourt

BATTLE

Dougan

THIRD

Quéant

LINE

Ytres

OLD BATTLEFIELD

OF THE SOMME

ARRAS

3rd Army

Albert

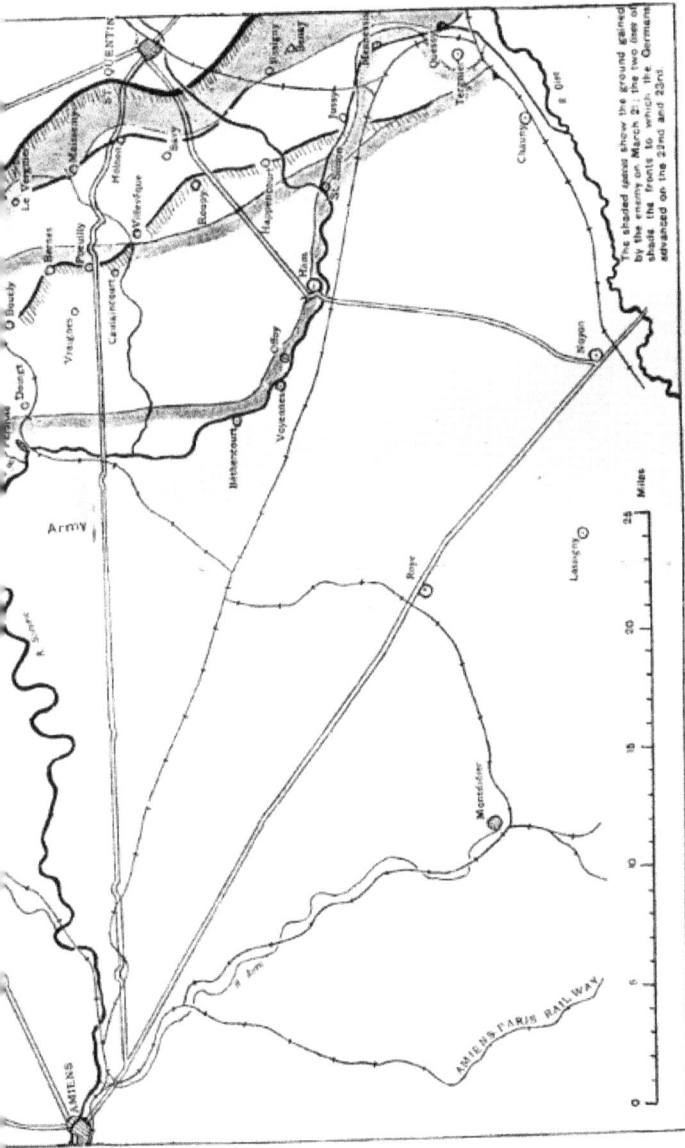

The Second Battle of the Somme: 1st Phase, March 21-23.—The Germans break through the British defence lines, and the British fall back to the Somme.

found their right flank turned. For, south of the Omignon, a gap had opened between the right wing of the 50th and the left of the 61st and 20th Divisions. Through it the Germans poured, and broke the third zone around Vaux and Beauvois.

That which the British Command most dreaded had come to pass. Our last reserves had been thrown in, and, save for one of Fayolle's French divisions, and some French cavalry now busily engaged at the Crozat Canal, there was no help available for the hard-pressed Fifth Army. The gap could not be stopped, so at all costs our front must withdraw. At 11 p.m. that night Gough gave orders to fall back to the bridgehead position east of the Somme, a position which, as we have seen, was not yet completed. Maxse's 18th Corps was to retire to the Somme line south of Voyennes, keeping touch with the 3rd Corps on the Crozat Canal. Watts's 19th Corps and Congreve's 7th Corps were to hold the Péronne bridgehead on a line running from Voyennes through Monchy Lagache to Vraignes, and thence continue in the third zone to the junction with the Third Army at Equancourt.

Byng had to fall back to conform, his front now running from Equancourt east of Metz-en-Couture, and then in the third zone to Henin-sur-Cojeul, whence the old battle zone was continued to Fampoux. His retreat was not seriously threatened, but it was otherwise with Gough. All through the thick night the divisions of the Fifth Army, now in the last stages of fatigue, retreated under constant enemy pressure, covered by rear-guards from the 20th, 50th, and 39th Divisions. In such a retirement complete order was impossible, and it was certain that gaps would be left in the new front. Such weak points appeared at Mory in the Third Army's centre, and at Ham in the area of the 18th Corps, and the morning was to give us news of them.

During the night Gough was faced with a momentous decision. The Crozat Canal line was yielding, and his right flank was in danger; he had fallen back to a position where the defences were weak and unfinished; he had intelligence that the whole German hinterland was packed with fresh troops; and he saw no hope of reinforcements for several days. His men, strung out on an immense front, had been fighting without rest for forty-eight hours. If he faced a general engagement on the morrow he might suffer decisive defeat. There seemed no course open to him but to abandon the Péronne bridgehead and fall back behind the Somme. It was a difficult decision, for, in the words of the official dispatch:

It greatly shortened the time available for clearing our troops and removable material from the east bank of the river, for completing the necessary final preparations, for the destruction of the river and canal bridges, for re-forming west of the river the divisions which had suffered most in the previous fighting, and generally for securing the adequate defence of the river line.

But the alternative was almost certain disaster, and beyond doubt in the circumstances his judgment was right. Accordingly, very early in the morning of Saturday, 23rd March, instructions were given to the 19th Corps to withdraw gradually to the river line, while the 7th Corps, on their left, were to take up position between Doingt and Nurlu. The latter front just covered Péronne, and had behind it, flowing from north to south, the little River Tortille.

The withdrawal began on Saturday morning, and was undertaken in the face of incessant attacks from an immensely superior enemy. That day was perhaps the most difficult in the whole annals of the British Army. Gaps, as we have seen, had already opened in the front taken up the night before, and the task of retreat was everywhere complicated by the enemy's presence at points in the rear.

It was open warfare with a vengeance, and often it seemed that the whole British line had lost cohesion, and had been jolted into a number of isolated detachments. Von Hutier began by increasing his hold west of the Crozat Canal. He forced a crossing at Jussy, and by some means or other got his tanks over. A little later, in spite of the stout resistance of the Canadian Cavalry Brigade, he had crossed at Mennessis, and by noon was advancing on the west bank. The French division had failed in their counterattack towards Tergnier, and all afternoon the enemy was slowly pressing in the 3rd Corps among the wooded uplands between the Somme and the Oise.

Farther north there was trouble at Ham, which the Germans entered in the early morning; and, owing to the bridges not being completely destroyed, they succeeded during the day in crossing the river there and at Pithon. In the afternoon the resistance of the 20th and 61st Divisions prevented them from advancing farther on the southern bank. The right wing of the 18th Corps was swinging slowly towards the Somme, righting delaying actions, in which the Ulster Division again distinguished itself.

The retreat of the 19th Corps succeeded better than might have been expected, considering the difficulties of a weak force retiring in daylight in the face of great numbers, and the 50th Division did marvellous work in covering the withdrawal. By 3.15 p.m. the whole corps was across the river, and most of the bridges had been destroyed. The water was low, the adjacent marshes dry, and the depression in which the stream ran was some sixty feet below the level of the downs on the eastern shore; but the position offered some degree of protection. The Germans tried to cross at Offoy and Bethencourt during the afternoon, but were repulsed; and all evening their troops, descending the bare slopes on the east, were heavily punished by our guns. North of Ham no German had crossed the Somme by nightfall.

Meanwhile Congreve, on the left, was in serious danger. The 7th Corps was holding a front just covering Péronne on the high ground towards Nurlu and Equancourt. During the morning its left withdrew from Nurlu to the line of the Canal du Nord north of Moislains. This caused a gap between it and the right of Fanshawe's 5th Corps in the Third Army, of which the enemy promptly took advantage. Gallant attempts to restore the position were made by divisions of the Third Army—the 47th (London), under Major-General Sir G. F. Gorringe, and a brigade of the 2nd, under Major-General Pereira; but the gap widened hourly. The result was that the 7th Corps, late in the afternoon, was forced back west of Péronne across the Tortille to the high ground around Bouchavesnes and south of Sailly-Saillisel. They were now back on the old Somme front held by us before the German retirement in March 1917.

Their extreme weakness made their line crack into fissures, which the Germans searched for and widened, so that ere night began their front was not established, and was still slowly giving ground. It was the beginning of that attempt to divide the Third and Fifth Armies which presently became the immediate strategic objective of the enemy. In this and subsequent fighting the debt of the British infantry to the Royal Air Force could not be overstated. So long as the light endured they kept at bay all enemy machines, which otherwise might have discerned the nakedness of the land.

This gap compelled the 5th Corps also to retire. Its right was forced back first to the Four Winds Farm, south of Ytres, and then, in spite of a great stand by the 47th Division, to a position east of Rocquigny. Farther north the rest of the Third Army had a day of desperate battles. Its centre lost Le Bucquière and Beugny after a long struggle, in which the 19th Division played a gallant part. At Vaulx Vraucourt the 41st

Division, under Major-General Sir S. T. B. Lawford, managed to hold its line against six separate assaults for which the enemy brought up cavalry and guns.

The gap at Mory was temporarily closed by the recapture of that village by the 40th Division, under Major-General John Ponsonby; and, west of St. Leger, Major-General Bridgford's 31st Division repulsed two German divisions. The evening saw the centre and left wing of the Third Army still standing firm, though in some danger from the retirement of its right flank. At Arras a curious thing had happened. That morning Otto von Below had designed a great attack upon our pivot there. Realising the danger, Byng had withdrawn his troops beforehand from the exposed position at Monchy. The enemy directed a violent bombardment on our old lines; but their infantry, when they advanced, found them empty. This completely upset the German plan, and the attack was postponed till the heavy guns could be brought up for the destruction of our new front.

That evening the German bulletins announced that the first stage of the great battle had ended, and that a large part of the British Army had been defeated. They claimed 25,000 prisoners and 400 guns. In three days they had advanced at the deepest point about nine miles. That morning, as if to signalise their triumph, they had begun the shelling of Paris with long-range guns—a battery of 8.4-inch pieces, emplaced some eight miles inside the German lines. A gun firing at a range of over seventy miles was a new thing in war, though its feasibility had long been known to the Allies. It was a *tour de force*, designed only to weaken the morale of the French capital, a task in which it most conspicuously failed.

But it was a warning to the Allies that Germany was devoting every energy to her final offensive, and would leave no method untried to break her foe. So far, she had succeeded greatly, but not beyond her expectations. Indeed, Ludendorff was some distance behind his programme. On the evening of the 23rd he had done little more than reach the positions which he had promised himself for the night of the 21st, and though he had worn the British line to a shadow, he had not yet broken it.

Nevertheless, on that Saturday evening, Sir Douglas Haig had food for anxious thought. He had arranged with the commanders of the First and Second Armies to organise a special force of reserve divisions, and he hoped soon to have the Canadian Corps for use on the Somme. Also, that afternoon Pétain had agreed to take over the front south of Péronne, with the result that the 3rd, 18th, and 19th Corps passed under Fayolle. But the adjustment of commands did not create fresh troops, and the French reserves in any strength could not appear for a day or two. In the meantime, parts of his front were obviously at cracking point. The Fifth Army was worn out, and, though for a moment the 3rd, 18th, and 19th Corps had found a sort of line, they were too weak to stand on it for long.

The flower of the German forces, the 1st and 2nd Guard Divisions, and the 5th and 6th Brandenburgers, were advancing against them. The 7th Corps was in desperate straits west of the Tortille, and was barely in touch with the right of the Third Army. *There* lay the worst danger, and any moment might bring news of a breach on a broad front. Giddy with lack of sleep, grey with fatigue, tortured by the ceaseless bombardment, summoned at almost every hour to repel attacks on flank and rear, the British troops had shown a fortitude beyond all human praise. But wars are fought with body as well as with spirit, and the body was breaking.

On Sunday morning, 24th March, the mist was as thick as ever. The battle of that day had two main features—a fight for the Somme crossings, and an effort to fill the breach between the Third and Fifth Armies. On the left of the Third Army there was little movement, and the serious pressure was all south of the Bapaume-Cambrai road. On the right of the Fifth Army, where the French had now two infantry divisions and one cavalry division in line, supported however by little artillery, the 20th and 36th British Divisions were forced back from Cugny and Eaucourt to the neighbourhood of Guiscard. This withdrawal, which was most difficult owing to the presence of the enemy on their flanks, was made possible by the brilliant work of the 6th Cavalry Brigade. The French just north of the Oise were gradually pressed behind Chauny, and in the evening, were withdrawn to the ridge above Crepigny, whence our line ran north-west, covering Guiscard and Libermont.

The 18th and 19th Corps battled all day for the Somme crossings. The enemy extended a gap at Ham, pressing back the 61st Division in a south-westerly direction towards the Libermont Canal. Here our gunners did wonderful work, often not limbering up and retiring till all our infantry had passed through them. Farther north a gap at Pargny was widened, so that the left flank of the 20th (Light) Division was in the air. The enemy reached Morchain, and the 20th withdrew to the canal. Beyond the gap the 8th Division, under Major-General

Heneker, the first British reserves to arrive in support, made a stout resistance on the river line.

Early in the morning the Germans had crossed at St. Christ and Bethencourt, but at these points had been held. The left of the 8th Division stood firm during the day; but its right, owing to the pressure from Pargny, had to be retired west of Morchain. The dry weather had seriously weakened the barrier of the Somme. It was now fordable at almost any point, and the undergrowth of the valley provided excellent cover for the German advance.

In all this confused and difficult fighting the work of the artillery and the cavalry was not less brilliant than that of the infantry divisions. In the 3rd Corps area especially, troops of the 2nd and 3rd Cavalry Divisions, mounted and dismounted covered every section of the retreat. So vital was the need of mounted troops that several Yeomanry regiments, which had recently been dismounted were hastily provided with horses. Without such assistance, in the words of the official dispatch:

> The enemy could scarcely have been prevented from breaking through the long and thinly held front of broken and wooded ground before the French reinforcements had had time to arrive.

By the evening the Somme line between Epenancourt and the Péronne bend was still held by us Péronne had fallen, and from there to north of the Bapaume-Cambrai road was fought the most critical action of the day. At dawn the Germans had reached Bus, Léchelle, and Le Mesnil, and during the morning they were in Sailly, Rancourt, and Cléry. This thrust compelled the evacuation of Bertincourt; but north of that village, though Mory fell, the Guards, under Major-General Geoffrey Feilding, and the 3rd and 31st Divisions managed to maintain a substantial front. Barastre and Rocquigny were held by the 17th and 47th Divisions till late in the afternoon, but the exposure of their right flank forced them to fall back in the evening.

For the breach between the two armies at the bend of the Somme was widening. Early in the afternoon the enemy entered Combles, and pressed over the high ground at Morval towards Lesboeufs. The left division of the Fifth Army, the 9th, struggled desperately just north of the river. Its South African Brigade at Marrières Wood, north of Cléry, repeated its exploit of two years before at Delville. It held the wood till 4.30 p.m., when its ammunition was gone and only 100

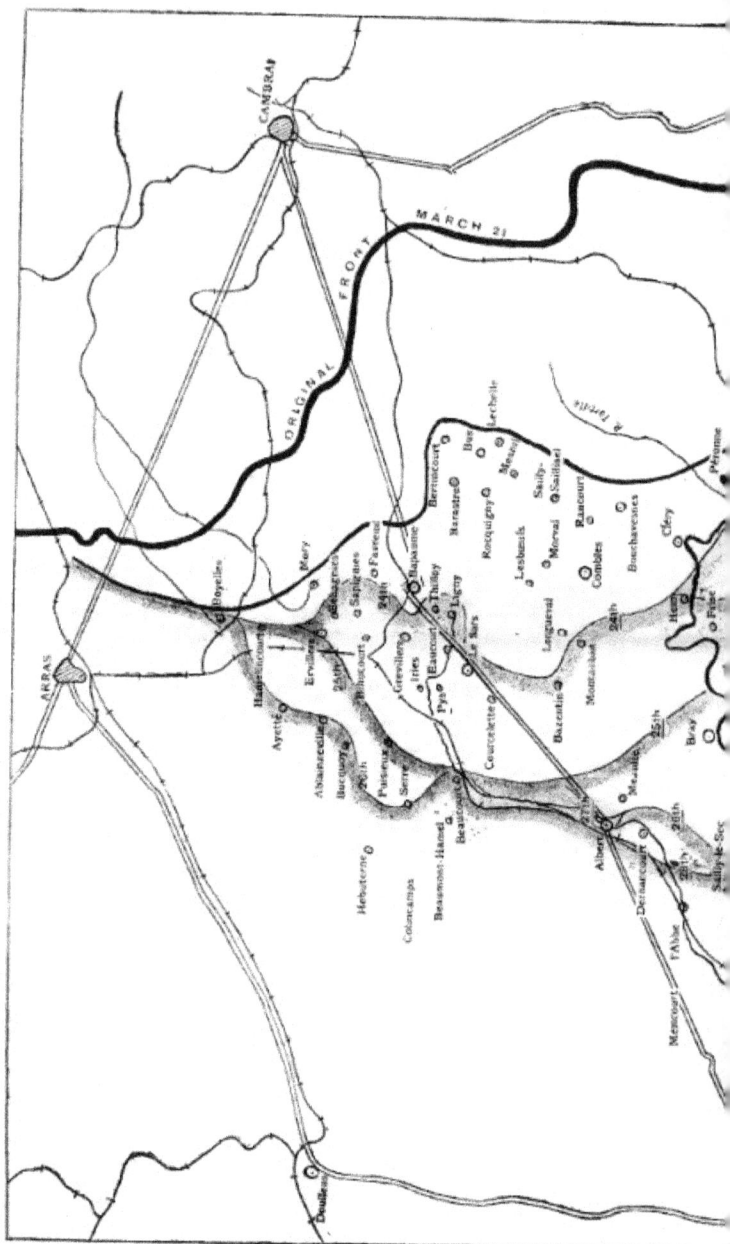

The Second Battle of the Somme: 2nd Phase, March 24-28.—The German advance across the Somme.
(The shaded lines show the Allied front at the close of each day, March 24th, 25th, 26th, 27th, 28th.)

men remained unwounded.

There was no other course than for the right and centre of the Third Army to make a comprehensive withdrawal. The 4th and 5th Corps were ordered to fall back to the line Bazentin-Le Sars-Grévillers-Ervillers. It was a task of supreme difficulty, for the enemy, working round their right flank, was already between them and their new positions, and it was made possible only by the heroic work of the machine gunners of the 63rd (Royal Naval) Division. The left of the Fifth Army was in worse case, for the remnants of the 9th and 21st Divisions were being pushed rapidly along the north bank of the Somme behind Cléry. At this moment the 35th Division, under Major-General Franks, which had arrived at Bray-sur-Somme, and various composite battalions scraped up in the Albert area, came to their relief, while the 1st Cavalry Division reached Montauban from the south. This enabled a line to be defended from the river at Hem through Trônes Wood to Longueval.

But the position at nightfall was very grave. The enemy had driven a deep and broad wedge into the centre of the British front. While the 19th Corps was still on the Somme south of Péronne, the 7th Corps was six miles farther west, and the 5th Corps had swung back precariously to conform. When the dark fell the line of the latter was Bazentin-High Wood-Eaucourt l'Abbaye-Ligny Thilloy. Bapaume had gone the way of Péronne, and we were well to the west of the front won in the First Battle of the Somme. Farther north, Harper's 4th Corps lay between La Barque and Ervillers. It was all a bad emergency line without prepared fortifications. Moreover, the two armies were not properly in touch, nor were the 4th and 5th Corps, nor were the divisions themselves. There were many gaps which, during the thick night, the enemy was diligently exploring.

Some adjustment of command was necessary, and Congreve's 7th Corps, now north of the Somme, was put under Byng. When the morning of Monday the 25th dawned, it became clear that the main German effort would be made between Ervillers and the river at Hem. During the night there had been strong assaults on the left of this front about Sapignies and Behagnies, and shortly after dawn an attack between Favreuil and Ervillers was repulsed. The 42nd Division, under Major-General Solly-Flood, retook Sapignies, and the stand of the 2nd Division at Ligny-Thilloy saved the situation during the morning.

But at noon the attack was renewed in great force, and the right of the 4th Corps, which had lost touch with the 5th Corps, was slowly bent back west of Grévillers and Bihucourt. Just north of the Somme the 7th Corps, though its left flank was in the air, succeeded in holding its ground in spite of the advance of five German divisions. But in the 5th Corps zone between Montauban and Ervillers it soon became clear that the front was crumbling. In spite of a most gallant stand by the 63rd Naval Division, under Major-General Lawrie, the various units, which were out of touch with each other, began to straggle back towards the Ancre. In the afternoon the enemy was in Courcelette, and pressing on to Pys and Irles, thereby turning the flank of the 4th Corps. At Beaucourt some of our men were actually west of the stream.

Orders were accordingly issued to take up the Ancre line. The right wing of the Third Army, now the 7th Corps, fell back to positions between Bray and Albert, just covering the latter place; the 5th Corps held the river bank from Albert to Beaumont Hamel; the 4th Corps withdrew to the line Bucquoy-Ablainzevelle, linking up with Haldane's 6th Corps at Boyelles. This left a gap between Beaumont Hamel and Serre, which promised trouble for the next day. Reinforcements, however, were now reaching the Third Army area, and the German thrust was weakening, partly from the fatigue of the divisions of attack and partly from the difficulties of transport over the old Somme battle-ground.

Meanwhile the rapid retreat of the Third Army had fatally compromised the situation beyond the Somme. Everywhere the line of the river south of Péronne had gone, all reserves had been drawn into the fight, and in the area of the 19th and 18th Corps there was no hope of immediate succour. Each hour our front grew longer and the weariness of our men greater. In the 3rd Corps area, however, the French were arriving. Guiscard had fallen during the night, and early on the morning of the 25th a strong attack developed against the Allied position on the spurs east of Noyon.

The French and British batteries north of the Oise Canal were withdrawn by 1 p.m. south of Appilly, with the help of dismounted troops of the Canadian Cavalry Brigade. All afternoon there was bitter fighting there, and by the evening the 18th Division had retaken the village of Baboeuf. But the Germans, pressing south-west from Guiscard, entered Noyon before the dark fell, and this compelled all our front east of the town to retire south of the Oise. During the night the withdrawal was successfully effected. The French were now appearing in such strength that it became possible to take the remnants of the 3rd Corps out of the line and send them north to help the Fifth Army.

That army, now consisting only of two corps, was all day in desperate straits. At Licourt there was a gap between the 18th and 19th Corps, which grew wider during the day. The enemy entered Nesle, and forced the 18th Corps back to the south bank of the Ingon River and west of the Libermont Canal, while the right of the 19th Corps was pressed back towards Chaulnes behind the blazing ruins of Marchélepot. The left wing up till midday was holding the east bank of the canal between Villers Carbonnel and Barleux, but this had now become an impossible salient.

Accordingly, during the evening, the 19th Corps was brought back to the line Hattencourt-Estrées-Frise, under cover of a counter-attack south of Biaches by the 39th Division. The gap between the two corps west of Nesle was ever broadening, and early in the night the Germans had reached Liancourt Wood, when a brigade of the 20th Division, brought up from the south and now reduced to 450 rifles, made a brilliant stand, and enabled the rest of the division to fall back towards Roye.

That evening the British front was disposed in a series of overlapping salients. The French in the old 3rd Corps area were farthest east; then the 18th and 19th Corps stood out in a long projection from Liancourt to Frise; while north of the Somme, in a still wider salient, the right wing of the Third Army rested on the Ancre. The enemy seemed to have every prospect of separating the British and French forces about Roye, the Fifth and Third Armies on the Somme, and the 5th and 4th Corps at Serre.

The moment was far too solemn for half measures. A divided command could not defend the long, lean front of the Allies against the organised might of Germany, directed by a single brain toward a single purpose. Hitherto we had only toyed with the problem. Versailles was a useful step, but no advisory council could provide the cure for disunion. One strong hand must be on the helm, and one only. It is fair to say that the opposition to a *generalissimo* had not come from one government alone; all the Allied Governments and staffs had fought shy of it. The British Prime Minister, while an enthusiastic advocate of Versailles, had stopped far short of the final step, and even the French Army chiefs were doubtful. But now the iron compulsion of fate had broken down the barriers.

On Sunday, the 24th, Lord Milner had arrived in Paris; and on

Retreat during the Spring Offensive

Monday he and M. Clemenceau and Sir Henry Wilson met Sir Douglas Haig and General Pétain at Doullens. That conference, held amid the confusion of retreat, marked in a real sense the turning-point of the war. The proposal for a supreme commander-in-chief, strongly urged by Clemenceau and Milner, was accepted by Pétain and welcomed by Haig. For the post there could be only one choice. Foch was by universal consent the master mind among the Allied generals. He was the most learned and scientific soldier in Europe, and had shown his greatness in the field at the Marne and First Ypres. For long his genius had been hampered, partly by professional jealousies, partly by the exponents of that political game which he whole-heartedly despised.

Not since November 1914 can it be said that he had been used as his qualities deserved. His guiding hand had been present at the Battle of the Somme; but during the first half of 1917 he had suffered from the confused relations between the army and the politicians. The Versailles Council had brought him again to the front; but he was born for greater things than mere staff work. Now the Allies in their extremity turned with one accord to the slight, grizzled, deep-eyed man of sixty-six, who during a laborious lifetime had made himself a finished master of war. Next day, Tuesday, the 26th, it was announced that Foch had assumed supreme control of the forces in the West. This narrative will record how nobly the new Constable of France fulfilled his trust.

The general-in-chief had been found; but on that Tuesday morning it looked as if presently he might have no armies to command. The situation just south of the Somme was all but desperate. Unless reserves could be found it seemed certain that the gossamer line of the 19th Corps must break. It must fall back still farther; and, if help did not come, the way to Amiens was open. On the 25th Gough had begun to collect a motley force, made up of stragglers, details returning to units, the personnel of a machine-gun school, army troops, tunnelling companies, and Canadian and American engineers; and on the 26th, under the command of Major-General Grant, the Chief Engineer of the Fifth Army, they prepared the old line of the Amiens defences from Mézières by Marcelcave to the Somme at Hamel.

Later, Brigadier-General Sandeman Carey, an officer of field artillery returning from leave, was put in charge, and commanded the detachment throughout the subsequent fighting. But the credit of the inception and organisation of the force belonged to Gough and the Fifth Army staff. These were the sole reserves available for this most vital section, and, since the 19th Corps could not be expected to hold any new enemy advance, orders were given to withdraw slowly from the Hattencourt-Frise line to the position Le Quesnoy-Rosières-Proyart, and to link up with the Third Army at Bray.

The Fifth Army was now fighting entirely on virgin soil, which no enemy had trod since the Western front was first established. The Third Army, in one part at least, was in the same case. During the morning of Tuesday, the 26th, the enemy poured through the gap between Beaumont Hamel and Puisieux, and occupied Colincamps with machine guns. These were silenced, however, by the field artillery of the 2nd Division, which galloped into action and engaged them with open sights. In the afternoon the New Zealand Division, under Major-General Sir A. H. Russell, which had just come up, retook Colincamps, and on their left a brigade of the 4th Australians, under Major-General Sinclair-Maclagan, filled the breach between Hebuterne and Bucquoy, thereby protecting the right flank of the 4th Corps. At Colincamps there appeared for the first time a weapon which was destined to play a great part in subsequent battles—the light British "whippet" tank.

Our front north of Albert was now more or less stable. On the right of the battle-ground we had to face a strong German thrust west and south-west from Nesle. The intention of the enemy was to divide the British and French forces, and by the speedy capture of Montdidier to prevent the detraining of the French reserves. The 18th Corps was now west and north of Rove, and from Hattencourt up to the Amiens-St. Quentin road the 19th Corps was being gradually driven back by repeated assaults. It was the strangest fighting. Both sides were utterly tired, and attacks and counter-attacks were carried out at a slow walk. Men fell down helpless from fatigue, and both sides took unwounded prisoners, who were simply paralyzed with weariness. This withdrawal, combined with the retreat of the French south-west of Roye, left a breach in the front, into which were flung the 36th and 30th Divisions, who had been taken out to rest on the previous day.

The Germans reached Erches, and, though their flank was turned, the 36th (Ulster) Division at Andechy managed to hold out till the afternoon of the next day, thereby compelling the enemy to check the speed of his advance. It was a matter of the most urgent need to stave him off from Montdidier as long as possible. Farther north, at Le Quesnoy, a hundred officers and men of the 20th Division, detailed to cover the withdrawal, kept the Germans at bay until six in the evening; only eleven survivors returned from this new Thermopylae.

At nightfall the gap had been partially closed, and touch had been found with the French, the line south of the Somme now running from Proyart by way of Rouvroy to Guerbigny. Von Hutier was now some five miles from Montdidier. The situation was still most anxious; but one thing had happened to disquiet the German High Command. Their front of assault was being narrowed. Fayolle's thrust from the south-west had shepherded the enemy north by west from the heights of Noyon. He no longer had the Oise to protect his left wing, and, when he reached Montdidier, he would have an exposed flank of some twenty miles.

But the British centre on the Somme was in evil case. In the opening stage of the retreat the Fifth Army had embarrassed the Third; it was now the turn of the Third Army to put the left of the Fifth in dire jeopardy. The 7th Corps, on Byng's right, had taken up the Bray-Albert line by the morning of the 26th, and that day, at Meaulte, the 9th Division had beaten off many attacks. But the local commander misunderstood Byng's plan. He thought that the Bray-Albert line was only a temporary halting place, and that it was his business to retire to the Ancre.

Accordingly, during the afternoon he fell back, and had gone too far before the Army Staff realised what had happened. The result was that that evening the 7th Corps rested on the Somme at Sailly-le-Sec, while the 19th Corps across the river were at Proyart, five miles farther east. This uncovered the flank of the Fifth Army, and gave the enemy the chance to cross and take it in rear. An emergency force of 350 men with Lewis guns and armoured cars was detailed to watch the fords.

The result of this blunder appeared early on Wednesday, the 27th. From 8.30 a.m. onwards the enemy attacked everywhere south of the Somme, and all day the British and the French toiled desperately to delay his progress to Montdidier, and to defend a line which would keep Amiens from bombardment. In the south von Hutier captured Lassigny and its heights. Farther north he took Davenescourt, and entered Montdidier. From Arvillers to Rosières the 20th, 30th, and 24th Divisions held their ground during the day, and the 8th Division defended Rosières against all attacks. Thence to the river, however, there was all but a disaster. The enemy crossed the Somme between Chipilly and Cerisy, and so turned our position at Proyart.

Heavily attacked in front also, the 19th Corps fell back, leaving

BRITISH TROOPS AT ROSIÈRES

Proyart, Framerville, and Morcourt in German hands. The enemy tried to push south in its rear, and troops of the 1st Cavalry Division were brought across the river from the Third Army to occupy Bouzencourt. Battalions of the 50th and the 8th Divisions (the latter also now engaged at Rosières) made a gallant stand southwest of Proyart, and the 66th Division counter-attacked at Framerville. The position at nightfall was that our front ran from Rosières east and north of Harbonnières, and then north-west to Bouzencourt. But it could not stand for long, for the enemy was still filtering across the river in the ill-omened gap.

North of the Somme that day the situation was better. During the night of the 26th-27th the enemy had entered Albert, and had won a footing in Aveluy Wood across the Ancre. During the 27th, however, he failed to increase his hold west of the stream, and was unable to debouch from Albert, where we held the line of the railway embankment. From midday onward, he attacked the 4th Corps between Bucquoy and Hamelincourt, and gained possession of Ablainzevelle and Ayette, but the 62nd Division, under Major-General Braithwaite, the 42nd, and the Guards maintained the rest of the front intact. Except on its right wing, the Third Army was now in a position of fair security, but it was aware that presently the storm would break on the Arras pivot.

On the morning of Thursday, the 28th, there began that stage in the battle in which the immediate enemy objective was the capture of Amiens. The Germans, as in 1870, delivered their main attack along the high ground to the south-west, split into shallow valleys by the streams of the Doms, the Avre, and the Luce, which with the Somme and the Ancre make up the Five Rivers of Picardy. It was difficult ground for the defence, for the streams in this dry spring were no barrier, and the narrows between the Luce and the Avre were a trap which might well be fatal to a weak army.

Ten miles west of the Avre ran the great Calais-Paris railway, the main route for the lateral communications of the Allies. Beyond it there was nothing but a single line till Beauvais was reached. If the enemy won the heights beyond the Avre he could at once put the trunk railway out of use. It had already been crippled by nightly German bombing raids; but guns west of Moreuil would make it wholly untenable. The same advance would bring the enemy within twelve miles of the centre of Amiens. If von Hutier could cut the line before the French reinforcements detrained, he would have a clear road to the city. It was true this his plan had partially miscarried. He had hoped to divide the British and French forces when he had still the Oise to guard his flank, and every day that success tarried made his situation more risky. But there was still time for a complete break through, if only he cut the Paris line before it could be used to bring up any serious reserves.

The capture of Amiens would follow, and the thin curtain of the British would be torn like tissue paper. But he must make haste, for his army had marched thirty-eight miles from their starting-point, were short of food and munitions, and a long way ahead of their heavy guns. The position was too like the days before the Marne to be quite free from disquiet; but, on the other hand, the French had then been retiring on their base, and now their retreat was in an eccentric direction.

The 28th was a critical day everywhere from Arras to the Oise. Let us look first at the much-harassed centre. During the night enemy bands worked southward from Cerisy and Morcourt, took Warfusée-Abancourt and Bayonvillers, and got astride the Amiens-St. Quentin road. This compelled the 19th Corps to swing back, pivoting on its right, to the line Vrély-Marcelcave, where the force which we may call "Carey's Detachment," with the 1st Cavalry Division in close support, continued the front to the river. It was presently clear that a more comprehensive retirement was necessary, for the position of the 18th Corps in the narrow salient between the Luce and the Avre could not be maintained. The Germans were attacking hard at Marcelcave; they were in Guillaucourt and pressing southward; and they had turned our right flank by the capture of Contoire.

The 61st Division, brought up in motor buses from the south, attempted to relieve the pressure by a counter-attack at Warfusée-Abancourt, but failed to stem the tide. Accordingly, we fell back through the 20th Division, which held the line Mézières-Démuin, and at nightfall were everywhere on the line of the old Amiens defences.

That day marked the end of the stand of the Fifth Army. The divisions which had suffered most were drawn out and sent to the Abbeville area to refit. Its commander, Sir Hubert Gough, was directed to supervise the construction of new defence lines in the rear, and the force between the Somme and the French was rechristened the Fourth Army, and put under the command of General Sir Henry Rawlinson and the old Fourth Army staff. The British line was once again wholly in the charge of Sir Douglas Haig. The new army, when constituted,

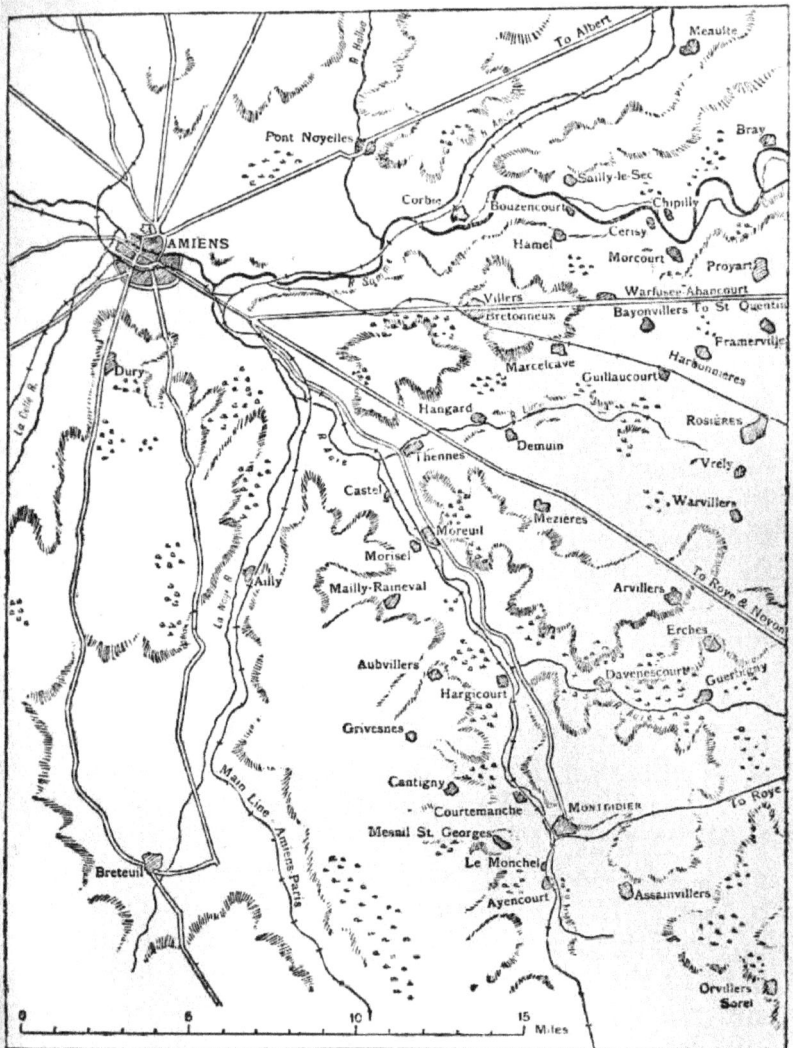

The Positions held for the Defence of Amiens and the Paris Railway.

held only the short line from the Somme to the Luce, and to begin with was composed of Carey's Detachment, some cavalry, and the few divisions which had come up during the battle.

Meantime Fayolle was hard pressed, and on his front various British units were also engaged. The day began with the line running from Warvillers by Arvillers to just west of Montdidier. It was steadily forced back to the Avre and the Doms; but south of Montdidier a counter-attack stayed the enemy progress and retook the villages of Courtemanche, Mesnil St. Georges, and Assainvillers, which had been lost. Farther north the French were driven out of Démuin and Moreuil. Between Montdidier and the Oise, at Pont l'Evêque, they counter-attacked successfully, driving the enemy back two miles on a front of six. So far, von Hutier had failed to get within range of the Paris railway, and the French reserves were coming up. Foch was busy collecting from his whole front a mass of manoeuvre, and the first fruits of his work appeared that day when a French Colonial Division came into line west of Montdidier. It was a proof to the enemy that his days of grace were fast vanishing.

He had another proof at the northern end of the battle-ground. Between seven and eight o'clock on the morning of the 28th Otto von Below hurled his weight on Arras. His guns had been brought up, and the attack originally staged for the 23rd was now delivered. The front of assault was across the valley of the Scarpe from the neighbourhood of Gavrelle to as far south as Puisieux. Its immediate object, as we learned from captured documents, was to recover Arras and the Vimy Ridge, and its larger purpose was to free the German armies from a front now growing too narrow for their comfort.

Von Below had three fresh divisions north of the Scarpe, besides the two in line; against Arras he had four divisions; while southward towards Serre no less than eleven divisions were disposed for the attack. The British forces were the 13th Corps north of the Scarpe, under Lieutenant-General Sir H. de Lisle, on the right of Horne's First Army; and from Arras to Bucquoy, Lieutenant-General Sir Charles Fergusson's 17th Corps and Lieutenant-General Sir Aylmer Haldane's 6th Corps.

The morning was fine, and the enemy had not his old advantage of fog. The advance was made after a short but very fierce bombardment, and was met by our guns firing under perfect conditions of weather. Indeed, before zero hour we had broken up with our artillery the masses assembling on Greenland Hill. Everywhere the enemy attacked

51

LIEUTENANT–GENERAL SIR HUBERT GOUGH
Commander of the Fifth Army on the Somme

with the greatest resolution, in some places in six lines shoulder to shoulder, offering superb targets for our gunners. The weight of the shock carried him through gaps in our outpost line, but he was firmly held long before he reached the battle zone, while the outpost garrisons turned their machine guns and caught him in rear.

North of the Scarpe the 4th Division, under Major-General Matheson, and the 56th (London) Division, under Major-General Dudgeon, and, south of the river, the 3rd Division and the 15th (Scottish) Division, under Major-General Reed, repelled the enemy—the two latter divisions fighting on the very ground where they had won renown at the Battle of Arras the year before. After midday the Germans began a new bombardment, and late in the afternoon attacked again north of the Scarpe, but with no better result. At the end of the day we had our battle zone untouched, and were able by counter-attacks to push out a new outpost line in front of it. The surviving garrisons of the old forward zone had for the most part fought their way back through the enemy to our lines.

Otto von Below's great effort was a complete and disastrous failure, and the spasmodic attacks on the rest of the Third Army front were no better fated. The Guards, the 31st, the 42nd, the 62nd, and the 4th Australian Divisions beat off all attacks from Boiry to Bucquoy. Only on the extreme right had we yielded a little ground, falling back south of Dernancourt to the line Méricourt-Sailly-le-Sec. The German check at Arras marked the end of the main battle so far as concerned the front north of the river. For a week and more there were local encounters, but Byng was now out of danger.

South of the Somme, however, things were still critical. On the morning of Friday, 29th March, the new Fourth Army had achieved some semblance of a line; but it was still desperately weak in men. Its immediate problem was to disengage its weary units, and the only reinforcements available were some of the divisions of the 3rd Corps, which had had only the scantiest period of rest. That was one danger; the other and the greater was the furious pressure on the French, for the enemy was beginning to put his chief weight into the attack between Moreuil and Noyon, where his communications were easier than in the devastated Somme battlefield, and it was still doubtful whether sufficient reserves for Fayolle would arrive in time.

On the 29th the Germans attacked from Démuin southward, and the French were driven out of Mézières, though in the Montdidier region they were able to retain the villages which they had recaptured

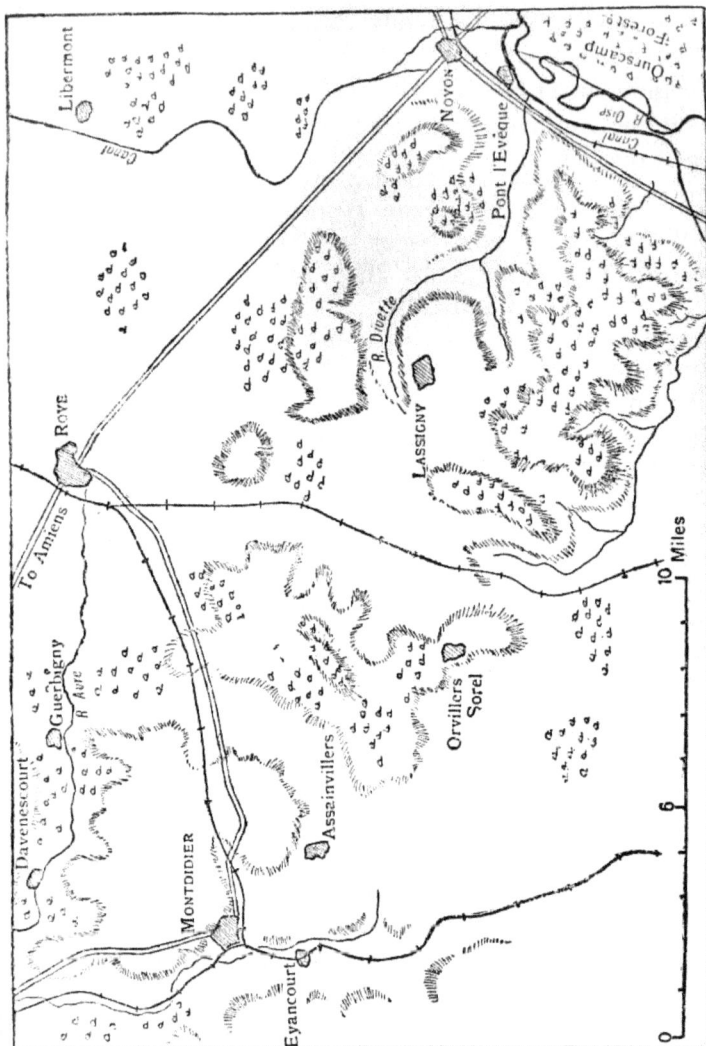

The Montdidier-Noyon Front and the Lassigny Heights.

on the previous day. During the night the Germans won Moreuil Wood, which we retook on the morning of the 30th; we lost Démuin, but later in the day recaptured it and Moreuil village. It was confused fighting, for the British were inextricably mixed up with the French, and the British cavalry have never been seen to finer advantage. The 1st, 2nd, and 3rd Cavalry Divisions and the Canadian Cavalry Brigade, together with the 66th, the 20th, and 50th Divisions, and the 3rd Australian Division, under Major-General Sir John Monash, though they had to yield ground, established a line from the Luce northward. South of that stream the front was still in a state of flux. The enemy won the ridge west of the Avre at Aubvillers, Cantigny, and Mesnil St. Georges, and retook Monchel and Ayencourt. Towards Lassigny the French stood firm, and even made some progress.

On Easter Sunday, the last day of March, the situation was grave, for the French reserves were still slow in coming. During the morning the Germans attacked between the Luce and the Avre, and captured Hangard, from which they were presently ejected. Farther south the Allies were driven back to the railway station at Moreuil; but a fine attack by the 8th Division enabled us to recapture the wood north-east of the town. On the heights of the Avre the French retook Grivesnes, and, south of Montdidier, they re-entered Monchel and Assainvillers. That day saw the end of the worst anxiety, for Fayolle had been strongly reinforced. On the 1st of April the British 8th Division and troops of the 2nd Cavalry Division won back some of the high ground north of Moreuil, and that evening the British forces there were relieved, the French taking over the front as far north as the village of Thennes, on the Luce.

Then for two days came a lull. On the 4th of April von Hutier made a last attempt to break through at the junction of the two armies. On the British front south of the Somme, from the river to Hangard, the assault was made at 7 a.m., and succeeded in driving back the left, (no longer Carey's Detachment, which had been relieved on 31st March), of the Fourth Army west of Hamel and Vaire Wood, which lay south-west of the village. From the Arras-St. Quentin road to the Luce the right wing stood firm. The pressure on the French, however, compelled it in the afternoon to withdraw a little in Hangard Wood.

Fayolle had to face a determined thrust by fifteen divisions, which virtually drove him out of the angle between the Luce and the Avre, and pressed him back to the west of the latter river behind the high ground on which stood the hamlets of Castel, Morisel, and Mailly-Raineval. Farther south his front held, and repulsed all attacks at Grivesnes. The Germans were now within a couple of miles of the Paris railway; but its importance was less great, for the French reserves had come into line. The British resistance on that day was highly creditable, and the dense masses of the enemy offered them the chance of a wholesale destruction. Most notable was the work of the gunners of the 3rd Australian Division north of the Somme, who from beyond the river protected our left flank at Hamel, and engaged the enemy over open sights.

On Friday, 5th April, the attack was renewed on the southern front, and for a moment, too, the battle flared up north of the Somme. Here the Germans advanced with ten divisions between Bucquoy and Dernancourt, but though they gained a little ground at these two places and at Beaumont Hamel, our line was never seriously shaken. Indeed, their losses were so utterly out of proportion to their gains that the day may be reckoned as an enemy defeat. South of the Somme he had no better fortune. There was severe righting around Hangard; but the Germans failed to advance anywhere, and on the ridge west of the Avre the French made considerable gains. On the southern front of the long salient, between Montdidier and Noyon, they advanced their line north of Orvillers Sorel and of Mont Renaud.

On Saturday, the 6th, enemy attacks south-west of Montdidier and in front of Noyon at Mont Renaud were repulsed; but it became necessary for the French to withdraw their troops from the ground they still retained on the right bank of the Oise. They retired across the river south of Chauny to the line Normezière-Pierremande. Two days later the extreme right of the battle-front fell back under strong enemy pressure to the Ailette.

The Second Battle of the Somme was at an end. The Allied front had been established, and the road to Amiens was for the moment closed, though the enemy held a position on the high ground west of the Avre and on the plateau east of Villers Bretonneux, from which, when he was ready, he could renew the attack. For the present he had exhausted his strength in the Somme area, and had thrown into the battle many weak divisions which had been already engaged. He had increased, too, the length of his front by thirty-five miles. The German High Command was now planning to achieve its main purpose by a blow in another quarter.

The Allied nations had faced the peril with an admirable calmness and courage. There was little recrimination, no hint of panic, and a

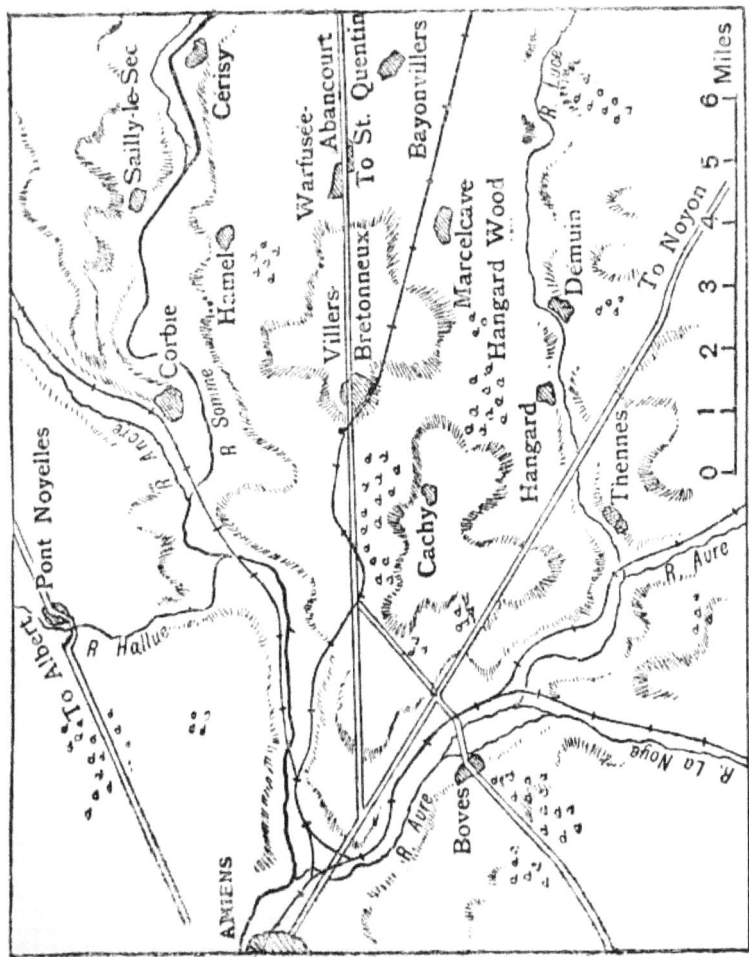

Villers-Bretonneux and the Ground between the Somme, Avre, and Luce.

very general drawing together of classes and a girding of loins to meet any demand which the future might bring. America increased her recruiting, and strained every nerve to quicken the dispatch of troops, so that she might soon stand in line with her Allies. France, unshaken by a menace which struck at her very heart, showed that quiet and almost prosaic resolution to win or perish which two years before had inspired her troops at Verdun.

In Britain the threats of industrial strikes disappeared as if by magic. The workers forewent their Easter holiday of their own accord in order to make up by an increased output for our lost guns and stores. It seemed as if the good spirit of 1914 had been reborn, when men spoke not of rights or interests, but of what service they might be privileged to give to their country. In January Sir Auckland Geddes had introduced his new man-power proposals; but by the end of March they seemed comically insufficient. On Wednesday, 10th April, by a majority of 223, the House of Commons passed a Bill raising the limit of military age to fifty, and giving the Government power to abolish the ordinary exemptions, and to extend conscription to Ireland. Two divisions and other units were transferred from Palestine to France, and a contingent from Salonica. Moreover, the old doctrine of the necessity of keeping a certain force inside our shores to protect them from invasion was summarily abandoned, and within a month from the 21st of March 355,000 men were sent across the Channel.

We may pause to consider this first stage in the great struggle, the first battle in the last German offensive. From the enemy point of view, it represented a qualified success. The Allied front was for the moment re-established, but it was deplorably weakened; and the Germans, though their losses were more than twice those of the Allies, had now a total superiority of some thirty divisions in the West, and a fresh mass of manoeuvre of at least twenty-five divisions. Ludendorff had not realised his full conception, but he had still the power to win if he had the skill. The first bout was over; but there were others to come, and the Allies were a long way from safety. The gate to Amiens had been shut, but the next blow might shatter it.

One thing was already clear—the splendour of the Allied performance. The fight had begun with an attack by sixty-four German divisions on thirty-two British. By the end of March seventy-three German divisions had engaged thirty-seven British. By 9th April the total British force in action had grown to forty-six divisions of infantry and three of cavalry, and against them more than eighty German divisions had been launched. The disparity was in reality far greater than two to one, for, owing to the German power of local concentration, in many parts of the field the odds had been three or four to one. After the second day we had no prepared lines on which to retire, and the rivers parallel to our front were useless from the drought. Again, and again a complete disaster was miraculously averted. Scratch forces, composed largely of non-combatants, held up storm-troops; cavalry did work that no cavalry had ever done before in the history of war; gunners broke every rule of the text-books. The retreat was in flat defiance of all precedent and law, and it succeeded only because of the stubborn valour of the British soldier.

★★★★★★

To realise the greatness of the battle it is instructive to compare it with Verdun. There, between February 21 and March 21, 1915, the French had to face 20½ German divisions. Between 21st March and 17th April, the British front was attacked by 102 and the French by 25 divisions.

★★★★★★

The cause of the defeat—for defeat it is, when two armies fall back thirty miles with heavy losses, and have the enemy's will imposed on them—was not any blunder of strategy on the part of the British High Command. Sir Douglas Haig, with the troops at his disposal, could not have done otherwise than he did. He could not keep adequate reserves at every point, and he was right not to thin the northern sections. It is true that there were no good alternate lines behind his front, but he had not had the time or the men to construct them. From no fault of his his third defensive zone was a farce, and the Péronne bridgehead too weak to be of service.

Nor can the situation be fairly blamed upon Pétain. He had good reason to believe that the Rheims area was threatened, and the enemy's exact intention could not be determined till the battle was joined. Finally, no fault can be found with the work of the commanders of the two armies or of the eight corps. It is hard to see how we could have continued to hold the Péronne bridgehead, and the failure to destroy the Somme bridges was due not to lack of foresight but to a trick of malevolent fortune, like the morning fogs and the dry marshes of the Somme and the Oise.

The one patent blunder in the whole battle, the premature withdrawal from the Bray-Albert line on 26th March, was such a misunderstanding as must happen in any great struggle. As for Sir Hubert

MEN WHO FELL COVERING THE RETREAT OF THE ARMY AT ALBERT
DURING THE HUN OFFENSIVE AT ALBERT IN 1918

Gough, who suffered most in repute, there was no single flaw in his conduct of the retirement. On the contrary, it was due to him and his staff that Carey's Detachment held the gap, and his courage and cheerfulness never failed him. The fight of the Fifth Army against incredible odds will remain one of the most glorious chapters in the history of British arms.

The cause of the defeat was simply that a long front had been imposed upon Sir Douglas Haig, and that he had not been given sufficient men wherewith to hold it. No doubt the British Staff underestimated the danger of the coming attack owing to their ignorance of the new German tactics; but they had never ceased to plead for more levies from home. The decision to extend to the Oise was not theirs, but that of the two governments. There were troops to spare in Britain, as the first weeks of the battle showed; and, beyond doubt, had these troops been available before the 21st of March the German thrust would have been parried at the start. It is a futile business to apportion blame amid the infinite accidents of war; but it is very certain that whatever discredit attached to the retreat from St. Quentin it did not fall upon the British soldier.

CHAPTER 2

The Battle of the Lys

Ludendorff, brought to a standstill on the Somme, was bound to cast about for a diversion. He was uneasy about the exposed left flank of his new salient, the point of which was Montdidier; and he could not permit the battle to decline into a stalemate, and so lose the initiative. His main purpose was unchanged, but he sought to achieve it by a new method. He would attack the British elsewhere, in a terrain where they were notoriously weak, and compel Foch to use up his reserves in defending it. Then, when our mass of manoeuvre had shrunk, he would strike again at the weakened door of Amiens.

This new effort could not have the *élan* and fury of the first. He could not again key up his troops to that mood of assured victory in which they had named the 21st of March "Michael's Day" and looked for the enemy's destruction within a week. Eighteen days had now gone, and the Allied line still held. A second enterprise must be a fresh effort, without the aid of any momentum carried over from the first.

But on Ludendorff's plan it was to be a strictly subsidiary operation, designed to prepare the way for his main task on the Somme. He proposed to allot only nine divisions for the initial stroke, and to choose a battle-ground where even a moderate force might obtain surprising results.

That battle-ground was the area just north of the La Bassée Canal. The German Staff were aware that it had already been thinned to supply ten divisions for the fighting in the south. It was at the moment weakly held, largely by troops exhausted in the Somme battle. Sir Douglas Haig had drawn from it, because the section from La Bassée to the Scarpe seemed to be more vital to the enemy's purpose, and because in the north it would be possible to give ground and retire behind certain inundated areas without putting the whole front in

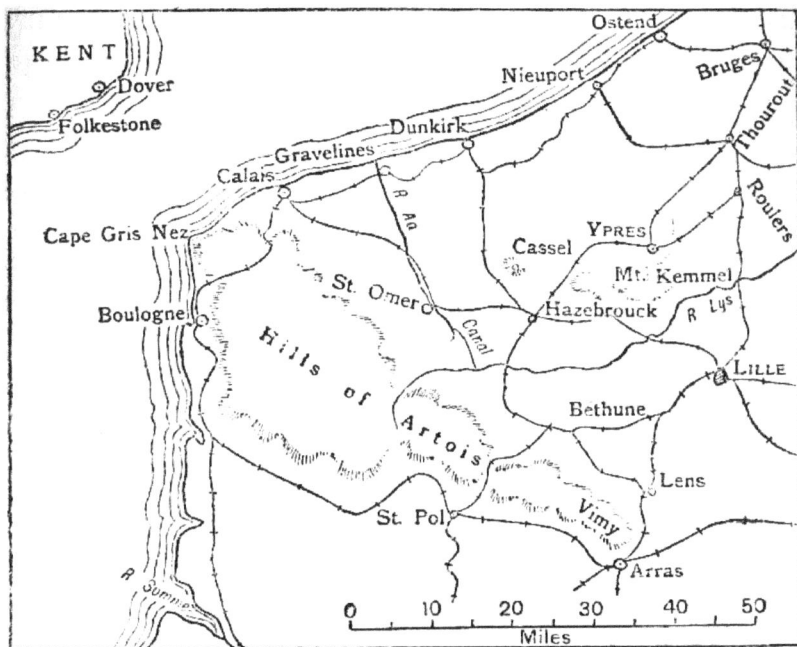

Sketch showing the main railway communications of the Ypres
front with the Channel ports; Hazebrouck junction; and the
alternative defence line of the river Aa to Arras.

such peril as would attend a retreat from Vimy.

But that northern section had many attractions for German eyes. It was far enough from the Amiens battle to put a heavy strain upon the Allied power of reinforcement. The Germans had the great city of Lille as a screen for their assembly. Certain nodal points of communication, like Béthune and Hazebrouck, lay at no great distance behind the British front. Again, any advance there threatened the Channel ports, and might be expected to work havoc with the British morale.

The one difficulty was the marshy land criss-crossed by dykes and canals, but the dry spring had done much to harden its water-logged soil. For a short, sharp thrust, calculated to confuse the Allied plans and absorb the Allied reserves, the place was well chosen. Above all, the British communications were bad, and the German were all but perfect. From Ostend to Douai and Cambrai ran a great double lateral line, served by many feeders from the east, and from Lille there rayed out a network of auxiliary routes. Behind the British was only the railway from St. Pol by Béthune and Hazebrouck to Calais and Dunkirk, much of it only a single line, and some of it too near and most of it too remote from the front trenches.

Ludendorff prepared his attack on a limited scale. Though the original nine divisions must be reinforced later, there was no intention of being drawn into a major action. His aim was to push through between La Bassée and Armentières, capture Béthune, and form a defensive flank along the Aire-La Bassée Canal. Then he would direct his main pressure northwest, aiming at the capture of Hazebrouck and the ridge of hills north of Bailleul. This would utterly dislocate the whole British front towards the coast, and compel a general retirement west of Dunkirk and the floods of the River Aa.

The British would be forced to fight hard to meet the peril, which directly menaced Calais and Boulogne; and when Foch had flung his last fresh troops into the breach, the time would be ripe for the final thrust for Amiens and the sea. It was intended to be a battle for a sharply-defined, though ambitious, objective, and Ludendorff had assigned to it just as many divisions as he could spare without weakening his forces for the major operation to follow.

The battle-ground, where we had fought incessantly during the first two years of the campaign, had certain clearly-marked physical features. The River Lys, less than a hundred feet wide, and with muddy banks and bottom, flows between Merville and Armentières in a dead-fiat plain. On the north bank there are the Forest of Nieppe and

British Cyclist Battalion

the line of hills running east and west from north of Flétre to Kemmel and Wytschaete—obstacles to an enemy advance, but, once captured, strategic points which would dominate the land to the north and west. South of the stream flat and boggy meadows stretch for ten miles to the La Bassée Canal, with, on the east, the Aubers ridge which shelters Lille. Clearly, Béthune, a junction on the British lateral railway, must be captured as the first objective, for till that was done the left flank would not be secure for the drive north-westward across the Lys to Merville and Hazebrouck.

The German Army opposite this area was the VI., under General von Quast. Its right extended to the Lys, whence the IV. Army continued to the sea. The latter was under General Sixt von Armin, who had resisted so stoutly at Passchendaele the autumn before, and he had as his Chief of Staff General von Lossberg, one of the ablest of German tacticians. Both armies were part of the group of the Crown Prince Rupprecht of Bavaria. The immediate reserves were not large, but they could be speedily supplemented from Ludendorff's mass of manoeuvre in the back areas.

The British front from the sea to Arras was held by the Second Army, under Sir Herbert Plumer, and the First Army, under Sir Henry Horne—the boundary between the two being the stream of the Lys. It will be remembered that as a result of the Third Battle of Ypres our line lay east of the Passchendaele heights, just west of Gheluvelt, and thence to the Lys, a mile or two west of Warneton, covering the Wytschaete-Messines ridge. It crossed the Lys two miles east of Armentières, and then fell back sharply to the west, just covering Neuve Chapelle and Festubert, till it reached the La Bassée Canal east of the slight rise at Givenchy.

The front north of the Lys was strongly placed, though the Passchendaele salient might prove a source of weakness; but on the south of the stream it had no natural defences save the dykes and runlets, though the ruins of the many farms and cottages gave it numerous strong points. The 2nd Corps, under Lieutenant-General Sir C. W. Jacob, held the Passchendaele area, with, on its right, the 22nd Corps, under Lieutenant-General Sir A. J. Godley. Just north of the Lys, covering the Wytschaete ridge, was the 9th Corps, under Lieutenant-General Sir A. Hamilton Gordon. On the left of the First Army were the 15th Corps, (on the second day of the battle the 15th Corps was transferred to the Second Army), under Lieutenant-General Sir J. P. Du Cane, and the 11th Corps, under Lieutenant-General Sir R. C. Haking. Beyond

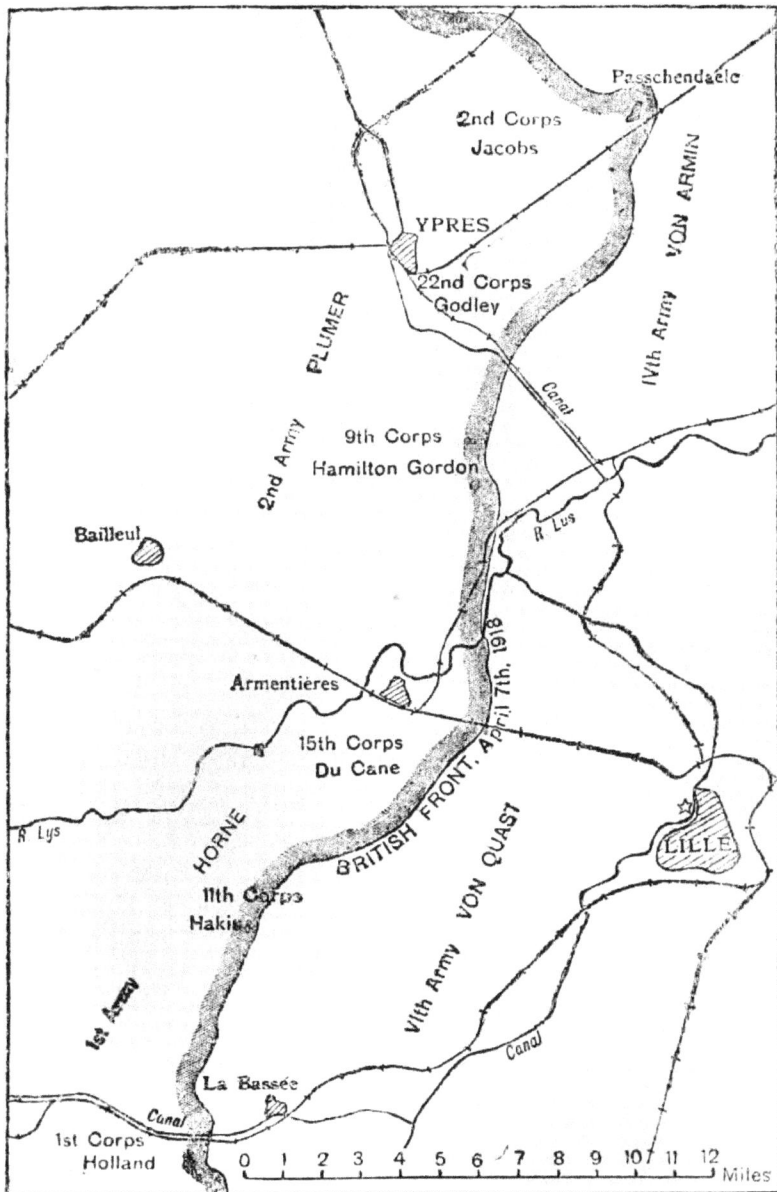

2nd Corps
Jacobs

Passchendaele

VIth Army VON ARMIN

YPRES

22nd Corps
Godley

PLUMER

2nd Army

9th Corps
Hamilton Gordon

Canal

R Lys

Bailleul

Armentières

15th Corps
Du Cane

BRITISH FRONT, April 7th, 1918

HORNE

R Lys

11th Corps
Haki...

VIth Army VON QUAST

LILLE

1st Army

Canal

La Bassée

Canal

1st Corps
Holland

0 1 2 3 4 5 6 7 8 9 10 11 12
Miles

The Opposing Armies north and south of the River Lys.

the La Bassée Canal lay the 1st Corps, under Lieutenant-General Sir Arthur Holland. The three corps directly threatened between Messines and La Bassée had seven divisions in line—from left to right, the 9th, 19th, 25th, 34th, 40th, 2nd Portuguese, and 55th.

The British front in this area on 7th April was in the unstable condition which attends readjustment. The two Portuguese divisions had been during the whole winter in a bad section, and needed rest, and it had been arranged that their relief should be completed by the morning of 10th April. But on the 7th only one of the Portuguese divisions had been withdrawn.

Of the seven British divisions, all but the 55th had been gravely weakened in the retreat from St. Quentin, and the 9th especially had gone through some of the severest fighting of the battle. In support there were the 51st and 50th Divisions, but both of these had suffered the same ordeal, and were very tired. It should be remembered that, out of the fifty-eight divisions which represented Sir Douglas Haig's total strength, forty-six had already been engaged in the southern battle. The commander-in-chief, who was aware that the enemy contemplated a stroke north of La Bassée, was also aware of its purpose. He knew that the enemy's main force was still concentrated east of Amiens, and he did not dare further to weaken that front. He had no alternative but to await an attack in the north with a line held by depleted divisions.

Sunday, the 7th April, was a mild spring day, with a thick fog in the morning hours. It passed quietly, but late in the evening an intense bombardment with gas shells began along the front between Lens and Armentières. The latter town had been consistently shelled by the Germans since the beginning of the year, and was no longer used by our troops. The gas bombardment continued during the 8th, and at 4 a.m. on the morning of Tuesday, the 9th, a furious preparation began, in which gas was mingled with high explosives. At about 7 a.m. the full weight of the German infantry assault fell upon the 15th and 11th Corps. The first to break was the 2nd Portuguese Division, which, stale from long inaction and indifferently led, was driven in at the first thrust. The flank of the 40th Division was turned, and the enemy streamed through the gap. The left of the 55th (West Lancashire) Division, under Major-General Jeudwine, was also turned.

The confusion of the fog and the gas made it hard for those behind to know what was happening; but the 51st and 50th Divisions were at once moved up behind Richebourg St. Vaast and Laventie, and cavalry

55TH DIVISION GAS CASUALTIES 10TH APRIL, 1918

and cyclists were sent forward to cover their deployment. By 10.15 a.m. the enemy was more than a mile in rear of the right battalion of the 40th Division, and that division was gradually forced back to a line facing south from Bois Grenier by Fleurbaix to the Lys at Sailly.

The whole centre had gone, though gallant machine-gun posts continued to resist long after the Germans had swept by them. The 55th Division had swung back in the same way, and formed a defensive flank facing north between Festubert and Le Touret. From Le Touret to the Lys was the gap which the 50th and 51st Divisions were labouring to stop; but the enemy progress had been so swift that we were forced out of all our prepared defences before we had the time to man them.

The events of that mad day were so tangled that it is hard to present them in a clear narrative. Let us take the centre first. The 1st King Edward's Horse and the 11th Cyclist Battalion managed to hold on for a time in Lacouture and Vieille Chapelle, and so enabled the 50th and 51st Divisions to take up position from Le Touret to Estaires along the east bank of the Lawe River. During the afternoon they were slowly forced towards the river crossings, and in the evening the Germans passed both streams at Estaires and Pont Riqueul, but were driven back again. When dark fell we still held the bridgeheads as far east as Sailly. In the north of the new salient the 40th Division had had a feverish day.

Before noon the enemy reached the Lys below Estaires, and intervened between it and the 50th Division. This compelled the right of the 40th early in the afternoon to withdraw across the river at Bac St. Maur. Its centre and left, assisted by troops of the 34th Division, continued to hold a very bad line from the Lys to our old front north of Bois Grenier; and the 12th Suffolks, though hopelessly outflanked, defended Fleurbaix till the evening. Meantime the Germans followed hard on our heels at Bac St. Maur. They crossed the river there about three o'clock in the afternoon, and pushed north as far as Croix du Bac. There the reserve brigade of the 25th Division held them for the moment, but could not prevent them from establishing a strong position north of the river.

Von Quast's advance had been cyclonic; but something was still wanting to complete his success. Unless he captured Béthune forthwith he would be cramped into too narrow a gate. But the 55th Division did not yield, though outnumbered by four to one. They had retired their left flank, but they still covered Béthune, and their right at

The German Offensive on the Lys (operations of April 9–17).

Givenchy stood like a rock. By noon the enemy had rushed the ruins; in the afternoon the Lancashire men had recovered them; in the evening they were again lost, and again in the night retaken.

This splendid defence was the determining event of the first stage of the battle. It was due, said the official dispatch:

> In great measure to the courage and determination displayed by our advanced posts. These held out with the utmost resolution though surrounded, pinning to the ground those parties of the enemy who had penetrated our defences, and preventing them from developing their attack. Among the many gallant deeds recorded of them, one instance is known of a machine gun which was kept in action although the German infantry had entered the rear compartment of the 'pill box' from which it was firing, the gun team holding up the enemy by revolver fire from the inner compartment.

All night there was intermittent fighting at the crossings of the Lawe and the Lys. Early on the morning of Wednesday, 10th April, after a heavy bombardment, the enemy attacked at Lestrem and Estaires. He won the farther bank at both places, but was driven back by counter-attacks. All day the 50th Division was in action, and the streets of Estaires saw bitter machinegun fighting. In the evening the town was lost, and the 50th Division retired to a position which had been hastily prepared to the north and west. East of Estaires the enemy enlarged the bridgehead he had won the night before, and forced the left of the 40th Division beyond Steenwerck—an advance of nearly four miles. He was broadening his salient by striking northward.

Meantime a new German Army had entered the battle. At 5.30 a.m. von Armin's infantry attacked north of the Lys from Frelinghien as far as Hill 60. The outposts of the 25th and 19th Divisions were driven in, and during the morning, under cover of the fog, the enemy filtered into our battle positions from Ploegsteert Wood to Messines, along the valleys of the Warnave and Douve streams. By noon he had taken Ploegsteert village and the southeast part of the wood, and had captured Messines, while farther north he had driven in our line as fax as Hollebeke, and was close on the crest of the Wytschaete ridge.

In the afternoon, however, the 9th (Scottish) Division brought him to a standstill. Its South African Brigade retook Messines, and during the evening cleared the Wytschaete ridge. This stand saved our northern flank, and gave us time to adjust our front to meet the grave situa-

Australian Troops

tion at Ploegsteert. Armentières was outflanked and clearly untenable, and during the afternoon the 34th Division, which held the place, retired to the left bank of the Lys, after destroying the bridges.

The situation on the Wednesday evening was, therefore, as follows. The German line ran from Hollebeke, east of Wytschaete, just east of Messines, through the south-east corner of Ploegsteert Wood, west of Ploegsteert village, south of Nieppe, north of Steenwerck, north and west of Estaires, east of Lestrem, east of the Lawe River, Le Touret, and Givenchy. It was a narrow front for a great advance, for the British pillars at Givenchy and the Messines ridge were still standing.

On Thursday, the 11th, von Quast and von Armin, with fresh reserves, attacked on the whole front. The 55th Division was unshaken, but in the centre the line of the Lawe stream was lost. The night before the enemy had won a footing on the western bank halfway between Locon and Lestrem, and during the day he was able to enlarge his holding and push out westward. This made impossible the position of the 50th Division north and west of Estaires, and during the afternoon they were driven back towards Merville.

The German masses, pressing on in close formation, had bulged out our front, and so lengthened the line to be held by the 50th. Gaps opened up through which the enemy pushed, and by 6 p.m. he was at Neuf Berquin, on the Estaires-Hazebrouck road, and, moving along the Lys, had entered Merville. Our front there was drawn back to the little stream of the Bourre just west of the town.

Farther east the 40th Division was forced well north of Steenwerck; but the 31st Division had arrived from the Somme, and, counter-attacking towards evening, recovered the villages of Le Verrier and La Becque. On their left the 34th Division was in serious danger. It was strongly attacked, and though it succeeded in holding Nieppe during the day, the pressure on the 25th Division from Ploegsteert left it in an untenable salient. That afternoon Messines was lost, but the 9th Division was still standing south of Hollebeke and on the Wytschaete ridge.

Plumer decided to rearrange his front, and early in the night he relinquished Nieppe, retiring to the neighbourhood of Pont d'Achelles. This involved the retirement of the 25th and 19th Divisions to a front about 1,000 yards east of Neuve Eglise and Wulverghem, and the abandonment of Hill 63. That night our front ran from Givenchy to Locon, west of Merville, west of Neuf Berquin, north of Steenwerck and Nieppe, east of Neuve Eglise and Wulverghem, west of Messines, and along the ridge just covering Wytschaete. The pillars still held.

Up to now the enemy had not used more than sixteen divisions. But on the morning of Friday, the 12th, he began to throw in his reserves at a furious pace. Elated by his unexpected success, he turned what was meant as a diversion into a major operation, and dreamed of Boulogne and Calais. It was Ludendorff's first blunder, and it was fatal. He used his mass of manoeuvre in an area where he had to begin *de novo*, and where he could not directly aid the great central thrust at Amiens. He lost the advantage of the cumulative blow, and abandoned the assets which he had won. If it succeeded, it would be a new plan, irrelevant to the first; if it failed, the first could only be resumed with impaired resources. Blindness seemed to have fallen for the moment on the German High Command—a blindness born of a too confident pride. It all but destroyed the British Army; but it saved the Allied front, and in the long run gave them the victory.

On Friday morning British reinforcements were arriving—the 3rd, 4th, 5th, 31st, 61st, and 1st Australian Divisions; but they could only gradually come into line, and we had still to face most critical days. Just before dawn the enemy broke through the left centre of the 51st Division near Pacaut, due south of Merville, and less than two miles from the La Bassée Canal. But for the brilliant work of our batteries, the Germans might have crossed the canal; and, as it was, they won a position on its eastern bank. The 3rd Division had now come up on the right of the 51st and the 61st Division on its left, and though both had been fighting for weeks south of Arras, they were able to steady the front between Locon and the Clarence River. At Merville itself, too, we held our ground; but the weight of the fresh German troops was felt in the pressure north of the Lys.

At 8 a.m. von Quast attacked on the front between the Estaires-Hazebrouck road and Steenwerck, and, in spite of gallant work by the 29th Division, under Major-General Cayley, which had come up in support, drove in our line at Doulieu and La Becque, and created an ugly gap south-west of Bailleul. This let through bodies of the enemy, who seized Merris and Outtersteene, north of the railway. The Germans were pushing direct for Hazebrouck, and were now close on Bailleul station. It was a grave moment; but in the evening any further advance was checked by a brigade of Major-General Pinney's 33rd Division, which, with a miscellaneous assortment of other troops, filled the breach. On the left of the British front there was no change during the day.

FIRING AT AIRCRAFT AT THE BATTLE OF LYS

The 49th (West Riding) Division, under Major-General Cameron, had come up on the right of the 34th, and these divisions and the 25th maintained the line south and south-east of Bailleul. The 19th and the 9th were still holding east of Wulverghem and Wytschaete. The result of the day had been that the enemy had curved out his front towards the north in a crescent, the maximum depth of which was about two miles.

Saturday, 13th April, saw a resolute continuance of the German attacks. These were aimed at the weakly-held gap in front of Bailleul, the first step towards Hazebrouck, and at the British positions at Neuve Eglise and Wulverghem, which were the key of Mont Kemmel. In the first area the 29th and 31st Divisions, both seriously depleted, held a front of 10,000 yards. Behind them the 1st Australian Division, under Major-General Sir H. B. Walker, was detraining, and it was imperative that the front should hold till it could appear in line. On the west of the gap the 4th Guards Brigade had arrived and taken over a front of 4,000 yards. Here the Germans launched their main assault, and in the foggy morning they were able to bring field guns up to point-blank range.

At first things went badly, and the village of Vieux Berquin fell. In the afternoon our line gave in parts, though outflanked garrisons continued to hold out to the end. For a moment it seemed as if the enemy had a clear path before him; but the resistance of the wearied troops had given the Australians time to organise positions east of the great Forest of Nieppe. By the evening they had taken over the section, and the gate of Hazebrouck was shut. The British endurance throughout this desperate day had been beyond praise. Sir Douglas Haig wrote:—

> No more brilliant exploit has taken place since the opening of the enemy's offensive, though gallant actions have been without number.

Meantime, in the second area the struggle was scarcely less bitter. Early on the Saturday morning the enemy forced his way into Neuve Eglise, but in the afternoon, he was driven out by troops of the 33rd and 49th Divisions, while the 34th and the rest of the 33rd were engaged between Méteren and La Crèche. In the evening the Germans won their way between La Crèche and Neuve Eglise, and so outflanked the left of the 34th Division. We could not continue on such a line, so during the night the 34th withdrew to the high ground called the Ravelsberg, between Bailleul and Neuve Eglise, without

GERMAN ASSAULT TROOPS

hindrance from the enemy. That night the Germans were again in Neuve Eglise, and after much confused fighting it passed finally into their hands on the following day.

The end of the week saw a slight stabilizing of the British front. The Germans had exhausted their first impetus, and, as had happened a fortnight before on the Somme, were pausing for breath. But the situation was still full of anxiety. The enemy had driven a great bulge into our line, which threatened two vital centres of our communications—Béthune, on the south, and Hazebrouck, on the north-west. He was on the edge, too, of the line of upland from Mont des Cats to Kemmel, which commanded all the northern plain toward the Channel. The French were sending troops, and we were hurrying up what we could spare; but with all our efforts we could not be otherwise than outnumbered, and, since the fight had become a major operation, we had to face continued drafts from the great German reserve.

On the 11th Sir Douglas Haig issued an order of the day in which he appealed to his men to endure to the last:

There is no other course open to us but to fight it out. Every position must be held to the last man; there must be no retirement. With our backs to the wall, and believing in the justice of our cause, each one of us must fight on to the end. The safety of our homes and the freedom of mankind depend alike upon the conduct of each one of us at this critical moment.

The British Commander-in-Chief was not addicted to rhetorical speech, and these grave words from one so silent had a profound effect upon the army and the nation. No less solemn was Lieutenant-General Sir Arthur Currie's charge to his troops before they entered the battle.

Looking back with pride on the unbroken record of your glorious achievements, asking you to realise that today the fate of the British Empire hangs in the balance, I place my trust in the Canadian Corps, knowing that where Canadians are engaged there can be no giving way. Under the orders of your devoted officers in the coming battle you will advance or fall where you stand facing the enemy.

To those who fall I say, 'You will not die, but step into immortality. Your mothers will not lament your fate, but will have been proud to have borne such sons. Your names will be revered for ever and ever by your grateful country, and God will take you unto Himself.'

Canadians, in this fateful hour I command you and I trust you to fight as you have ever fought, with all your strength, with all your determination, with all your tranquil courage. On many a hard-fought field of battle you have overcome this enemy. With God's help you shall achieve victory once more.

On Sunday, the 14th, the struggle continued at Neuve Eglise, which fell; at Bailleul and Merville, where our line was maintained; and east of Robecq, where we improved our position and took prisoners. Next morning the 19th Division repelled an attack at Wytschaete, and late in the afternoon the battle flared up south of Bailleul. Three fresh German divisions, including the Bavarian Alpine Corps, attacked our front on the Ravelsberg, and after heavy fighting seized the east end of the ridge and worked their way westward. At seven in the evening they had the whole height, and Bailleul was doomed. We fell back to a line between Méteren and Dranoutre, and at 9 p.m. the Germans entered the town.

Meantime, in order to delay any attack which, the enemy might make in the north, we had begun to evacuate the Ypres salient. By the morning of the 13th the Passchendaele ridge was held only by out-posts, and by the morning of the 16th the 2nd Corps had withdrawn approximately to the old position a mile east of the town from which the Third Battle of Ypres had started. Our front now ran along the Steenbeek River, and by the Westhoek ridge to Wytschaete. This gave us a strong position, and enabled us to economise men. The retreat was not disturbed; but on the morning of Tuesday, the 16th, our front at Wytschaete and Spanbroekmolen was attacked, with the result that the enemy captured both places, and forced us back to a line south of Lindenhoek.

That day, too, he secured a footing in Méteren. The first French troops had now arrived, and by a counter-attack that evening they regained Méteren, while the 9th Division temporarily reoccupied Wytschaete. But it was not for long, and by the morning of the 17th the enemy held both villages. This meant that the northern pillar of our defence had gone, for we were now everywhere off the ridge, and the time had come for von Armin to advance on Mont Kemmel.

We may pause to consider the nature of the phase into which the battle had now developed. The enemy had definitely set himself to se-cure a decision in this area, and his immediate aim was, by the capture

GERMAN COLUMN ADVANCING

of Béthune, Hazebrouck, and the Kemmel range, to drive Haig back to a front pivoting upon Arras, and running to the sea by St. Omer and the line of the River Aa. Such a front would have been strong so far as natural defences went, but it would have produced certain disagreeable consequences for the British Command.

Dunkirk would be in the enemy's hands, and he would be many miles nearer the Narrows of the Channel. He would be only some ten miles distant from Calais, and could render that port useless with his big guns. The British would have no good lateral communications except those passing along the coast. A new and awkward salient would be created at Arras, and the Vimy Ridge would probably become untenable. Finally, the British would be desperately circumscribed in the area left them to manoeuvre in, and any fresh German advance would mean the loss of the Channel ports.

To effect this design, Ludendorff had to secure certain immediate objectives. The first was Béthune; the second was the Kemmel range, which would give him Hazebrouck, for the direct advance on that town by way of Merville presented difficulties. There was a third objective, which, if attained, would give him all he desired. This was an advance north of the Ypres salient, which would turn the Kemmel range and drive the 2nd Corps and the Belgians in confusion through narrow necks of retreat with a great loss in men and guns. Five more divisions had arrived from Russia, giving the Germans a total of 204 in the West, as against 166 of the Allies.

It was true that 128 had been engaged in heavy fighting since 21st March, and that of these sixty had been employed twice and ten thrice. But Ludendorff had still twenty-two fresh divisions in reserve, and many of those which he had withdrawn under his system of *roulement* were now sufficiently rested to return to the line. It was all in flat defiance of his old plan, and was fatally mortgaging the resources for his future strategy; but that was small comfort to the British Army, now worn to a shadow by a month's struggle against preposterous odds.

The next two days were perhaps the most critical of the whole battle. The enemy had reached his greatest strength, and the British troops were not yet reinforced at any point within sight of security. On the morning of Wednesday, the 17th, von Armin launched his attack north of the Ypres salient against the Belgians astride the Ypres-Staden railway. On a front of 4,000 yards he used twenty-one battalions, drawn principally from the 58th Saxon, the 6th Bavarian, and the 2nd Naval Divisions—all troops of proved quality. It began at 8.30

a.m. without any preliminary bombardment, and at the first shock the Belgian line was pierced at one point, and bodies of the enemy pressed through towards Bixschoote. But the Belgian reinforcements struck in upon the right flank of the advance, drove it into marshy ground, and completely defeated it. Over 700 prisoners were taken, and some 2,000 Germans were killed—an exploit immensely to the credit of troops who had lived for long in a stagnant and difficult section, and perhaps the most successful counterstroke so far in the Lys battle.

The same morning von Armin's left assaulted the wooded slopes of Kemmel, for the possession of the Wytschaete ridge now gave him observation over all the country to the west. At the same time strong subsidiary attacks were made in the Méteren and Merris area. After an intense bombardment the German infantry advanced with great resolution from their new positions at Neuve Eglise and Wulverghem. They were repulsed at all points with heavy losses by the 34th, 49th, and 19th Divisions. At Méteren and Merris they fared no better, for the 33rd and the 1st Australian Divisions stood firm on that front. The first two of the German plans had been foiled.

But next day, Thursday, the 18th, came a more serious threat, this time on the southern flank of the salient towards Béthune. After a long bombardment, von Quast attacked on almost the whole front between Merville and Givenchy. The enemy in previous fighting had gained the eastern bank of the La Bassée Canal, at the point where it is crossed by the road from Hinges to Merville, and on the night of the 17th he took the village of Riez du Vinage. Between that point and Givenchy, he had six divisions of assault, and at the Hinges bridge he was massed to the extent of nine or ten bayonets to the yard.

His first attempt, made just at dawn, was to reach the canal bank on a broad front; but his troops were mown down by the fire of our batteries on the other side, directed by observation from the little mound of Bernenchon. In his second attempt he came down the Merville road, reached the canal, and launched his pontoons. But he never crossed. The fire of the 4th Division broke up his troops into something like a rout, and before the daylight had fully come the enterprise had failed utterly, with immense slaughter. It was for the Germans the most futile and costly incident of the battle.

At Robecq there was an attack by one division, easily repulsed by the 61st, and at Givenchy an attempt by no less than three. The latter was for the time a critical affair, and some of our advanced posts changed hands many times during the day. The pillar, however,

AUSTRALIAN TROOPS

stood firm, and by the evening the 1st Division, under Major-General Strickland, had recovered every yard of ground that had been lost. This action was the end of the first and principal phase of the battle, and so severely had the Germans suffered in the past two days that for nearly a week quiet reigned on our front.

We were able to improve our position by local counter-attacks at Festubert and between the Lawe and Clarence Rivers, and to relieve some of the divisions which had suffered most. The French had already come into line about Méteren and Spanbroekmolen, and by the morning of Sunday, the 21st, had taken over the whole section between these points, which was the front of assault against Mont Kemmel.

★★★★★★

Since 21st March the British Army had engaged alone 79 German divisions, the French alone 24, and 23 divisions had been engaged by both French and British. Of the British 79, 28 had been fought twice and 1 thrice; of the French 24, 4 had been fought twice; of the joint 23, 15 had been engaged twice and 1 thrice. The British had therefore had 109 fights with German divisions alone, and the French 28 alone. Taking all the engagements together, the British had had 149 and the French 68 fights with German divisions.

★★★★★★

There were signs about this time that Ludendorff's mind was growing anxious about his main offensive on the Somme. The attack on Villers Bretonneux on 23rd April, which we shall presently consider, was clearly meant as a preparation for the final movement on Amiens. The Allies had added to their total strength by bringing troops from Britain, from Italy, and from Egypt; but these did little more than replace the month's heavy wastage. Nine British divisions had been reduced to *cadres*, and the number of fighting divisions was only fifty-one. Foch had already used up part of his mass of manoeuvre, and the Germans had at the moment a numerical superiority of considerably over a quarter of a million men.

It was beyond doubt the part of wisdom for Ludendorff to break off the battle on the Lys and use his still formidable reserve to secure a decision in the main area. But it is a characteristic of strategical blunders that they compel their authors to pursue them to their last consequences, and make it impossible for them to retrace their steps. Ludendorff had dipped too deeply in the north to withdraw easily. He had incurred huge losses without gaining any real strategical objective, and he could not bring himself to write off these losses without another effort to pluck the fruit which was so near his grasp. Accordingly, he continued the northern fight, and struck again for Kemmel Hill.

Kemmel is the isolated eastern outlier of the range behind Bailleul. If the Germans secured it they would broaden their comfortless salient and win direct observation over the northern plain. They would make our front at Ypres, if not untenable, at least insecure, and they would prepare the way for an advance westward along the ridge to Hazebrouck. An attack at the moment had one special attraction for them, for in front of Kemmel was the junction of the British and French lines, which they regarded as the weakest spot in the front. The French, as we have seen, lay from Méteren to the Messines-Kemmel road, halfway between Kemmel and Wytschaete, with, on their left, the British 9th Corps.

On the morning of Thursday, 25th April, seventeen days since the battle began, the enemy violently bombarded the whole front from Méteren to the Ypres-Comines Canal. At 5 a.m. he attacked with nine divisions, five of which were fresh. His aim was to capture Kemmel by a direct assault on the French, and by a simultaneous attack upon the British right south of Wytschaete to turn their flank and separate the two forces. At first, he succeeded. At ten in the morning he had worked his way round the lower slopes, and taken Kemmel village and the hill itself, though isolated French troops still held out in both places. In the British area the 9th and 49th Divisions were heavily engaged west of Wytschaete.

Before midday the right of the 9th was driven back to Vierstraat, but we still retained the Grand Bois on the slopes north of Wytschaete village. In the afternoon the 21st Division, farther north, was also attacked, and by the evening the whole line in this area had been forced back to positions running from Hill 60 by Voormezeele, and north of Vierstraat to the hamlet of La Clytte, on the Poperinghe-Kemmel road, where we linked up with the French.

By next morning supports had arrived, and an attempt was made to recapture the lost ground. The 25th Division, along with French troops and elements of the 21st and 49th Divisions, re-entered Kemmel village, but found themselves unable to maintain it against flanking fire from the northern slopes of the hill. Then followed the second wave of the German assault. It failed to make ground owing to the gallant resistance of the 49th Division, under Major-General Black-

86

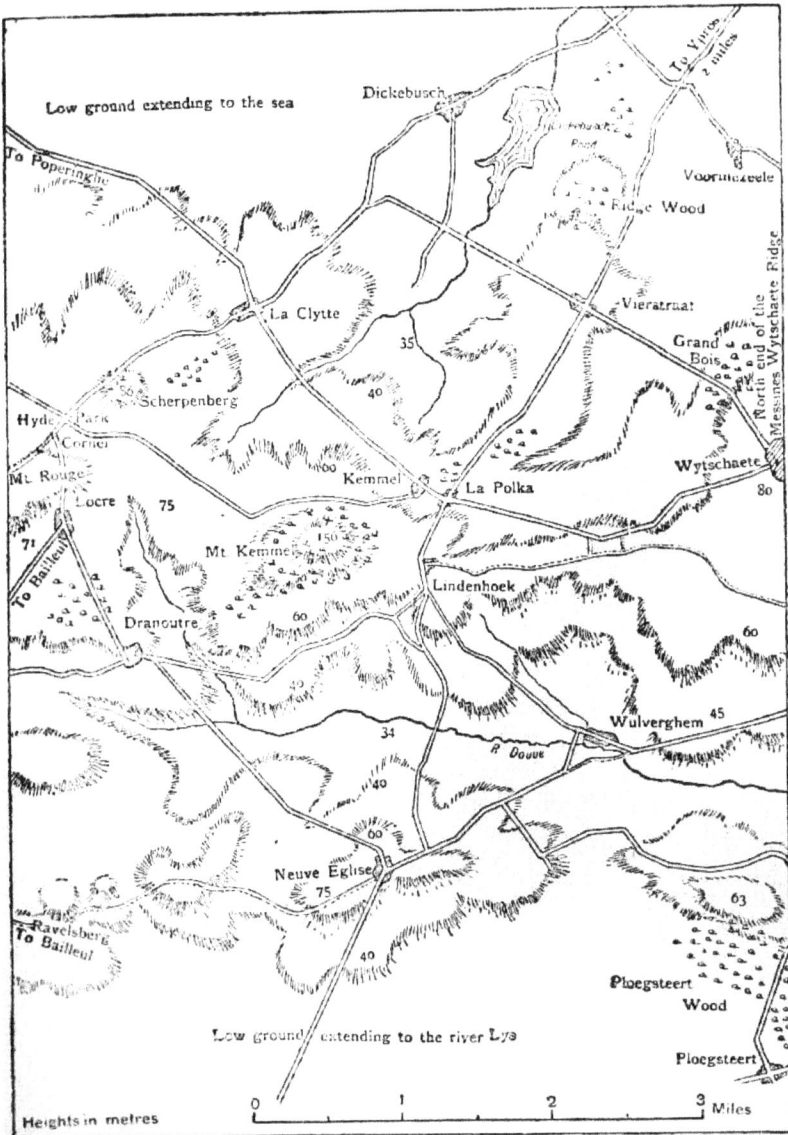

Low ground extending to the sea

Dickebusch

To Vimy 2 miles

To Poperinghe

Voormezeele

Ridge Wood

La Clytte

Vieratraat

35

Grand Bois

40

Scherpenberg

North end of the Messines Wytschaete Ridge

Hyde Park Corner

Wytschaete

Kemmel

80

Mt. Rouge

La Polka

Locre

75

Mt. Kemmel

150

71

To Bailleul

60

Lindenhoek

60

Dranoutre

Wulverghem

45

34

40

40

60

Neuve Eglise

63

75

To Ravelsberg

To Bailleul

40

Ploegsteert Wood

Low ground extending to the river Lys

Ploegsteert

Heights in metres

0   1   2   3 Miles

Scene of the Fighting about Mount Kemmel.

lock, and of the 21st, 30th, 39th, and 9th Divisions, all four of which had been fighting for five weeks without rest.

That afternoon the French recaptured Locre, on the saddle between Kemmel Hill and the heights to the west. Our line in that quarter now ran just below the eastern slopes of the Scherpenberg, east of Locre, and thence south of St. Jans Cappel to Méteren. The loss of Kemmel and the threat to Voormezeele made it necessary to adjust our front in the Ypres salient. Accordingly, that night we withdrew to a line running from Pilckem to Voormezeele by way of Wieltje and the west end of the Zillebeke lake.

In the afternoon of the 27th the Germans captured Voormezeele, but were driven out by a counter-attack early in the night. On the 28th the French were heavily in action around Locre, but there was no material change in the situation. On the morning of Monday, 29th April, after an intense bombardment, the enemy attacked the French and British positions from west of Dranoutre to Voormezeele. The Allied front at the moment ran around the eastern base of Mont Rouge, just covering Locre, across the low saddle of the range to the meadows in front of La Clytte, and thence by Voormezeele to the Ypres-Comines Canal.

The British right was in the neighbourhood of the cross-roads which we called Hyde Park Corner, on the saddle between the Scherpenberg and Mont Rouge. There lay the 25th Division as far as the little stream which runs from Kemmel to the Dickebusch lake. On its left was the 49th Division as far as Voormezeele, and beyond it the 21st Division to the canal. The enemy made three main assaults—first against the French, to carry Locre and Mont Rouge; the second at the junction of the French and the 25th Division, aimed at turning the Scherpenberg; and the third between the 49th and 21st Divisions, to turn the obstacle called Ridge Wood.

The infantry attack was launched at 5 a.m. in a dense mist by at least eleven divisions—six against the French, and five against the British. It was delivered in mass formation, the density being from six to eight bayonets to the yard. At first by its sheer weight it succeeded. The Germans entered Locre, and even reached Hyde Park Corner, which all but gave them their objective. Then came the French counterstroke, which completely checked them, and drove them back at points nearly a mile beyond the line from which they had started. On the British front no ground was gained at all.

The three divisions in line, with the assistance of troops of the 30th

German tank

and 39th Divisions, not only stood firm, but in some cases advanced to meet the oncoming Germans and drove them back with the bayonet. A second attack at 6 a.m. was equally disastrous. At the end of the day Locre remained in German hands, but it was retaken by the French the following morning. Farther north the Belgians had been attacked on the Ypres-Staden railway, but had repulsed the enemy with the same vigour that they had shown on the 17th. The result of this action was a complete and most costly German repulse. The enemy attacked with some 80,000 men, and his casualties were at least a quarter of his strength.

The fight of 29th April was the last episode in the Battle of the Lys. Thereafter there were only local actions. On 1st May the French made a slight advance north-east of Locre. On the night of 3rd May the British improved their position north-east of Hinges. On the 4th the enemy opened an intense bombardment between Méteren and Ypres, which, as we learned later, was intended as a preparation for a serious attack. But the weather interfered, and still more our counter-bombardment. On the 8th an attack between Voormezeele and La Clytte was easily repulsed.

On the night of 10th May, and on the 11th, the French gained ground in the Kemmel area, and on the night of the 12th we made a successful gas attack on the Lens-La Bassée front. On the 19th we straightened out a slight salient north-west of Merville. On the 27th the French between Locre and Voormezeele were attacked by four divisions, but the little ground they lost was recovered on the following morning. By that day the centre of gravity had moved from the Lys and the Somme to the Aisne.

It remains to record the events of these weeks in the Amiens area. During the Battle of the Lys we had had to face there only local attacks directed mainly at Hangard, where the Fourth Army linked up with the French. On the morning of 23rd April, however, the enemy attacked the Fourth Army with four divisions on the line between the Somme and the Ancre. His bombardment began at 3.30 a.m., and at 6.30, under cover of fog, the new German tanks broke through our line south-east of Villers Bretonneux. His aim was to secure the high ground between the Somme and the Luce as a base for a movement against Amiens. For the first time British and German tanks came into the conflict, and the honours were wholly with the former. Villers Bretonneux fell, but the advance was checked at the wood west of the village by a counter-attack of the 8th Division. South of the village

BRITISH WHIPPET TANK

our heavy tanks destroyed the enemy's tanks advancing on Cachy.

At 10 p.m. that night came the British counterattack, conducted by a brigade of the 18th Division and two brigades of the 4th and 5th Australians. That the counterstroke should have been so prompt showed the resource and audacity of the British Command. The Australians cut their way through thick belts of wire, and advanced with complete precision over country which had not been previously reconnoitred. At daybreak on the 24th Villers Bretonneux was all but surrounded, and during the morning troops of the 8th Division fought their way through its streets. That afternoon it was wholly in our hands, together with 1,000 prisoners.

At the same time seven of our "whippet" tanks, debouching from north of Cachy, attacked the enemy on the ridge between Villers Bretonneux and Hangard Wood. The ridge was held by machine-gun groups in shell-holes, while on the eastern slopes three German battalions were forming up in the open for attack. The "whippets" moved from shell-hole to shell-hole, destroying the machine-gun groups, and then proceeded to disperse the infantry. One was destroyed by shell fire; the others returned with a total casualty list of five. It was a wonderful performance, for the "whippets" left their base, three and a half miles from the seat of action, after 11 a.m., and were home before 3 p.m., having fought over a distance of ten miles. Twenty men with five casualties to themselves had inflicted 400 losses on the enemy, and completely broken up a German brigade. It was a triumphant proof of the value of the light tank in a counter-offensive.

This brilliant affair seemed to damp the enemy's ardour on the Somme. During May there was little to record. On the night of the 5th, and again on the night of the 7th, we advanced our line southwest of Morlancourt, between the Somme and the Ancre. On the 14th the enemy attacked the new front without success. Meantime, the French on the 9th had captured the park at Grivesnes, north-west of Montdidier, and on the 11th had repulsed an attack south-west of Mailly-Raineval. On the 14th they advanced south of Hailles, and secured a wood on the west bank of the Avre. On the 19th the 2nd Australians took Ville-sur-Ancre, and improved their front in the angle of the two rivers. The enemy's quiescence in May was more marked on the Amiens front than even in the north.

The Battle of the Lys was for the enemy a tactical success but a strategic failure. He achieved no one of his principal aims, and in the struggle, he weakened his chances of a future offensive by squandering

Whippet Tank

some of his best reserves. By the end of April, he had employed in that one northern area thirty-five fresh divisions and nine which had been already in action. These troops were the cream of his army, and could not be replaced. He had caused to the British front since 21st March something like a quarter of a million casualties, but his own losses were far greater. Moreover, an odd feature had appeared in the last stages of the Lys battle. The Germans seemed to have forgotten their tactics of infiltration, and to have fallen back upon their old methods of mass and shock.

The weakness of the new tactics was becoming clear. They could be used only with specially trained troops and with fresh troops; they put too great a strain upon wearied divisions and raw levies. Therefore, as the enemy's losses grew, his tactics would deteriorate in the same proportion. There were other signs of stress. The 1919 class had been long ago absorbed in the line, and there was evidence that the 1920 class, the last resource of Germany's manhood, was beginning to appear in the field depots.

Nevertheless, at the close of May the immediate strength of Germany was still far superior to that of the Allies. They had on their whole front 168 divisions, and the enemy had 208. He had a reserve of at least eighty divisions which he could use for a new blow. The Americans were arriving; but it would be two months yet before, by normal calculations, they could make any notable difference in the battle. Foch had expended much of his reserve, and the British Army, actively engaged for nine weeks, was very tired. A new blow was impending, but the exact terrain was hard to guess.

There were signs of a revival of the battle on the Lys. There was the continuing threat to Amiens. Much pontoon and bridging material had been brought to Flanders from Russia, and it looked as if another attempt might be made to turn the Allied flank on the Yser. From Italy, too, came news that the omens pointed to a great Austrian attack astride the Brenta, and it was reasonable to assume that Germany might assist in the operations. Lastly, there was the dangerous southern flank of the main salient, where an assault had been anticipated before 21st March.

Foch had no easy problem before him. With heroic parsimony he must nurse his scanty reserves, and at the same time be prepared to face at any moment a new assault in any one of four sections of his long front. The darkest clouds of March and April had dispersed; but the air was still heavy with doubt, and the issues of the battle were still uncertain. It is such a season that tries the nerve of a general far more highly than a fight against odds. The May days passed in a tense expectancy, and then, in the last week of the month, the doubt was resolved. For very early on the morning of the 27th the storm broke on the Chemin des Dames; by the evening the French gains in three great actions had vanished like smoke, and the enemy was across the Aisne. On the second day he was beyond the Vesle, and on the third his vanguard was looking down from the heights of the Tardenois on the waters of the Marne.

CHAPTER 3

Zeebrugge and Ostend

In the midst of the great struggle in Flanders, where the British Army was fighting desperately for breathing space, and daily the enemy crept nearer the Channel ports, there came suddenly good news from the sea. It had no immediate bearing upon the land war, but it was a pledge to an anxious people that they had not lost their ancient prowess on the waters. For long there had been a murmur abroad that the British Fleet was content with defensive achievements, and had forgotten its old spirit of attack. But a new man had appeared who had the Elizabethan tradition of inspired audacity. Sir Roger Keyes had been one of the most trusted of Sir Rosslyn Wemyss's lieutenants in the Dardanelles campaign, and, like his leader, he interpreted generously the limits of what was possible to the British sailor. His appointment, first to the Plans Department of the Admiralty, and then, in succession to Admiral Bacon, to the command of the Dover Patrol, augured well for a new phase of initiative and daring.

The events of the winter at sea had not been many. The loss of a convoy of eleven vessels in the North Sea on October 17, 1917, had been followed by the destruction on 11th December in the same waters of a convoy of fourteen. On the evening of 3rd November there was a brilliant little action in the Kattegat, where we sank a German auxiliary cruiser and ten patrol boats. On 17th November our light cruisers were in action in the Heligoland Bight, and two enemy ships were damaged.

On January 14, 1918, late in the evening, Yarmouth suffered her third bombardment from the sea. In the last week of that month the south end of the Dardanelles witnessed a curious affair. About 5.30 a.m. on Sunday, 20th January, the British destroyer *Lizard*, being at the moment off the north-east point of Imbros, discovered the German

96

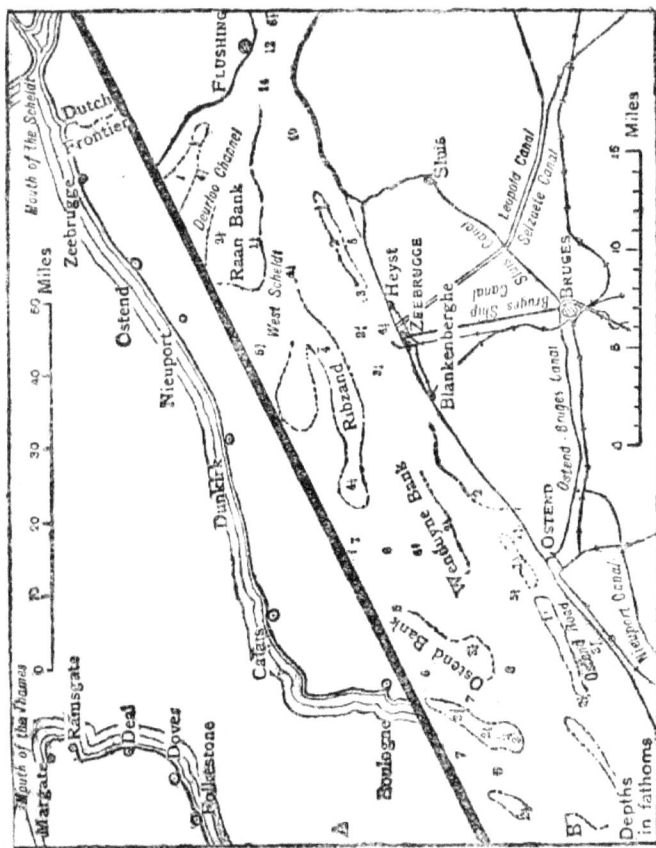

A. Ostend, Zeebrugge, and the North Sea Coast from Dover Straits to the Scheldt.

B. Sea Approaches and Canal Connections of Ostend and Zeebrugge.

cruiser *Breslau*, with the *Goeben* a mile astern, making for the harbour where British monitors were lying all unprepared. She engaged the enemy at a range of 11,000 yards, and came under heavy fire, so that she was unable to get within torpedoing distance.

Another destroyer, *Tigress*, came to her aid, and the two attempted to shield the monitors by smoke screens. But their efforts were in vain, and the monitors *Raglan* and *M*. 28 were speedily sunk, before the former could get her 14-inch American guns into action. The enemy then turned south, followed by *Lizard* and *Tigress*, and at 7 a.m. *Breslau* ran into a minefield, struck several mines, and promptly sank. Four Turkish destroyers appeared, accompanied by an old cruiser, and these *Lizard* and *Tigress* engaged and drove up the straits.

Goeben continued southward till she found the attentions of our aircraft unpleasant, when she put about to return. In the act she struck a mine, which made her settle down aft and gave her a list of some fifteen degrees. The Turkish destroyers returned to protect her, and she managed to creep inside the straits, followed by *Lizard* and *Tigress*, and assiduously bombed by British seaplanes. Her captain ran her ashore in the Narrows to the west of Nagara Point, where she lay for some days under the menace of our aircraft, till she was eventually tinkered up and refloated.

The opening of the German offensive on 21st March had been attended, as we have seen, with the bombardment of Dunkirk from the sea. The bombarding force was engaged by two British and three French destroyers, with apparently the loss of several enemy craft. Meantime, a plan had been maturing to get rid of the intolerable menace presented by the use of the Flanders ports as German bases. A year before Lord Jellicoe had declared his hope that the problem of the Belgian coast was not insoluble; it was now the business of Sir Roger Keyes to find the solution.

The strategical importance of closing up Zeebrugge and Ostend was patent. There nested the German destroyer flotillas which raided the Narrow Seas and occupied most of the time of the Dover Patrol. Our chief weapon against the U-boat was the destroyer, and the presence of German craft in these ports withdrew a large number of British destroyers from the anti-submarine campaign. Could Zeebrugge and Ostend be put out of action, the German naval base would be pushed back three hundred miles to Emden, and the East Coast ports would become the natural bases from which to deal with the attacks by enemy surface craft on the Channel. It would not cut off the main

Bird's-eye view of the successful British raid upon the German submarine base at Zeebrugge.
Note position of blocking cruisers and how the Daffodil held the Vindictive against the mole

bases of the U-boats, but it would release the forces of the Dover Patrol to hunt them down, and it would facilitate the construction of a new Channel mine barrage.

A plan had been under consideration since November 1917, and the advent of Sir Roger Keyes brought it rapidly to completion. Its purpose was to block the end of the Bruges Canal at Zeebrugge and the entrance of Ostend harbour—an operation such as in the Spanish-American War Lieutenant Hobson had attempted at Santiago. To understand the details, it is necessary to examine the topography of the two places.

Zeebrugge is not a port so much as the sea end of the Bruges Canal, and in the canal the enemy submarines found perfect harbourage. Its mouth is flanked by two short piers or sea walls with a lighthouse at the end of each, and half a mile up the canal are the lock gates. In those difficult seas the entrance would be soon blocked by silted sand unless some breakwater was constructed to protect it. So, a large mole had been built in a curve to the west of the channel—a mole about eighty yards wide and a mile long. At the land end, to allow for the flow of the tide, there were five hundred yards of viaduct on piles.

The Mole, as the vital defence of the harbour, had a normal garrison of a thousand men, and bristled with machine guns, while all the coast was studded with long-range heavy artillery. On the Mole were the railway station and many newly built sheds for military and naval stores. The Ostend harbour was less elaborate. It was also the mouth of a canal to Bruges, but there was no mole as a flank guard. The problem for Sir Roger Keyes in both cases was to sink ships inside the canal, so that, aided by the silt of the tides, they should block the entrance. It is no light task to clear an obstruction from a Channel port; about Christmas 1916 a rice-laden tramp sank in Boulogne harbour, and shut the place for a month. Could the operation be achieved the results were certain; but, in view of the strong defence, it seemed a desperate adventure, especially among the intricacies of Zeebrugge. As it turned out, Ostend was the more difficult problem, for the very complexity of its safeguards made Zeebrugge vulnerable.

The plan for Ostend was simply to get ships into the harbour and sink them far enough in to do the maximum of damage. It was a feat depending on secrecy and dash. At Zeebrugge the scheme was more elaborate. Three cruisers packed with concrete were to get as near the lock gates as possible before being sunk. To create a diversion, other vessels were to attack the Mole from its sea side, land men to engage

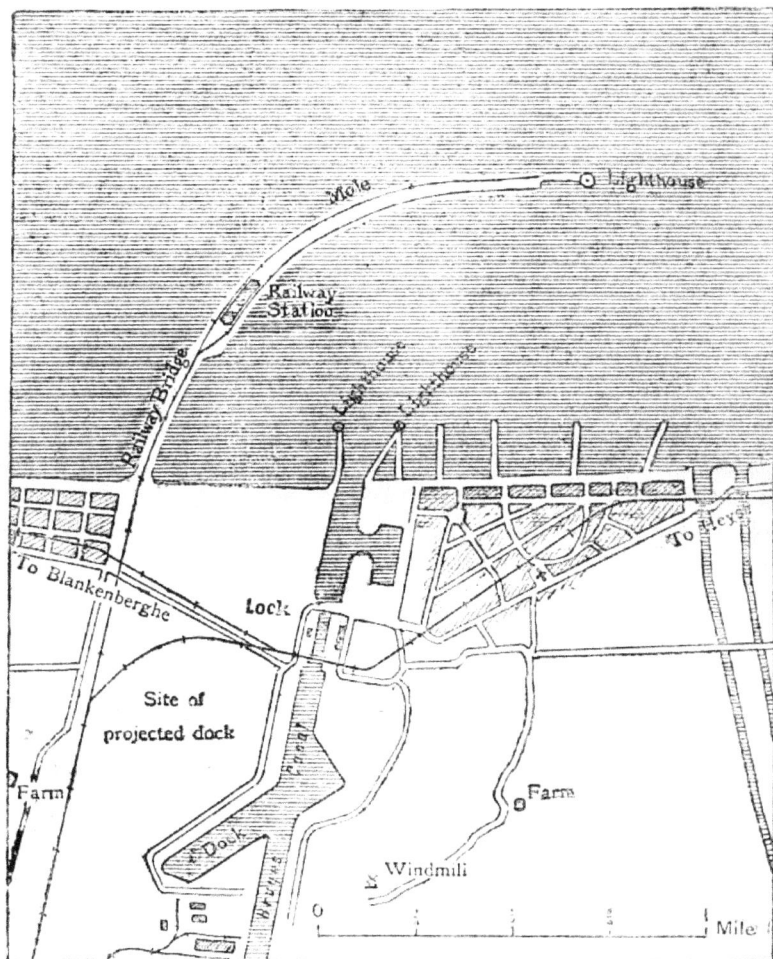

Zeebrugge.

the enemy garrison and prevent the guns there being used against the blockships. At the same time, by means of a submarine laden with explosives, it was proposed to blow up the viaduct, which would isolate the German garrison on the Mole. The Zeebrugge attack was, therefore, planned in three stages—the attack on the Mole, the simultaneous attack on the viaduct, and the later entry of the block-ships into the canal mouth.

★★★★★★

In the expedition to Ostend in 1798, under Captain H. R. Popham, R.N., troops were landed under General Eyre Coote to blow up the sluice-gates of the Bruges Canal. They succeeded in doing this, but could not re-embark through stress of weather, and were compelled to surrender.

★★★★★★

Twice Sir Roger Keyes's flotilla started, and twice it put back to port. It needed special weather conditions for success—an overcast sky, a drift of haze, a light wind, and a short sea. On Monday, 22nd April, the eve of St. George's Day, the omens were favourable, and in the late afternoon, three hours before sunset, the expedition started, timed to reach Zeebrugge by midnight. It was a singular Armada. There were five old cruisers to act as block-ships—*Intrepid, Iphigenia,* and *Thetis* for Zeebrugge, and *Brilliant* and *Sirius* for Ostend. A small cruiser, *Vindictive* (5,600 tons, with a broadside of six 6-inch guns), was designed for the attack on the Mole, assisted by two Liverpool ferryboats, *Daffodil* and *Iris.*

There were also a flotilla of monitors, motor launches, and fast coastal motor boats for special purposes. Admiral Tyrwhitt's destroyers from Harwich covered the operations from the north, and there were present light covering forces from the Dover Patrol. The operations were commanded by Sir Roger Keyes in the destroyer *Warwick,* and he had also with him the destroyers *North Star* and *Phoebe.* The men for the block-ships and the landing-parties were bluejackets and marines, picked from a great number who had volunteered for the work. They were armed as for a land battle, with grenades and flamethrowers as well as rifles and bayonets; *Vindictive* carried machine guns, Stokes mortars, and howitzers; and elaborate preparations had been made for the creation of an artificial fog to cover the attack.

It was a prodigious hazard to approach a hostile coast where navigation was difficult at the best of times, without lights, without knowledge of what new minefields the enemy might have laid, and at the mercy of a change in the weather which would expose the little fleet to every gun on the Flanders shore. There was only an hour and a half for the whole operation, for the shore batteries had a range of sixteen miles, and the return voyage must start at 1.30, to be out of danger before dawn. All went well on the outward voyage.

Presently *Sirius* and *Brilliant* changed course for Ostend, and the smokescreen, provided by the smaller craft, rolled landwards with the north-east wind ahead of the cruisers. Meantime the monitors and seaplanes had gone to work, bombarding the coast defences, as they had done often before. This device apparently deceived the enemy. He did not man the Mole, and his gunners retired to their bomb-proof shelters on shore, knowing well that in face of the smoke-screen they could not reply effectively to our fire. It was a case where an artillery "preparation" lulled instead of awakening the enemy's suspicions.

But fifteen minutes before *Vindictive* reached the Mole the wind changed to the south-west, and rolled back the smoke-screen so that the whole harbour was clear to our eyes and we to the enemy's. Instantly the darkness was made bright with star-shells and searchlights, and from the Mole and the shore an intense fire greeted our vessels. The action had begun, and Sir Roger Keyes signalled "St. George for England," to which *Vindictive* replied, "May we give the dragon's tail a damned good twist."

There was no time to be lost, and *Vindictive* , under Captain A. F. B. Carpenter, laid her nose against the concrete sea wall of the Mole. Her port side had been fitted with "brows"—light hinged drawbridges which could drop their ends on the wall. A sudden sea had risen, which made the operation difficult; so, after *Vindictive* had let go an anchor she signalled *Daffodil* to lie against her stern and keep it in position, while *Iris* went forward to make fast to the Mole ahead of her. All the time a tornado of fire was beating on the three vessels, and to land men under such conditions might well have seemed impossible. But the marines and bluejackets, under their gallant leaders, Colonel Elliot and Captain Halahan (both of whom fell), swarmed over the splintering gangways, and dropped on to the shell-swept wall.

★★★★★★

Lieutenant-Commander Hilton Young, who was present in *Vindictive*, has this grim recollection:—

> Coming round to a starboard battery I stumbled over something at the foot of one of the wooden ramps leading to the landing platform. As well as I could see in the

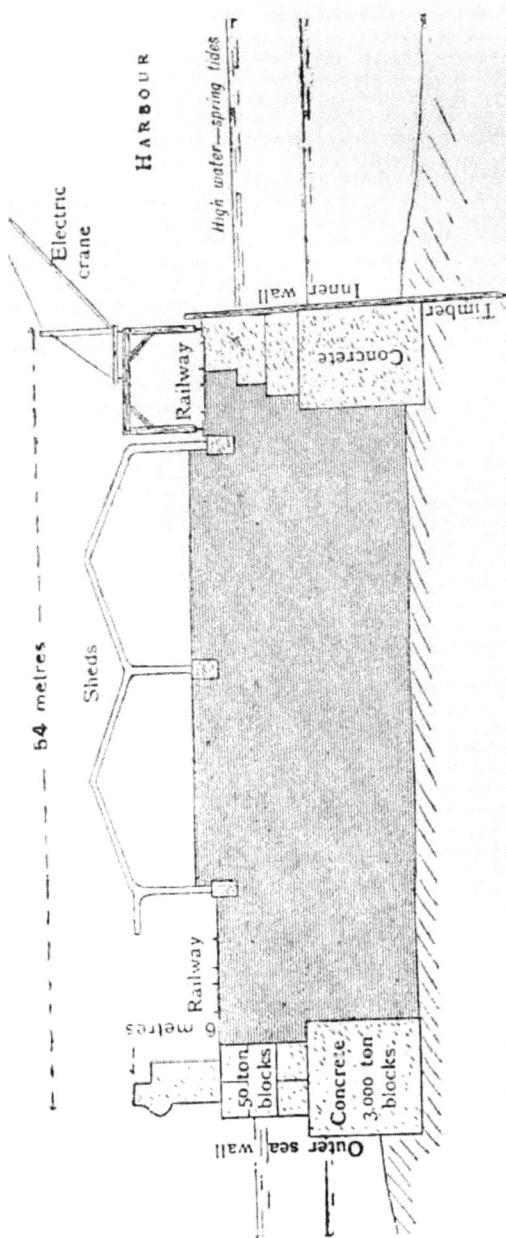

Cross-section of the Mole at Zeebrugge, showing the difficulty of landing over the high outer sea wall.

dark there was a platoon of marines still waiting there, crouched on the deck. A marine officer looked down from the landing platform.

'Aren't these folk going over?' I asked.

'Those are all gone,' he said.

★★★★★★

Daffodil, which should have landed her own men after berthing *Vindictive*, was compelled to remain on the latter's starboard, pressing her into position, while her men crossed *Vindictive* to join the storming-party; and *Iris*, which should have made fast ahead of *Vindictive*, found her grapnels too small, and had to fall in astern.

The storming-parties moved along the Mole, finding no Germans, but subject to the same withering fire from the shore end. Steadily, methodically, they blew up one building after another. A German destroyer lay on the harbour side of the Mole, and was promptly blown up by our bombs. And then suddenly ahead of them a vast column of flame leapt into the air, and they knew that the viaduct had gone. An old submarine, C 3 (Lieutenant R. D. Sandford), had steered straight for the viaduct under the enemy's searchlights and under constant fire—an anxious task, for the thing was full of explosives. The viaduct itself was crowded with the enemy, who watched the little vessel approaching as if stupefied by its audacity. Apparently, they thought that it was trying to get through the viaduct into the harbour. Lieutenant Sandford rammed his boat into the hole left for the tide in the steel curtain, touched the button, got into a skiff, and won clear away. There was no more gallant exploit in all that marvellous night.

The landing-parties on the Mole pushed on to the ragged edge of what had once been the viaduct, steadily pursuing the work of destruction. The lighthouse was taken, and there Wing-Commander Brock, who had organised the smoke-screen, was last seen desperately wounded, but still fighting. Suddenly the German fire seemed to be concentrated more on the harbour, and as they looked eastward they saw the reason. The block-ships were steering straight for the canal. *Thetis* (Commander Sneyd) went first to show the way, but she had the misfortune to foul her propeller in the defence nets. She signalled a warning to the others, and then, pounded at by the shore batteries, was sunk in the channel some hundreds of yards from the canal mouth.

Meantime *Intrepid* (Lieutenant Bonham-Carter), with every gun in action, and belching smoke like a volcano, steered into the canal, and, resting her nose on the mud of the western bank, blew up

H.M.S. "VINDICTIVE" SUNK AT OSTEND. MAY. 9TH. 1918.

and settled down neatly athwart the channel. *Iphigenia* (Lieutenant Billyard-Leake) followed, a little confused by *Intrepid's* smoke, rammed a dredger, and continued, dredger and all, on her consort's heels. She beached on the eastern side, swung across the canal, and was blown up. The crews of these vessels retired in every kind of small craft, and, for the most part, were picked up by the destroyers sheltering behind the smoke-screen.

The signal arranged for re-embarkation had been a blast from *Vindictive's* siren. But *Vindictive* had long ago lost her siren, so *Daffodil* did the best she could with her hooter. What was left of the landing-parties clambered aboard; *Daffodil* towed *Vindictive* loose, and the flotilla turned for home. The intensity of the German fire redoubled, but the changed wind now served us well, and the smoke clouds cloaked our departure. The 120 heavy guns between Zeebrugge and Ostend did not find their mark, and the raiders, led by the twisted and battered *Vindictive*, were presently in English waters.

The Ostend operation was less successful, for there the block-ships could not be assisted by any containing action, such as that on the Zeebrugge Mole, to distract the enemy. Our motor boats lit flares on the ends of the piers, and concealed them from the shore end by a smoke-screen. Unhappily, the veer of the wind blew aside the screen and revealed the flares, which the enemy promptly extinguished by gunfire. *Brilliant* and *Sirius* failed to find the entrance to the harbour, and were compelled to sink themselves four hundred yards east of the piers and more than a mile from the true canal mouth.

By the morning of St. George's Day, the main part of the great venture had been successfully accomplished. Zeebrugge and the Bruges Canal were blocked, and it did not appear how, under the constant assaults of our airplanes, they could ever be cleared. The quality of the British Navy had been triumphantly vindicated, and in the darkest days of the war on land the hard-pressed Allies were given assurance that the Fleet was still master of the seas, and the final barrier to a German victory. For the gallantry of all concerned—the marines on the Mole, the crews of the block-ships and of *Vindictive* and her consorts, the men in the picket boats and motor launches—no words of praise are adequate.

The affair will rank in history among the classic exploits of sea warfare. But in admiration for the human quality shown, the technical brilliance of the feat should not be forgotten. From its nature it could not be rehearsed. It demanded a number of conditions which

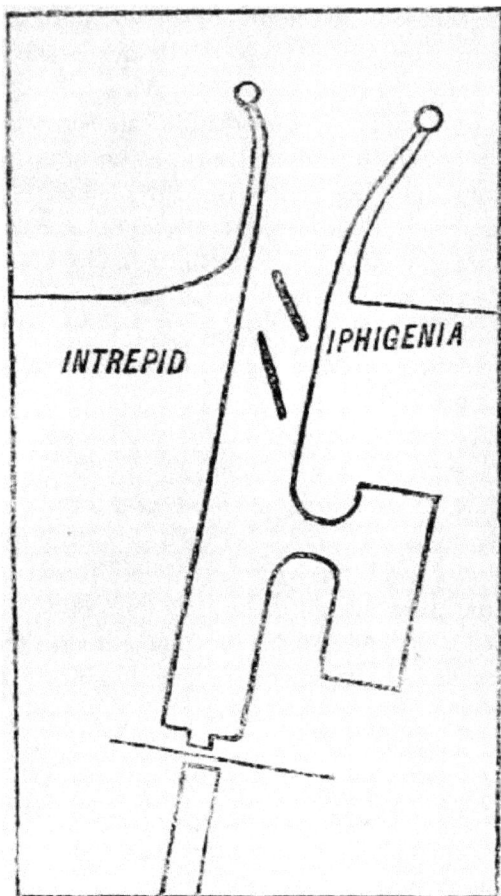

Tracing from an aerial reconnaissance photograph, showing where the block-ships
sank in the canal entrance
at Zeebrugge.

involved for their concomitance an indefinite period of waiting, and in such a continued tension secrecy on the one hand and ardour on the other are not easy to preserve. It required an intricate plan, worked out to minute details, any one of which was at the mercy of unforeseeable accident. Sir Roger Keyes succeeded by taking every human precaution, and then trusting to the luck of the navy; and it is hard to know whether the more to admire his admirable caution or his admirable hardihood.

The saga of the Flanders coast was not finished. To be forewarned is not always to be forearmed. A surprise so audacious may be achieved that it is confidently assumed that it cannot be repeated; but the mere fact of this assumption may be the occasion of a second surprise. The Germans at Ostend had removed all guiding marks for attacking ships, had cut gaps in the piers to prevent a repetition of the landing on Zeebrugge Mole, and had a flotilla of nine destroyers watching the bit of coast. A second attack there was to the enemy unthinkable, and therefore Sir Roger Keyes attempted it.

The second affair was planned as methodically as the first. It was under the command of Commodore Hubert Lynes, who had been in charge on the night of 22nd-23rd April. About midnight on Thursday, 9th May, he left the British coast with a number of monitors, destroyers, and motor boats, and the old *Vindictive,* now on her last voyage. Sir Roger Keyes was also present in the *Warwick.* It was a windless spring night, with a quiet sea and a sky lit with faint stars. The commodore's destroyer hurried ahead, laid a light buoy, and then fell back, while *Vindictive* and the other block-ships in the charge of the smaller craft approached the shore. They saw before them a beacon burning, a flare which one of our coastal motor boats had hung in the rigging of the sunken *Sirius.*

There was no preliminary bombardment till fifteen minutes before the block-ships were due at the harbour mouth. At that moment two motor boats dashed in and torpedoed the ends of the high wooden piers, and on the signal the airplanes watching in the heavens began their bombardment, and the great shells from our monitors shrieked into the town. Our smoke clouds were loosed, and blinded the searchlights and the observation of the German batteries. And on their heels, came the real thing, a dense sea fog, which blanketed everything, and forced our destroyers to use their sirens to keep in touch.

The block-ships were hard put to it to find the entrance. They wandered east and west in a hell of fire from the shore, groping for the

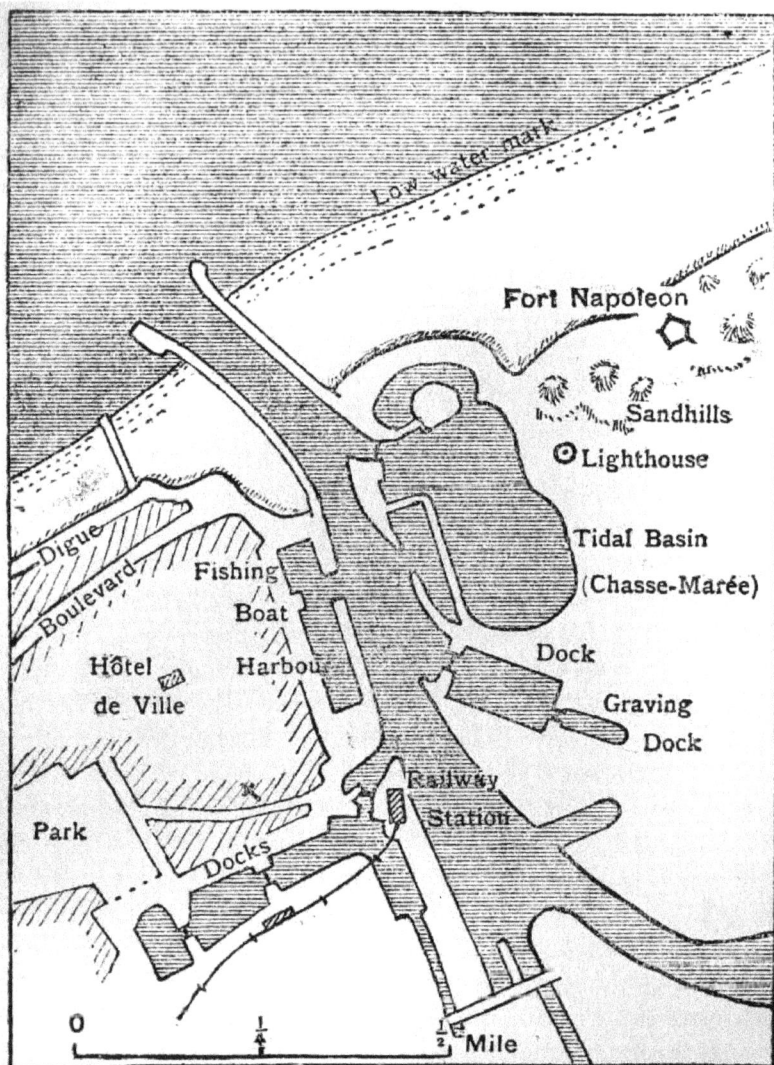

Low water mark

Fort Napoleon

Sandhills

⊙ Lighthouse

Tidal Basin

(Chasse-Marée)

Digue

Boulevard

Fishing

Boat

Harbour

Hôtel
de Ville

Dock

Graving
Dock

Railway
Station

Park

Docks

0   ¼   ½ Mile

Ostend Harbour.

harbour mouth. A motor boat managed to plant a flare between the piers, and *Vindictive* steamed in. She was not the main block-ship—her draught was too great for the purpose—but the hope of success now lay alone with her. The enemy batteries had found her, and she was terribly wounded, while the machine guns on the piers raked her decks. She laid her nose to the eastern pier, and was preparing to swing across the channel when a shell destroyed her conning-tower.

It appeared that she could not swing farther round, and there was nothing for it but to sink her, lying at an angle of forty degrees to the eastern pier. There remained a narrow passage between her and the western pier, too narrow to be used by destroyers or the larger sub-marines. Most of her crew were got off in motor launches, and at 2.30 on the morning of Friday, the 10th, the recall rockets went up and the flotilla turned for home. The nine German destroyers had been dis-creet, and had not shown themselves throughout the action. *Vindictive* had been triumphant in her death as in her life, and the second of the two great West Flanders bases was now lost to the enemy.

Zeebrugge and Ostend were the last nails in the coffin of the Ger-man Navy. It seemed incredible that along with the great German land attack in France and Flanders there should not be some attempt at action by the ships from Kiel and Wilhelmshaven. If Germany was staking everything on victory, surely, she must stake her Fleet. It did not come. The British reserves were ferried across the Channel with-out interference. Then Britain herself attacked by sea two most vital bases and ruined them irrevocably, and still the great battleships gave no sign.

At the moment it was a mystery, but six months later that mystery was explained. The German Fleet had ceased to be more than a name. The sleepless activity of Sir David Beatty had paralyzed its heart. In the first six months of 1918 over a hundred surface craft were lost in the Bight of Heligoland. Minelayers, minesweepers, patrol boats—they were being driven from the seas; they mutinied, and the mutiny was suppressed; but the spirit and discipline necessary for the most arduous of human tasks had gone from their men. The use of foul weapons like the submarine had ruined the morale of sailors who had done gal-lantly at Coronel and the Dogger Bank and Jutland. The ancient law of Poseidon cannot be broken without disaster to the breaker. Already the British Admiralty knew what the German *Marineamt* only dimly guessed, that the first order given to prepare for a fleet action would for the German Navy be the signal for revolution.

Chapter 4

The Third Battle of the Aisne

The success of their armies in the West had during April and May keyed the German people to a high pitch of confidence. All talk of democracy and the liberalising of the constitution had been silenced by the shouts of triumph. For the moment the High Command were again the idols of the populace, and the Hohenzollerns shared in their glory. A "German peace" would be made before the leaves fell, and those who had been most clamorous for a peace by negotiation were the speediest and noisiest in their recantation. It would be easy to cull from the writings and speeches of German leaders an anthology of vainglory.

"The thing is over," said Hindenburg on 25th March.

Helfferich said on 24th April:—

We have put a ring about the British islands," a ring which every day is drawn closer, and we shall bring the war to a decision in the west of France and on the waters about England.

On the same day, in answer to President Wilson, he declared:

He shall have it, force to the utmost, force without stint or limit.

In the Prussian Diet Count Yorck von Wartenberg announced:

We have had enough of stretching out the hand of peace. It was not by renunciation and agreement, but by power of arms that the state of Frederick and Bismarck was made great.

The *Vorwaerts* joined in the *paean*.

We welcome this victory in the West with special joy, because we believe that it must destroy for the Western peoples the last remnants of blindness and false hopes of success. The psycho-

GENERALFELDMARSCHALL PAUL VON HINDENBURG

logical moment has now arrived when their war-will must collapse.

But the most interesting testimony, perhaps, came from a curious little book published in the spring, in which deputies of all parties, except the Minority Socialists, expounded their faith. "The fundamental condition for all of us," said one socialist, "is that Germany shall remain the conqueror in the world's war."

"The peace in the East," said another, "has broken up the coalition against us."

A member of the Centre wrote:

The war, was never anything else but an economic duel between Germany and England, and the result must be a greater Germany, with ample economic and territorial guarantees.

The National Liberals clamoured for indemnities.

For reasons alike of law and morality it is evident that the German people must be better off after the war than before.

As for the Pan-Germans, they wanted everything—the Meuse, Belgium, the Balkans, colossal payments.

The interests of Germany must be satisfied without any consideration for the interests of foreign peoples.

And all agreed that the only way to these good things was by a decisive field victory. This unanimity of press and platform was scarcely an index to the feeling of the average German citizen. The truth was that he was very weary. He considered that he had done enough *"pour chauffer la gloire"* and he no longer thrilled to the flamboyant dispatches of the High Command and the Emperor's grandiosities. He wanted peace above all things—after victory, if possible, but peace in any case—a dangerous mood for a conquering Power. Moreover, his nerve was being shaken by the daring air raids which the British Independent Air Force was now conducting as far afield as Cologne.

Hitherto he had rejoiced at the bombing of Paris and London, but it had been the boast of his rulers that war would never enter the German frontiers, and this looked unpleasantly like a failure of the promise. There were doubting Thomases also in high places. Kuhlmann had never concealed his opinion that the victory in the West which Ludendorff had guaranteed could not be attained. He had not quite the confidence of his colleagues in the tardiness of America, and he had

THIRD BATTLE OF THE MARNE

ugly premonitions that his diplomacy in the East had been less triumphant than he had at first imagined. He would have preferred to stand on the defensive in the West, husband the German reserves, and finish the work in Russia. For it was now becoming clear that the iron fist in the Ukraine was too rough to reap the fruits which he had looked for, and that Bolshevism, which he had alternately flattered and bullied, was like to be a broken reed for German statecraft to lean upon.

But Ludendorff had put his hand to the plough, and there could be no turning back. The stagnation of May was not part of his plan, but a sheer necessity to enable him to fill up the gaps in his ranks. He had lost something over half a million of men—not, indeed, more than he had bargained for, but in that bargain, he had assumed a success which was still denied him. By the last week of May he had replaced more than 70 *per cent,* of his losses from men returned from hospitals and the first part of the 1920 class. He had still a real superiority in numbers over his antagonists; he had the strategic initiative and the priceless advantage of interior lines.

He had not changed his main purpose. He still aimed at separating the British and French armies, and for him the vital terrain was still the Somme. But he did not consider that the time was ripe for the final blow, and he resolved to repeat his Lys experiment, and strike first in a different area, with the object of exhausting Foch's reserves and stripping bare his centre. There were many inducements to this course. Repeated blows at widely separated sections would compel the moving of Allied supports round the big outer edge of the salient; would certainly give him local successes; and might, in the precarious position of the Allies, supply just that finishing stroke which would disintegrate their entire defence.

He and his colleagues had always Russia in mind. He had treated the Russian front in this way, and by-and-by had come the Revolution when the heart and limbs of Russia failed her. Might not the sentimental democracies of the West be driven down the same road? He had still some five months of campaigning before him, and he did not believe that America would prove a serious factor in the war before the winter. His time limits were inexorable, but the allowance seemed still sufficient.

The new terrain must be of the same type as the Lys—that is, it must be sufficiently remote from the centre to make reinforcement difficult, and it must threaten some vital possession of the Allies. He found such an area in the Heights of the Aisne. (The British Staff from the month of April onward had been confident that the next German blow would be in this area.) It was the nearest point to Paris; it was a path to the Marne; and an advance beyond that river would cut the Paris-Châlons railways and imperil the whole French front in Champagne. He could concentrate troops for the attack in the angle of the salient, so that, as on 21st March, the Allies could not guess his intention. And, having renewed his shock troops, he could once again use the deadly tactics of March, to which Foch as yet seemed to have found no answer.

About the 20th of May the army group of the Crown Prince had mustered some forty divisions for the attempt, twenty-five for the first wave and fifteen in reserve. The two armies allotted to the task were: on the right, the VII. Army, under von Boehn; and, on the left, the I. Army, under Fritz von Below. They lay between the Ailette and Rheims, wholly to the north and east of the plateau; while on the heights was part of the group of Franchet d'Esperey, the French Sixth Army, under General Maistre, with only the 11th Corps of four divisions in line.

On the French right lay the British 9th Corps, under Lieutenant-General Sir A. Hamilton-Gordon, which had been recently withdrawn from Flanders. It held the California Plateau and Craonne, and extended as far south as Berméricourt, with three divisions in line—the 50th, 8th, and 21st, and the 25th in reserve on the left wing. Around Rheims lay the French Fifth Army, with, on its right, General Gouraud's Fourth Army extending into Champagne.

The British divisions, which were depleted and tired after their two months' struggle, had been brought to the section to rest. The weakness of the Allied front—seven divisions to hold a line of thirty miles—was no fault of the High Command, but due simply to the exigencies of the great battle. If a force is outnumbered it must be content to be thin at many points, and the Aisne was not the only, or, so far as could be judged, the most critical area on the Western front.

We have seen that Ludendorff began the Lys battle with an attack of nine divisions, a modest complement suitable for a subsidiary operation. We have seen, too, that he was gradually drawn by unexpected success into a gross expenditure of men. The new plan marked a further weakening in the rigour of his first strategy. A thirty-mile front and twenty-five divisions of assault were on a scale too great for a legitimate diversion. He still held to his main plan, but he was fumbling in his methods, and he had chosen an ill place for one prone to

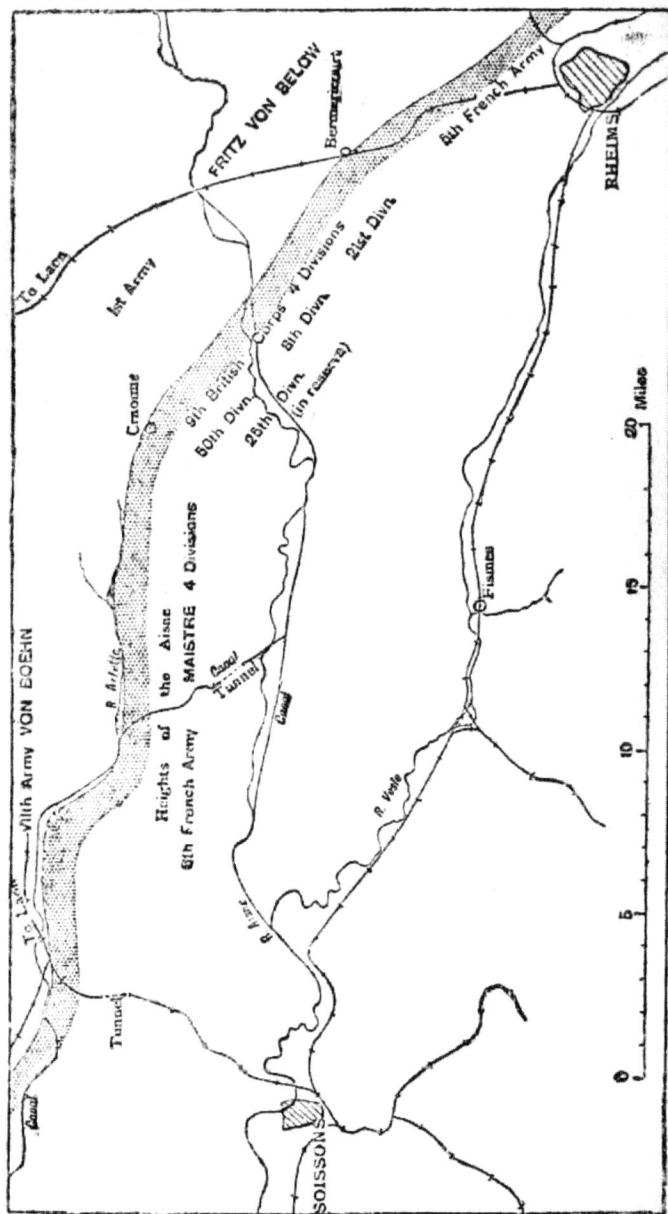

The Opposing Armies on the Front from the Aisne Heights to Rheims (May 1918).

temptation. For Paris lay in the south-west beyond the forests, and the lure of a capital city is hard to resist for the soldier, and harder for the politicians behind him.

Ludendorff employed many of the same troops, including three divisions of the Prussian Guard, as had led the assault on 21st March. Both in the secrecy of his concentration, (first news of the impending attack came from prisoners taken by the French on the 26th), and in the precision of his new tactics he far exceeded his previous record. Never, perhaps, during the whole campaign did the great German war machine move so noiselessly and so fast. On the evening of Sunday, 26th May, all was quiet in the threatened area. Then at one o'clock on the morning of Monday, the 27th, a sharp bombardment began everywhere from the Ailette to the suburbs of Rheims.

At four o'clock the infantry advanced, and in an hour or two had swept the French from the crest of the ridge. The odds were too desperate, and the four weak French divisions were smothered under weight of numbers and artillery. The 11th Corps early in the morning was back on the southern slopes of the heights, and by the afternoon was on the Aisne itself, five miles from its old positions.

By 8 a.m. three French divisions from reserve had attempted to hold a line on the southern bank of the river covering the crossings. They were swept aside, and the vanguard of von Conta's corps crossed by the French bridges, and before nightfall had reached the Vesle: a total advance of twelve miles, and far beyond anything that had been accomplished on 21st March. By the evening the French front ran from the Ailette, near Leuilly, by Neuville-sur-Margival to the Aisne at Condé, and then in a crescent on the southern bank by Braisne, Quincy, and Mont-Notre-Dame to south of Fismes. Large numbers of prisoners and an immense store of booty had fallen into von Boehn's hands.

At first Fritz von Below fared less well against the British 9th Corps. It was forced back to its second position, but resisted gallantly for most of the day. It will be remembered that the 8th Division had held the line of the Somme on 24th March against the Brandenburgers, and a month later had shared in the fighting at Villers Bretonneux; that the 21st had fought at Epéhy and at Voormezeele; that the 25th had been in action in March on the Bapaume-Cambrai road, and in April at Ploegsteert Wood, at Neuve Eglise, and at Kemmel; and that the 50th had been engaged throughout the St. Quentin retreat, and most furiously on the Lys on 9th April.

GERMAN TROOPS ATTACKING

The 21st, between Cormicy and Berméricourt, with a French Colonial Division on its right, held its ground throughout the day. The 8th, around Berry-au-Bac, stood firm till the afternoon, when the pressure on the west forced it across the river. The 50th, at Craonne, had the hardest task of all, for the retreat of the French uncovered its left flank, and it was slowly driven back to the Aisne, after making a heroic effort to recapture the Craonne plateau. That evening the line of the 9th Corps ran from Berméricourt westward through Cormicy and Bouffignereux, to link up precariously with the French north-east of Fismes.

The battle had now reached the district of the Tardenois, that upland which is the watershed between Aisne and Marne. The countryside is broken up into many hollows, but the centre is open and full of excellent roads. On the west and southwest lie big patches of forest, of which the great wood of Villers-Cotterets is the chief. It is cut in the middle by the stream of the Ourcq, flowing westward, and farther east by the long and shallow valley of the Vesle. On the south it breaks down sharply to the Marne, and an enemy coming from the north by the plateau commands all the flatter southern shore.

It was Ludendorff's desire to push for the Marne at his best speed; but the difficulty lay with his flanks. So long as Soissons and Rheims held he would be forced by every day's advance into a narrowing salient. His advantage was that the French line had been completely broken, and that some days must elapse before serious resistance could be made to his triumphant centre. At all costs he must broaden the salient, and on the 28th he succeeded in forcing back the containing Allied wings.

On his right he drove the French to the line Venizel-Serches-Lesges, and on his left, he compelled the British 9th Corps to retire to positions running well south of the Vesle by Crugny to Muizon. (That night the British 19th Division was brought up in 'buses to the Ardre valley to fill a gap in the French line). In the centre the French were south of Lhuys and Chéry and Courville. He did more, for on his extreme right, between the Aisne and the Ailette, he captured Sancy, and won a line from Pont-St. Mard by Terny to Bray. He was now on the heights overlooking Soissons from the north and close on the town in the river flats to the east.

That day an event happened which might well have given food for thought to the German Command. American troops had been before this date engaged in minor actions in Lorraine, but now for the first

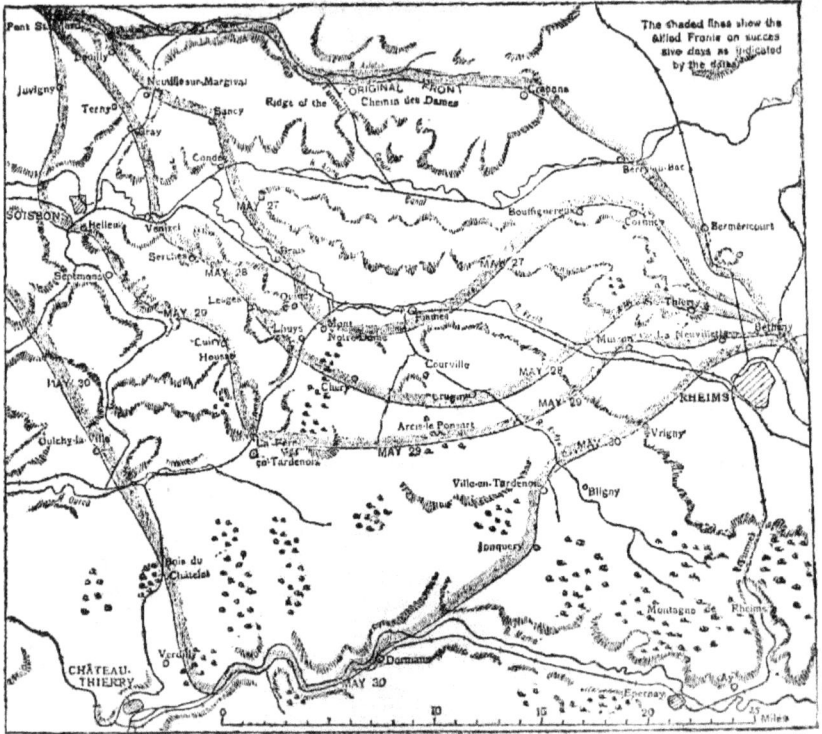

The German Advance to the Marne (May 27-30, 1918).

time they took part in the main battle. The 1st United States Division, brigaded with the Third French Army, attacked in the Montdidier section, and took the village of Cantigny, along with 170 prisoners. Three furious counter-attacks by the enemy failed to retake the place. It was much that a new division should thus neatly and efficiently carry out an offensive, but that they should be able to consolidate and hold their gains was a real achievement and a happy augury for the future.

On Wednesday, the 29th, the broadening of the salient began in earnest, and Soissons fell. All the day before it had been hotly shelled, and in some places set on fire; and on the morning of the 29th the enemy, strengthened by fresh divisions, pushed in from the east and entered its streets. They were driven out after severe fighting, but returned to the attack in the afternoon, and compelled the French to retire to the plateau west and south of the town. Fritz von Below, on the German left, had also increased his forces, and succeeded in pressing the British and French troops on the Allied right off the upland of St. Thierry. That day there was a general falling back everywhere, and at night the Allied line ran from La Neuvillette north of Rheims, well to the south of Crugny, south of Arcis le Ponsart, through the station of Fère-en-Tardenois, and then north-west by Cuiry-Housse, Septmonts, and Belleu, to the west of Soissons, and so to Juvigny and Pont St. Mard.

Next day the German centre made a strong forward thrust. It was the second main attack of the battle, and its aims were to reach the Marne, and to destroy the two pillars of the Allied front at Soissons and Rheims. The first was immediately successful. During the morning the German vanguard appeared on the hills above the Marne between Château-Thierry and Dormans, and by the evening the enemy was in possession of some ten miles of the north bank of the river. He was less fortunate on his flanks. He failed entirely to debouch from Soissons. In the east La Neuvillette fell, and he won a foothold in Bétheny, but he was checked in front of Rheims. That night the Allied front lay from Rheims by Vrigny, Ville-en-Tardenois, and Jonquery to Dormans; then along the right bank of the Marne to just east of Château-Thierry; then north-west by Oulchy-la-Ville, Missy-au-Bois, and Tartiers to the original line at Pontoise.

The enemy had now cause to consider his position. His achievement had been brilliant—an advance of over thirty miles in seventy-two hours, the occupation of ten miles of the Marne shore, between 30,000 and 40,000 prisoners, and some 400 guns. But there were anxious elements in his success. He had used up most of the fresh divi-

A British P.O.W. in the Spring Offensive

sions of the crown prince's reserve, and though Prince Rupprecht had twenty more, and the Duke of Wurtemberg and General von Gallwitz at least four fresh divisions to spare, it would be unwise to squander the total mass of manoeuvre in what had been intended as a diversion. But the position won was such that it offered no safe resting-place; the battle must be continued, or the gains must be relinquished.

It is a good working rule that a salient on a formed front should not be in depth more than a third of its base. But von Boehn had far exceeded this proportion, and he found himself forced through too narrow a gate. There was nothing for it but to carry away the gate-posts—to halt the centre while the flanks came into line.

The more dangerous wing was the German right, which followed roughly the high road from Soissons to Château-Thierry. If von Boehn could press out in that direction he would enlarge the borders of his salient, and, by outflanking the Soissons heights, break down that vital gate-post. Accordingly, on the morning of the 31st he performed the military operation known as "forming front to a flank." He drove back the French from the southern bank of the Oise and Aisne Canal between Guny and Noyon, and he pressed down the valley of the Ourcq as far as Neuilly St. Front. North of that point his front ran by Vierzy to Missy, and south of it through Bois-du-Châtelet and Verdilly to the north-east of Château-Thierry.

Next day, Saturday, 1st June, it was the turn of Fritz von Below, who attacked at Rheims with tanks on the left flank of the German salient and at first made ground. A French counterattack later in the day drove him back and captured four of his tanks. North-west of Soissons von Boehn made a half-hearted effort, and south-west of the town the French won back some ground, and checked further enemy progress down by the south bank of the Aisne. On Sunday, 2nd June, both German armies made a resolute attempt to break the gate-posts. Von Below, with five divisions, attacked at Vrigny, south-west of Rheims, but failed to advance. Von Boehn drove hard against the western flank, occupied the northern part of Château-Thierry and the high riverside ground as far as Chézy-sur-Marne, and enlarged his holding farther north in the neighbourhood of Chézy-en-Borzois'.

But he made no progress down the Ourcq, for the French had brought up reserves in that area, and had found a line which they could defend. Just east of the great forest of Villers-Cotterets runs the little River Savières, in a deep gorge with precipitous sides. It falls into the Ourcq at Troesnes, whence an irregular line of heights stretches

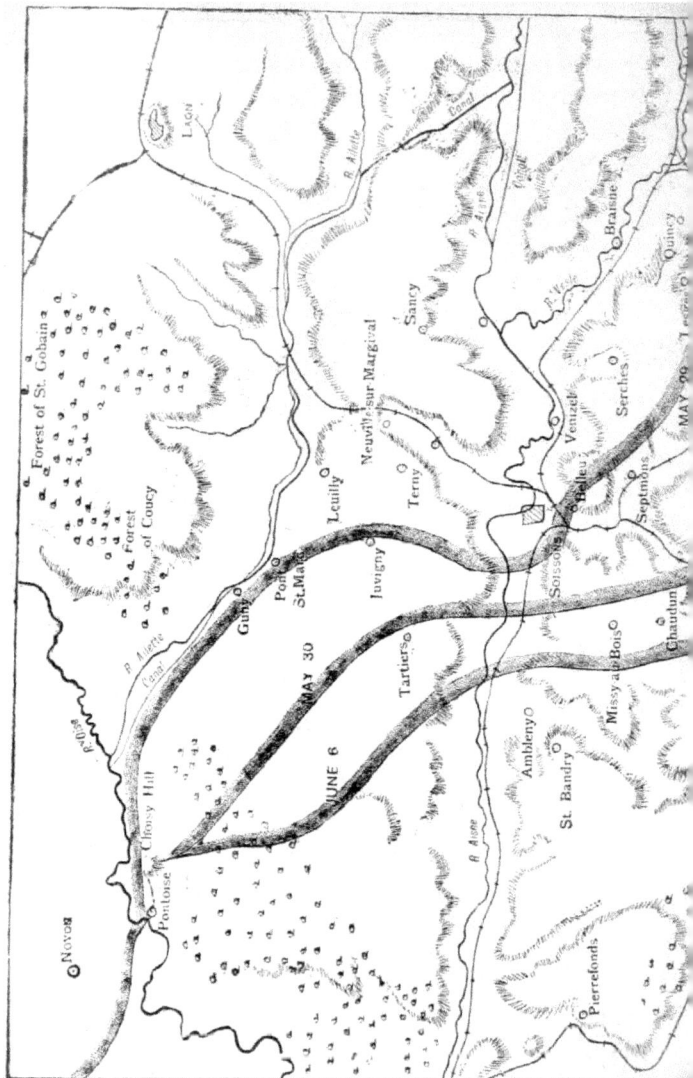

The German Attempt to widen the Marne Salient to the Westward.

southward in front of Passy and Torcy. All this line, which was of some strength, was recaptured by the French by the Sunday evening, with the exception of the hamlet of Faverolles, where the Germans had still a footing. That day marked the farthest limit of von Boehn's success in this area, for, though he continued his efforts for another week, he made comparatively small progress.

The crown prince had used forty-one divisions in the week's battle, and had practically exhausted his own reserves, but he had not drawn upon the resources of the neighbouring group commanders. The situation was still very grave, for the French line had been greatly lengthened, it bristled with vulnerable points, and there was scanty room to manoeuvre. Paris was dangerously near the new front, and the loss of Paris meant far more than the loss of a capital. Earlier in the campaign the great city might have fallen without bringing upon the Allies irreparable disaster. But in the past two years it was in the environs of Paris that many of the chief new munition factories had arisen. If these were lost the Allied strength would be grievously crippled, and after four years of war it was doubtful whether France had the power to replace them.

On Monday, the 3rd, there was heavy fighting around Torcy, where the Germans tried to push down the little valley of the Clignon; between Troesnes and Faverolles; and on the Chaudun plateau, southwest of Soissons, where von Boehn was endeavouring to turn the Villers-Cotterets forest by its northern end. The struggle was bitter; but the French reaction had clearly begun, and on their extreme left they recovered the southern part of the hill of Choisy, which overlooks the Oise. On the Tuesday there was a lull, and on Wednesday, the 5th, the French repulsed an attempt to cross the Oise near Mont Lagache.

American troops had come into action on the western and southern side of the salient, and counter-attacked with success west of Torcy at the wood of Neuilly-la-Poterie, and defeated an attempt to ford the Marne at Jaulgonne, north-east of Château-Thierry. On Thursday, the 6th, the Germans were forced back a mile at Torcy, and that night the British 19th Division retook the village of Bligny, eight miles to the south-west of Rheims.

★★★★★★

The general commanding the French Fifth Army paid the following tribute to the British 9th Corps: "They have enabled us to establish a barrier against which the hostile waves have beaten and shattered themselves. This none of the French who

GERMAN STORMTROOPERS

witnessed it will ever forget."

★★★★★★

On the 7th the French and Americans took Neuilly-la-Poterie and Bouresches, and the French captured the important Hill 204 above Château-Thierry, Von Boehn had exhausted his strength, and had called a halt; and, according to their practice in such lulls, the Germans announced the results of their victory—55,000 prisoners and 650 guns. They were clearly preparing a blow elsewhere, and Foch waited anxiously for news of it.

It came on the morning of Sunday, the 9th, and, as had been expected, from another army. This time it was the turn of von Hutier. It had proved impossible to carry away the gate-posts by means of the two armies already engaged, so it was necessary to bring the force on their right into action. At midnight on the 8th an intense bombardment began in the Montdidier-Noyon section, and at dawn on the 9th von Hutier attacked with fifteen divisions on a front of twenty-five miles. In the next three days three more divisions were drawn in, and of the eighteen five were from the reserve of Prince Rupprecht.

The Allied front between Montdidier and Noyon had for its main feature the group of low hills south of Lassigny, between the stream of the Matz and the Oise. West of the Matz the line ran through an open country of ploughland and rolling downs. East of it the front curved round the northern skirts of the hills, which were thickly wooded and rose to some 400 feet above the surrounding levels. They formed a continuous ridge except at their western end, where one summit was separated by a sharp valley, with the village of Gury at its northern end.

If von Hutier could thrust down the Matz he would turn the uplands, and so get rid of the main natural obstacle between him and Compiegne. The main strategic object of Ludendorff was now to secure the front Compiegne-Château-Thierry, from which he could threaten Paris. Already his greater scheme, though not consciously relinquished, was growing dim, and the lure of the capital was overmastering him. Further, he had to release von Boehn from the awkward narrows in which he was wedged.

On most of the front of attack von Hutier failed, for there was no element of surprise, and Foch was ready for him. But in the centre along the Matz there was a local success. The enemy advanced some three miles, took the isolated hill above Gury, and got as far as the village of Ressons, in the south. Next day the three miles became six, and the Germans were in Marquéglise and Elincourt, in the centre;

GERMAN INFANTRY AT THE THIRD BATTLE OF THE MARNE

on their left they entered the Bois de Thiescourt; and on their right, took the villages of Méry, Belloy, and St. Maur. The extreme French left, between Rubescourt and Courcelles, stood firm.

That evening the French front ran from Mesnil St. Georges, in the west, by Le Ployron, Courcelles, Marest, Montigny, and La Bernardie, to the south of Cannectancourt. The battle was one of dogged resistance, and, for the enemy, slow and costly progress, very different to the Aisne action a fortnight before. But Foch could not afford to take risks, so that night he shortened his line by evacuating the salient south of Noyon, between Nampcel and Montigny. Measures were also taken for the defence of Paris should the enemy advance continue.

It was blazing June weather, the ground was bone-dry, and all the conditions favoured the attackers. But a new thing had begun to appear in the campaign. The enemy continued his former tactics, but they were less successful. The French were notably quick in counter-attack, and this discomfited the shock—troops in their infiltration, for it is small use finding weak spots in a front if you are checked before you can take advantage of them. The French reserves were still scanty, and the defence was still heavily outnumbered, but the odds were not so fantastic as in March and April, and in their hundreds of thousands America was landing her troops. Already some of them had been in the line, and at Cantigny and Château-Thierry had shown their brilliant quality.

The battle-front was now gigantic, not less than 100 miles from Mesnil St. Georges to Rheims. For the remainder of the month there was a ding-dong struggle, no side gaining any real advantage, for both were near the end of their endurance. On the 11th the French retook Méry and Belloy, and advanced their line nearly two miles on a front of four between Gournay and Courcelles. Farther east they pressed back the enemy from the Matz River, and repulsed a German attack along the Ribecourt-Compiègne road. That same day, between the Ourcq and the Marne, the Americans made a fine advance at Belleau Wood, and took 300 prisoners.

On the 12th the Germans had some success between Ribecourt and Marest, and took the latter village, as well as Chevincourt and Machemont and Melicocq. Just south of the Aisne they made another advance—two miles on a front of three—and reached the outskirts of Ambleny and St. Bandry. The only French gain was at Melicocq, where they won the southern bank of the Matz from Marest to the Oise. On the 13th the enemy made a great effort between Courcelles

The German Attempt in June to advance on the Montdidier–Soissons Front.

and Méry, and again between Bouresches and Belleau, but failed utterly with heavy losses. That day von Hutier's subsidiary operation may be said to have closed, and closed without any serious gain. He had squandered twenty odd divisions, and the fresh reserves left to Prince Rupprecht were again no more than twenty. The tide of assault in the west was slowly ebbing.

Having failed on his right flank, the Crown Prince made a final effort on his left. On 18th June Fritz von Below attacked at Rheims on a front of ten miles, between Vrigny, on the south-west, and the fort of La Pompelle, on the south-east of the city. He hoped to take Rheims, but he underrated the defence, and used only three divisions. The place was a vital road junction for the Allies, and, though encircled on three sides, it had held out most stoutly during the battle, much aided by the fact that the Allies held the great massif of the Montagne de Rheims to the south and south-west. Von Below's attempt was futile, but the fiasco seems to have impressed the German Staff with the necessity of a serious effort against the Montagne if they were to make any headway beyond the Marne. Of this impression we shall presently see the fruits.

For the better part of a month silence fell on the battle-front, broken only by local attacks of the French and British, which in every case were successful, for the enemy was holding most of his front thinly with indifferent troops. He was preparing another blow, as all the omens indicated, and it was likely that this blow would be his last. It was certain that it would be on a great scale, and would be delivered with desperate resolution, for the summer days were slipping by, and Germany waited the fulfilment of Ludendorff's pledge. So far, in three great actions, he had strategically failed. He had taken heavy toll of the Allies; but he had himself suffered colossally, and his casualties were now mounting fast to the limit which he had named as the price of victory.

The climax of the battle—and of the war—was approaching, and Foch faced it with an easier mind; for he saw his army growing daily as the Americans came into line, and he could now spend more lavishly since he was sure of his ultimate reserves. More important still, he had solved the problem of how to meet the new German tactics, and was ready with a method of his own in which this great master of modern war had borrowed from his opponents, and glorified and transformed the borrowings.

CHAPTER 5

The Second Battle of the Marne

A defensive need not be stagnant and supine. It may be as vigilant and aggressive as any attack. From 21st March to the middle of July the mind of Foch was working intensely on the problem before him. He had to repel from day to day Ludendorff's hordes, and conserve and nurse his own mass of manoeuvre; but he had also to discover the answer to the new German tactics, and frame his own tactical plan against the day of *revanche*. Hints of his solution appeared in the June fighting on the Matz and in the Italian resistance on the Piave, and by midsummer his scheme was complete.

The gist of his tactical reply lay in three points: first, the organisation of his outpost line in great depth, not unlike von Armin's device at Third Ypres, so that the first enemy shock might spend itself in the void; second, a highly-complex use of artillery to break up a concentration once it was located; and, third, a system of rapid counterattacks to check "infiltration" at the start. That was for the defence. For his own advance, when the time for it came, he had recast Ludendorff's tactics in a better form, and had subordinated them to a strategical plan of far greater boldness and ingenuity than anything as yet originated by the German General Staff. For these tactics he had a weapon of supreme value in his new light tanks, which, modelled on the British "whippet," were now appearing in large quantities on the French front. Already, in local counter-attacks on the Aisne, they had proved their merit; they were soon to paralyze the enemy's defence in a decisive battle.

But no plan is effective without numbers to execute it, and for the first time Foch had numbers at his command. The achievements of America in war finance, in ship construction, and in production of *matériel* were adequate to the seriousness of her purpose, and there could be no higher praise. Already her levies of men had passed the two million point, and their preliminary training had been expedited to such a degree that soon after midsummer she was landing in France every five weeks as many troops as the sum of Germany's annual recruitment. The retreat from St. Quentin had been for the Allies a blessing in disguise, for it had induced America to perform one of the most miraculous exploits in history.

In April 117,212 American soldiers had landed in Europe; in May, 224,345; in June, 276,372; and of the total of 617,929 more than half had been carried in British ships. The rate was increasing, too, with every week. Moreover, America had shown the most admirable generosity and good sense in the use made of her forces. She naturally looked forward to great American armies in France commanded, like the French and the British, by her own generals.

But in order to facilitate training it was desirable to postpone the realisation of this ideal, and she consented to brigade her men with French and British troops. The American divisional unit, (an American division numbered 30,000 men), was maintained, but it served for the present under French or British Army and corps commanders. For a month or two it was inevitable that the number of American troops capable of being used in the first line would be only a small proportion of the total in France. (There were at the moment twelve American divisions in the line in France.) But the presence of these great potential reserves had the inestimable advantage that it enabled Foch to use his seasoned troops boldly, since material for replacing them was mounting up daily.

It is hard to tell how far Germany was aware of the full danger awaiting her in this addition to the Allied strength. Whatever her General Staff may have thought, her politicians and her press gave no sign that they realised its gravity. Sneers at America were the stock-in-trade of every German newspaper and most German orators. The great American Army could not swim or fly, therefore it would never arrive; the Americans only shouted to keep warm, and would bring everything to market except their own skins; the bravos of the West were no better than Falstaff's men in buckram; only the wastrel and the degenerate ever enlisted in the ranks—such are a few phrases culled from writers of established reputation.

The financiers told the people that it was fortunate that America had entered the war, since she was the only country from which a big indemnity could be extracted. Even in July 1918 the boasting

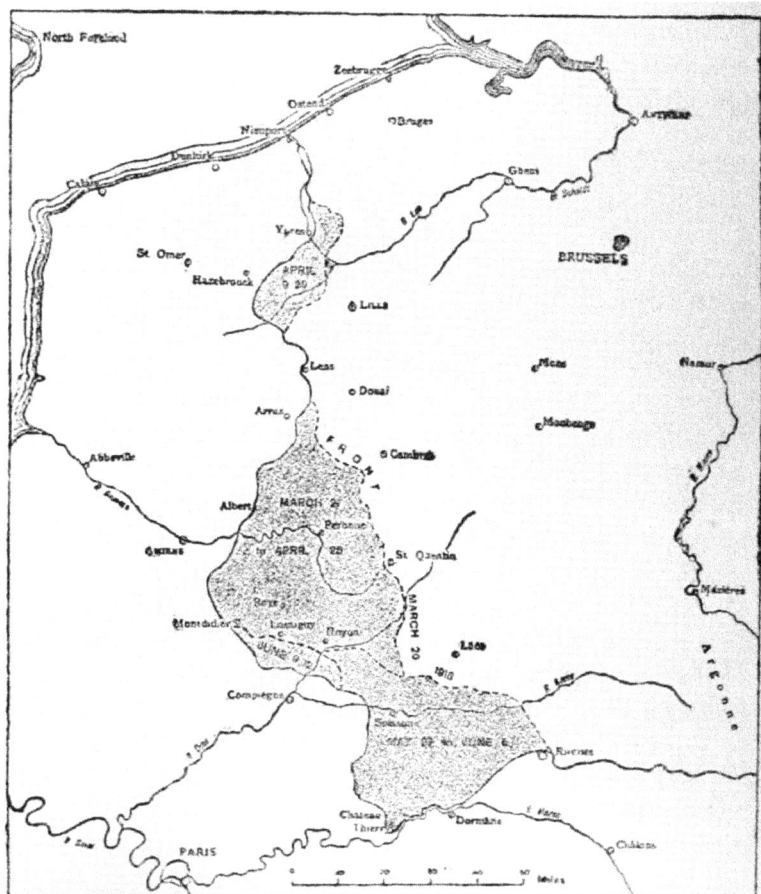

North Foreland · Zeebrugge · Ostend · Nieuport · Bruges · Dunkirk · Ghent · Calais · Scheldt · Antwerp · Ypres · St. Omer · Hazebrouck · APRIL 9-29 · Lille · BRUSSELS · Lens · Mons · Namur · Arras · Douai · Maubeuge · Abbeville · FRONT · Cambrai · Albert · MARCH 21 · Péronne · AMIENS · to APRIL 29 · St. Quentin · Roye · Montdidier · Lassigny · Noyon · MARCH 20 · Laon · 1918 · JUNE 9-13 · Mézières · Compiègne · ARGONNE · Soissons · MAY 27 to JUNE 6 · Rheims · PARIS · Château Thierry · Dormans · Châlons

Sketch Map showing the Front from the Sea to the Argonne on March 20, 1918—the ground won by the enemy from March 21 to the beginning of July—the three Salients thus formed, and the new Front on the eve of the final German effort and the Allied Counter-attack.

continued. One German journal during that month declared that the American millions would be found to be only "soldiers of a child's game, mostly made of paper cuttings;" and on 4th July the *Deutsche Tageszeitung* wrote:

> Today, on the anniversary of the American Day of Independence, the Entente will fill the world with sounding praises of this help. America herself will produce a world of bluff in the shape of phrases, threats, and assertions—all bluff, pure bluff, celebrated in Paris by a review.

A blindness from the gods had fallen upon the people, and this was to be followed hot-foot by Nemesis, the avenger.

Ludendorff was an experienced soldier, and less easily deceived. But he considered that he had still a chance of winning the victory which he had promised his people. He had waited six weeks—the same time as elapsed between the Battle of the Lys and the Third Battle of the Aisne—and he had collected every reserve from every front on which there were German troops. He had brought a new army, the IX., under von Eben, (he was succeeded on the 9th of August by von Carlowitz), from the East, to act as an "army of pursuit" when the Allied front was broken. His plan was to strike out from the awkward salient in which von Boehn had been entrapped, and to press beyond the Marne and cut the great lateral railway from Paris to Nancy.

At the same time von Mudra (who had succeeded Fritz von Below) with the I. Army, and von Einem with the III. Army, were to strike east of Rheims between Prunay and the Argonne. If these operations succeeded, Rheims and the Montagne de Rheims would fall, and the French front would be divided into two parts which would never again be joined. Then, sweeping westward, with the help of von Eben, von Boehn would march on Paris down the valley of the Marne. Foch would hurry up his scanty reserves—Ludendorff believed that they were all but exhausted, and that the Americans were too untrained to be dangerous—to the threatened point, and at that moment von Hutier and von der Marwitz would break through the Amiens-Montdidier front and descend on the capital from the north.

Then would Haig be finally cut off from Pétain, and Pétain would be broken in two, and victory, complete and cataclysmic, would follow. The Germans christened the coming battle the *Friedensturm*, the action which would bring about a "German peace."

The enemy was so confident that he made little secret of his plans.

THE SECOND BATTLE OF THE MARNE

From deserters and prisoners Foch gathered the main details long before the assault was launched. His problem was not an easy one, for he had vital objectives, like Paris and the Nancy railway, far too near his front. It was not likely that von Boehn could advance far unless he broadened his salient; but the attack of von Mudra and von Einem east of Rheims was a grave matter, for, if they succeeded, all the difficulties of the salient would vanish, and the disadvantage of position would lie wholly with the French. He resolved to meet the shock as best he could, and at the right moment to use every atom of reserve strength to strike at the enemy's nerve centre, as a wary boxer, when his antagonist has overreached himself, aims at the "mark."

It was a bold decision, for the Allied *generalissimo* had followed Montrose's maxim, and *"put it to the touch to win or lose it all."* If he failed it would be hard to save Paris. But if he succeeded—To a watcher of the auspices the German front on the map wore a look of happy omen, for it had that shape of a sickle, with the handle in Champagne and the centre of the blade on the Ourcq, which it had borne on the crucial day of September 9, 1914. That day Foch had struck and shattered the first German dream; now, after four years, he played for the same tremendous stake among the same hills and forests.

Foch had planned on a majestic scale a battle of the Napoleonic type. All the cherished stages of the great Emperor were provided for. The advance guard should take the first shock, make clear the enemy's intention, and pin him down to a definite field of action. Next, at the right moment, a blow should be delivered at the enemy's weakest flank. Last should come the thrust against the now embarrassed centre, and whatever the gods might send thereafter in the way of fortune. To carry out this scheme it was essential that the Germans should not repeat their performance at the Third Battle of the Aisne, and drive back the French too far. Some retirement was inevitable, but it must be calculated and defined.

In von Boehn's area it would be all to the good that the apex of the German salient should extend well south of the Marne till it became as deep as it was broad; it would only make the conditions better for the next stage. But the gateposts must stand, and at all costs the salient must not be widened. The critical area was east of Rheims. There the enemy must be held in the battle positions, for if he pressed too far he would render Rheims and the Montagne untenable, and instead of an ugly salient would create a broad arc curving securely into Champagne.

SENEGELESE INFANTRY AT THE SECOND BATTLE OF THE MARNE

Between Dormans, on the Marne, and Rheims Foch had the Ninth Army, under Berthelot, who had for nearly two years been chief of the Allied Mission in Rumania. With Berthelot at the Montagne de Rheims was the Italian 2nd Corps, containing picked Alpini battalions. On his left, from Dormans to Faverolles, lay the Sixth Army, under Dégoutte, who, in April 1917, had commanded the Moroccan Division at Moronvilliers. Between Faverolles and Soissons lay the Tenth Army, under Mangin. Mangin, it will be remembered, had been the hero of the winter battles at Verdun in 1916, and had commanded the Sixth Army at the Second Battle of the Aisne.

After that for many months he had been lost in obscure commands; but now he was to vindicate his claim to rank among the greatest Allied generals. East of Rheims, holding the gate of Champagne, was the Fourth Army, under Gouraud. With him was the 42nd American Division, known as the "Rainbow," since it was drawn from every State. With Dégoutte was the 1st American Corps, under General Liggett, numbering six divisions—the 1st, 2nd, 3rd, and 4th of the Regular Army, the 26th National Guard from the New England States, and the 28th National Guard from Pennsylvania, together with various units of marines.

Ludendorff, seeking a final decision, did not unduly limit his objectives. He wanted no less than the line of the Marne between Epernay and Châlons as the fruit of the first day's advance. The attack was arranged in two sections—on a front of twenty-seven miles, between Fossoy, south-east of Château-Thierry, and Vrigny; and on a front of twenty-six miles east of Rheims, between Prunay and the Main de Massiges. In each area he used fifteen divisions for the first wave, twenty-three of them fresh divisions from his general reserve, and seven of them borrowed from Prince Rupprecht's group. He had a large number of tanks, which he allotted to the area east of Rheims, where the low downs of Champagne made the going easier for machines which had not the skill of the Allied type in covering rough country.

At midnight on Sunday, 14th July, Paris was awakened by the sound of great guns. At first, she thought it an air raid, but the blaze in the eastern sky showed that business was afoot on the battlefield. She waited for news with a solemn mind, for she knew that the last phase had begun of the struggle for her possession. The "preparation" lasted till four o'clock; but before the dawn broke the Germans were aware of a new feature in the bombardment.

The French guns were replying, and with amazing skill were

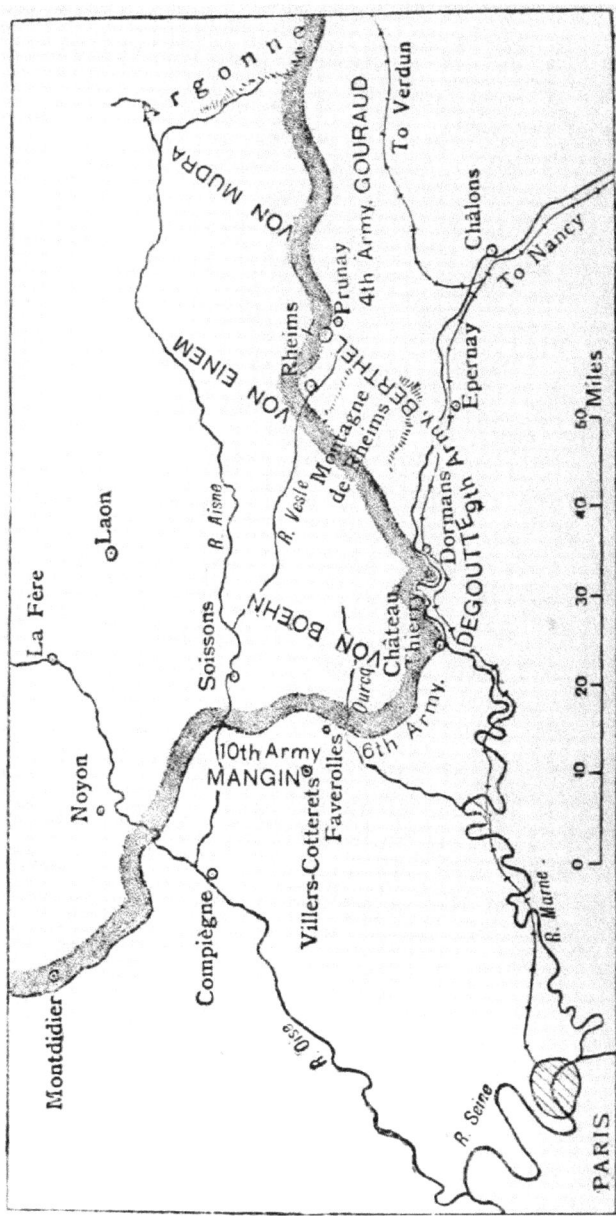

The German Front from Montdidier to Champagne, July 14, 1918.

searching out their batteries and assembly trenches, so that when zero hour came the attacking infantry in many parts of the line were already disorganised. Foch's intelligence service had done its work; he had profited by the enemy's bravado, and he read their plans like an open book.

About 4 a.m., just at dawn, the German infantry crossed the parapets. Von Boehn was instantly successful, for it was no part of Foch's plan to resist too doggedly at the apex of the salient. The Germans passed the Marne at various points between Château-Thierry and Dormans, reached the crest of the hills on the south shore, and extended to the valley where lay the villages of St. Agnan and La Chapelle. It was an advance of from one to three miles on a front of twenty-two. That evening von Boehn 's line lay from Fossoy, south of the Marne and three miles east of Château-Thierry, by Mezy, St. Agnan, La Chapelle, Comblizy, north of Mareuil le Port, through Chatillon, north of Belval, through Cuitron and Clairizet to the Bois de Vrigny.

It was a substantial advance; but one thing it had utterly failed to achieve. It had not widened the salient. No impression had been made upon the French front in the Montagne de Rheims region, and the gatepost on the west at Château-Thierry stood like a strong tower. In the former area the Italian 2nd Corps, fighting among thick woods in the upper glen of the Ardre, barred the way to Epernay by the Nanteuil-Hautvillers road. In the latter area the Americans formed the right wing of Dégoutte's army, and at Vaux and Fossoy they first checked and then rolled back the German wave, clearing that part of the south bank of the river, and taking 600 prisoners.

These were the troops who, according to the German belief, would not land in Europe unless they could swim like fishes or fly like birds. Like the doubting noble of Samaria, the Germans had declared:

If the Lord would make windows in heaven, might this thing be.

But the inconceivable had been brought to pass. Birnam Wood had come to Dunsinane.

East of Rheims von Mudra and von Einem made no headway at all. They were opposed by one who was not only a *paladin* of chivalry, but a great and wily tactician. Gouraud's counter-bombardment dislocated the German attack before it began; his deep outpost zone caused it to spend itself idly with heavy losses; his swift counterattacks checked the "infiltration" before it could be set going. Ground was, indeed, given up north of Souain and Prosnes, and between Tahure

144

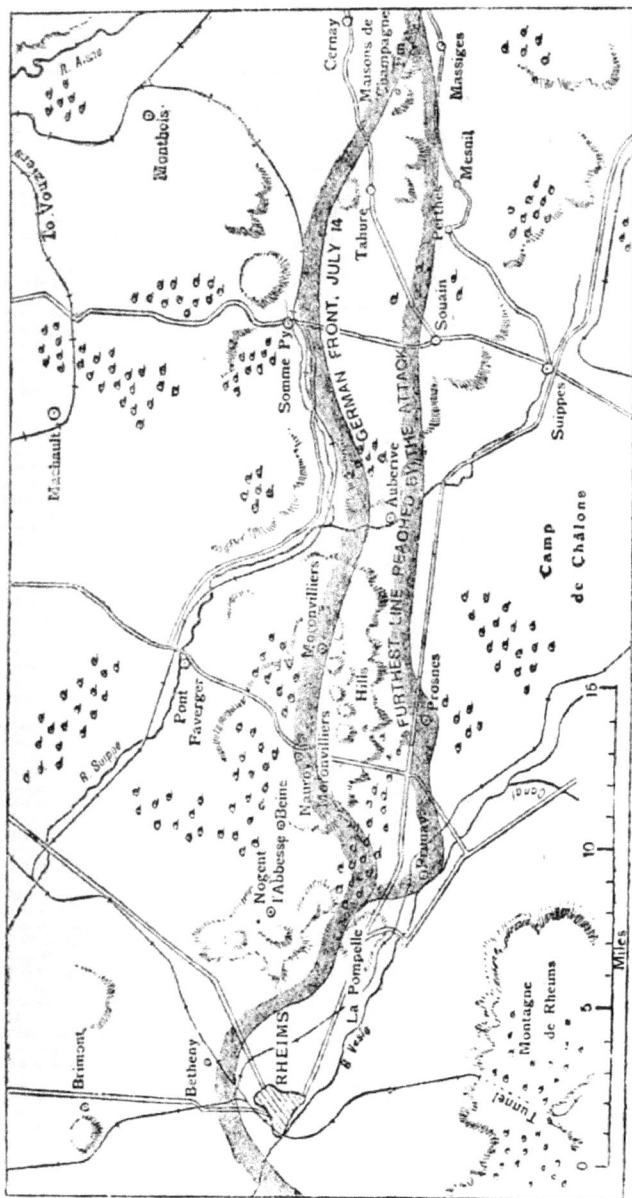

The German Offensive east of Rheims.

and Massiges on the old Champagne battle-ground, and the Germans entered Prunay. But not a French gun was lost, and Gouraud's battle zone was untouched. The German tanks were all stopped by anti-tank guns or land mines. The French losses were trifling: only 3,000 men passed that day through Gouraud's casualty stations. It was indeed such a situation as had faced Nivelle at the end of the first day of the Second Battle of the Aisne. But the failure was far graver for Ludendorff, for he was staking all on an immediate victory.

Nevertheless, the end was not yet. The Germans had still at least sixty divisions in reserve, and they were battling for dear life. The unsuccess of the first day must be redeemed, and at any cost Epernay must be reached and the Montagne isolated. Could this be done, there was still time to form a new front on the western flank and push down the Marne to Paris. The French south of the river in the St. Agnan valley had lost their power of direct observation, and so could not use their guns effectively against the German bridges. The danger point was the road to Epernay up the Marne valley, and all day on the 16th Berthelot was hotly engaged. He fell back 4,000 yards, but in the evening his centre was still holding on the line Festigny-Œeuilly-Belval.

Further west the French had better fortune, for in the afternoon they counter-attacked between Comblizy and St. Agnan, won the ridge overlooking the Marne, and proceeded to make havoc among the German pontoons. In Champagne that day there was no advance. Von Mudra and von Einem were utterly exhausted. On the fringes of the Montagne the French and Italian troops on Berthelot's right maintained their positions. The day closed with ill omens for the enemy. Since the French on the St. Agnan ridge could sweep the river crossings, it would be hard for von Boehn to maintain his eight divisions beyond the river.

Yet on Wednesday, the 17th, he still persisted. There was hard fighting on Berthelot's right wing, where the Italian 2nd Corps was engaged on the Upper Ardre, and the Germans made progress at the Bois de Courton and towards Nanteuil. The Italians, however, by a brilliant counter-attack retook the village of Clairizet. South of the Marne the French centre was pressed further up the river; but by the evening it had retaken Montvoisin and the high ground to the west between that place and Festigny. Von Boehn made a great effort to win back the ridge just south of the Marne, but failed; and all day the battle swung backwards and forwards without material result. But by the evening the eight German divisions were very weary, and their communications across the river were in serious jeopardy. They had shot their bolt, and at the farthest point had advanced some six miles from their old battle-ground.

The time had now come for Foch's counterstroke. He had resolved to thrust with all his available reserves against the weak enemy flank between Soissons and Château-Thierry. It offered a superb mark. In the first place, von Boehn was fighting with his head turned the wrong way, and in case of a flank attack must make hasty and difficult adjustments. In the second place, the German communications were parallel to their front. The great road from Soissons by Fère-en-Tardenois to Rheims, with its branches running south to the Marne, was the main feeder of the whole German line in the salient. If that were cut anywhere north of Rozoy supply would be gravely hampered.

Moreover, all the railway communications between the salient and the north depended upon the junction of Soissons. If that junction were captured or rendered unusable, the Marne front would suddenly find itself some thirty miles from a railhead. It is inconceivable that the German Staff should not have been alive to such a risk, and the only explanation is that they believed that Foch had no serious reinforcements. At the moment, between Soissons and Château-Thierry, von Boehn had only eight divisions in line and six in support; but he had large reserves inside the salient, and the new IX. Army, under von Eben, was forming in the rear for its advance on Paris.

When Foch decided to stake everything on his attack, he took one of those risks without which no great victory was ever won. Prince Rupprecht had still his twenty-two fresh divisions threatening the Amiens gate, and more than one French commander viewed the hazard with grave perturbation. There were anxious consultations between Foch, Pétain, and Fayolle, who commanded the group of armies. But the general most intimately concerned, Sir Douglas Haig, had no doubts. He was prepared to weaken his own line rather than cripple Foch's great bid for a decision. He gladly consented to the withdrawal of the eight French divisions from Flanders, and he sent a British corps to fight under Mangin and Berthelot.

Ever since the Third Battle of the Aisne had died away Mangin had been engaged in preparing a jumping-off ground for his assault. By many local attacks he had worked his way out of the gully between Ambleny and St. Pierre Aigle, and, farther south, had reached the east bank of the Savières. He wanted to be clear of the forest and the ravines, and to have a starting-point on the edge of the plateau. From

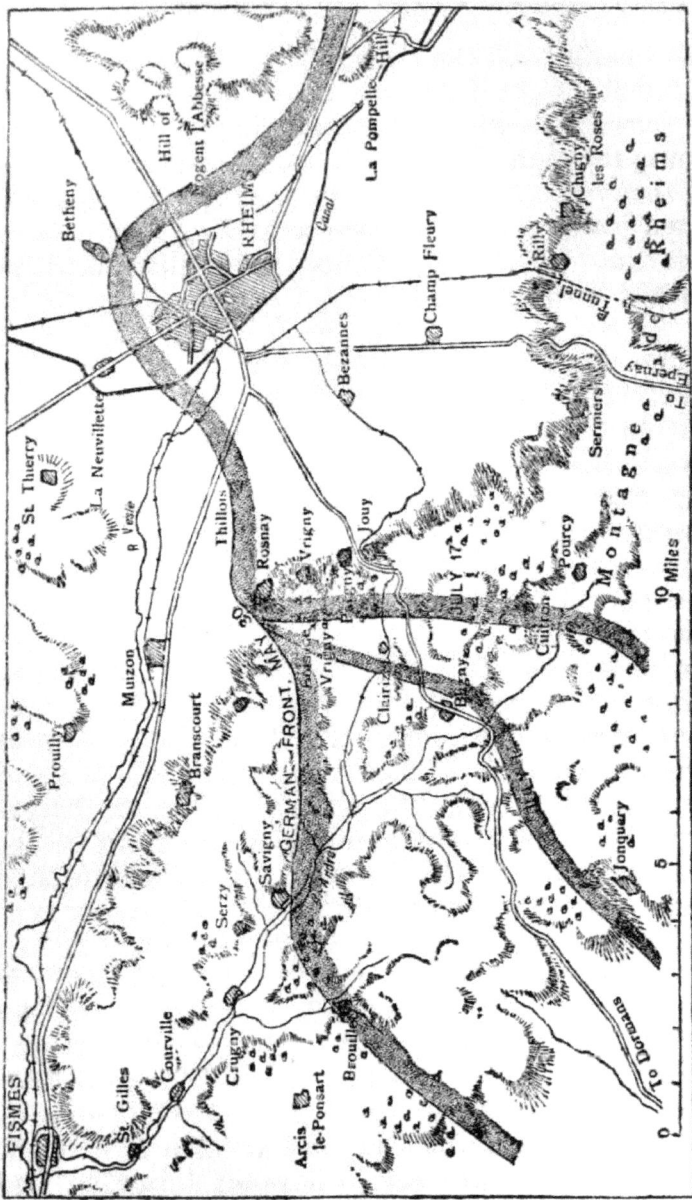

The Ardre Valley and the Montagne de Rheims Position.

Longpont there runs eastward from the forest for twenty miles a high and narrow ridge, culminating in the heights north of Grand Rozoy. This gave him an avenue for his advance, for if he could win its eastern end he would command not only the vale of the Ourcq, but the whole plateau eastward towards the Vesle.

By the morning of Thursday, the 18th, there had been a readjustment of the French forces. Mangin's Tenth Army, which was to conduct the main operations, was in its old place between the Aisne and Faverolles, on the Savières; but Dégoutte's Sixth Army, which had been holding the line from Faverolles to St. Agnan, drew in its right to Vaux, a mile west of Château-Thierry, and the gap between it and Berthelot was filled by the French reserve army, the Fifth, under de Mitry.

Mangin's reinforcements were assembled during the 17th in the shade of the Villers-Cotterets forest. The morning of the 18th dawned, after a night of thunderstorms and furious winds. There was no gun fired on the northern section, but at 4.30 out from the shelter of the woods came a great fleet of French "mosquito" tanks; and behind them, on a front of thirty-five miles, Mangin's army and Dégoutte's left wing crossed the parapets. (Dégoutte had begun an artillery "preparation" at 3.30 which lasted for an hour and a half.) During that time his pickets were working forward into the German outpost zone. The tactics of Cambrai had been faithfully followed.

From Fontenoy, on the Aisne, to Belleau, six miles north-west of Château-Thierry, was the front of action, and before the puzzled enemy could realise his danger the French and Americans were through his first defences. At the First Battle of the Marne Foch's generals had told him that they could no longer hold on. "You cannot hold on!" he replied. "Then I will attack." He was the incarnate spirit of the offensive, and that spirit, kept in leash for four arduous months, had grown with its confinement till, transmitted to every soldier of his command, it had become a devouring fire.

The advance of the 18th was like a great bound forward. The chief work was done by Mangin's left wing, which swept through the villages of Pernant and Mercin, and by half-past ten in the morning held the crown of the Montagne de Paris, half a league from the streets of Soissons, and within two miles of the vital railway junction. Farther south, his centre reached Berzy-le-Sec, on the edge of the great Soissons-Fère-en-Tardenois road, which was now cut. His right wing took Léchelle, Vierzy, and the Bois de Mauloy. Dégoutte by the

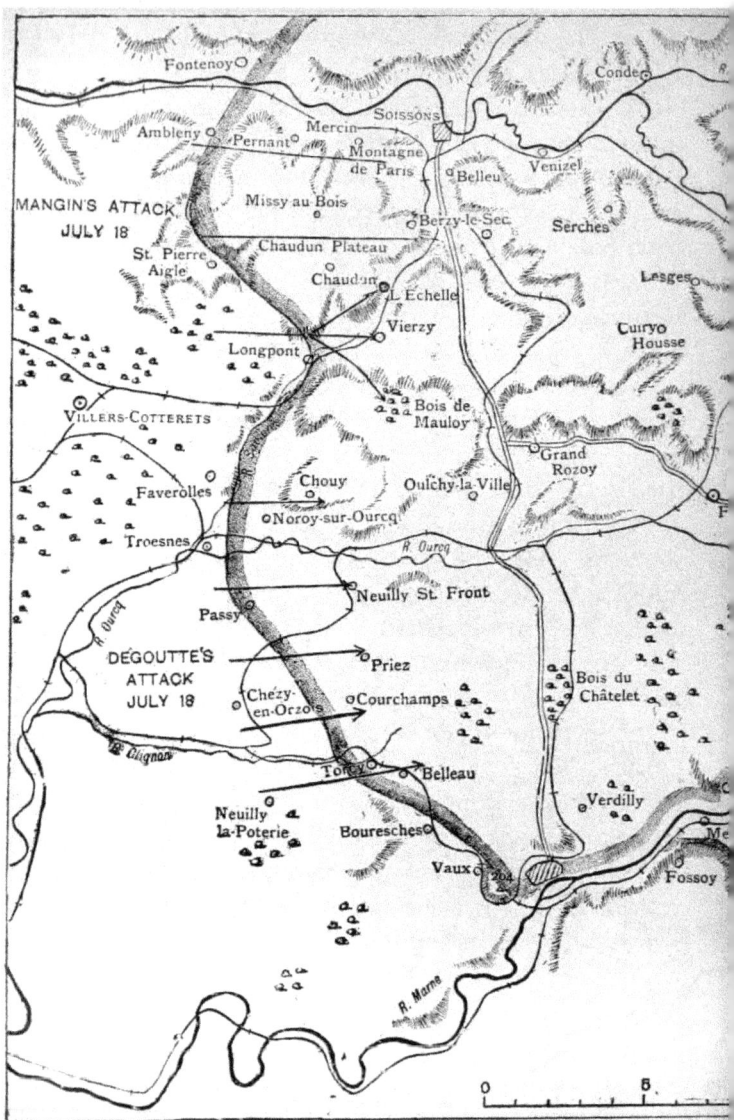

The German Advance on the Marne in July

Berry-au-Bac

Cormicy

Bermericourt

Canal

R. Vesle

St. Thierry

Mont Notre-Dame

La Neuvillette

Bethuny

Chery

Courville

Crugny

RHEIMS

Arcis-le-Ponsart

Vrigny

Clairizet

R. Ardre

Ville-en-Tardenois

Bligny

JULY 15

Cuitron

JULY 17

Jonquery

Nanteuil

Bois de Courton

JULY 15

Belval

JULY 4

Chatillon

JULY 15

JULY 16

JULY 17

FRONT. JULY

Dormans

Mareuil le Port

Œuilly

Montvoisin

Festigny

JULY 15

Comblizy

EPERNAY

La Chapelle

St. Agnan

French Counter-attack.

JULY 16

Forest of

Enghien

15   20   25 Miles

e Beginning of the Allied Counter-attack.

evening held the front Chouy-Neuilly St. Front, and thence by Priez and Courchamps to Belleau, though an enemy salient remained about Noroy-sur-Ourcq. His American troops took Courchamps, Torcy, and Belleau.

Sixteen thousand prisoners fell to the French, and some fifty guns; and at one point, Mangin had advanced as much as eight miles—the longest advance as yet made in one day by the Allies in the West. Foch had narrowed the German salient, crumpled its western flank, and destroyed its communications. He had wrested the initiative from the enemy, and brought the *Friedensturm* to a dismal close.

He had done more, though at the time no eye could pierce the future and read the full implications of his victory. Moments of high crisis slip past unnoticed; it is only the historian in later years who can point to a half-hour in a crowded day and say that then was decided the fate of a cause or a people. As the wounded trickled back through the tossing woods of Villers Cotterets, spectators noted a strange exaltation in their faces. When the news reached Paris, the city breathed a relief which was scarcely justified with the enemy still so strongly posted at her gates. But the instinct was right. The decisive blow had been struck. Foch was still far from his Appomattox, but he had won his Gettysburg. He had paralyzed the nerve-centre of the enemy, and driven him down the first stage of the road to defeat. When the Allies breasted the Montagne de Paris on that July morning, they had, without knowing it, won the Second Battle of the Marne, and, with it, the war. Four months earlier Ludendorff had stood as the apparent dictator of Europe; four months later he and his master were fleeing to a dishonoured exile.

The battles of 1918 that led to the end of the First World War are to be found in the second volume of *1918: Catastrophe to Victory*—'*The Allied Hundred Day's Offensive*'.

Appendix: Sir Douglas Haig's Sixth Dispatch

The Retreat from St. Quentin, and the Battle of the Lys.

War Office,
21st October 1918.

The following dispatch has been received by the Secretary of State for War from Field-Marshal Sir Douglas Haig, K.T., G.C.B., G.C.V.O., Commanding-in-Chief, British Armies in France:—

General Headquarters,
20th July 1918.

My Lord,

I have the honour to submit the following report upon the operations of the Forces under my Command during the period following the actions in the vicinity of Cambrai in the first week of December 1917.

General Situation.

(1) The broad facts of the change which took place in the general war situation at the close of 1917, and the causes which led to it, have long been well known, and need be referred to but shortly.

The disappearance of Russia as a belligerent country on the side of the Entente Powers had set free the great bulk of the German and Austrian divisions on the Eastern front. Already, at the beginning of November 1917, the transfer of German divisions from the Russian to the Western front had begun. It became certain that the movement would be continued steadily until numerical superiority lay with the enemy.

It was to be expected, moreover, that large numbers of guns and munitions formerly in the possession of the Russian Armies would fall into the hands of our enemies, and at some future date would be turned against the Allies.

Although the growing Army of the United States of America might be expected eventually to restore the balance in our favour, a considerable period of time would be required to enable that army to develop its full strength. While it would be possible for Germany to complete her new dispositions early in the new year, the forces which America could send to France before the season would permit active operations to be recommenced would not be large.

TRANSITION FROM AN OFFENSIVE TO A DEFENSIVE POLICY.

(2) In view of the situation described above, it became necessary to change the policy governing the conduct of the operations of the British Armies in France. Orders accordingly were issued early in December having for their object immediate preparation to meet a strong and sustained hostile offensive. In other words, a defensive policy was adopted, and all necessary arrangements consequent thereon were put in hand with the least possible delay.

EXTENSION OF THE BRITISH FRONT.

(3) Since the month of September 1917, pursuant to a decision taken by the British Government towards the end of that month, negotiations had been proceeding with the French authorities regarding the extension of the front held by the British Armies. After considerable discussion on the subject it was finally decided that the British should relieve the French troops on my right as far as the vicinity of the village of Barisis, immediately south of the River Oise. The additional front to be taken over by me amounted to over twenty-eight miles.

This relief, which was to have taken place in December, was delayed until January in consequence of the further development of the Cambrai battle. In the meantime, the French forces which had co-operated so successfully on the left of the British in Flanders had been withdrawn, and French troops again assumed responsibility for the coastal sector at Nieuport.

By the end of January 1918, the relief of the French as far as Barisis had been completed without incident. At that date the British Armies were holding some 125 miles of active front.

MAN-POWER AND TRAINING.

(4) The strenuous efforts made by the British forces during 1917 had left the Army at a low ebb in regard both to training and numbers. It was therefore of the first importance, in view of the expected Ger-

man offensive, to fill up the ranks as rapidly as possible and provide ample facilities for training.

So far as the second of these requirements was concerned, two factors materially affected the situation. Firstly, training had hitherto been primarily devoted to preparation for offensive operations. Secondly, the necessity for maintaining the front line systems of defence and the construction of new lines on ground recently captured from the enemy had precluded the development of rear line systems to any great degree.

Under the new conditions the early construction of these latter systems, involving the employment of every available man on the work, became a matter of vital importance. In consequence, it was difficult to carry out any elaborate course of training in defensive tactics. On the other hand, in the course of the strenuous fighting in 1916 and 1917, great developments had taken place in the methods of conducting a defensive battle. It was essential that the lessons learned therein should be assimilated rapidly and thoroughly by all ranks.

At the same time a change took place in the organisation of the forces. Under instructions from the Army Council, the reorganisation of divisions from a 13 battalion to a 10 battalion basis was completed during the month of February. Apart from the reduction in fighting strength involved by this reorganisation, the fighting efficiency of units was to some extent affected. An unfamiliar grouping of units was introduced thereby, necessitating new methods of tactical handling of the troops and the discarding of old methods to which subordinate commanders had been accustomed.

The difficulties with which we were faced were accentuated by the increase in the British front described in the preceding paragraph. Meanwhile, in marked contrast to our own position, the large reserves in the Western theatre, which the enemy was able to create for himself by the transfer of numerous divisions from the East, enabled him to carry out extensive training with units completed to establishment.

Preparations for Defence.

(5) Orders issued early in December, as stated above, had defined the defensive policy to be adopted and the methods of defence. A vast amount of work was required to be done in the construction of defences, old systems had to be remodelled and new systems created. The construction of new communications and the extension of old, more especially in the area south-east of Arras which the enemy had

devastated in his retirement last year, involved the building of a number of additional roads and the laying out of railways, both narrow and normal gauge. Work of this nature was particularly necessary on the Somme battlefield and in the area recently taken over from the French.

All available men of the fighting units, with the exception of a very small proportion undergoing training, and all labour units were employed on these tasks. Though the time and labour available were in no way adequate if, as was suspected, the enemy intended to commence his offensive operations in the early spring, a large portion of the work was in fact completed before the enemy launched his great attack. That so much was accomplished is due to the untiring energy of all ranks of the fighting units, the Transportation Service, and the Labour Corps.

Arrangements for Co-Operation with the French.

(6) In addition to our own defensive schemes, completion of arrangements for the closest possible co-operation with the French was recognised to be a matter of great importance and urgency. A comprehensive investigation was undertaken into the various problems connected with the co-operations of the two allied forces. Plans were drawn up in combination with the French military authorities and were worked out in great detail to meet the different situations which might arise on different parts of the Allied front. Measures were taken to ensure the smooth and rapid execution of these plans.

Among the many problems studied by the Allied Staffs, those involved by a hostile offensive on the line of the Somme River and the passage of that river by the enemy had been worked out. The plans applicable to such a situation had been drawn up and were ready to be put into execution when required.

Operations During the Winter.

(7) In order to ensure the greatest possible concentration of effort upon training, reorganisation and defences, and also in order to allow my divisions the maximum amount of rest after the continuous fighting of 1917, only such minor enterprises were undertaken by the British forces during the winter months as were essential to keep us informed regarding the dispositions and intentions of the German forces opposed to us. Special attention was directed to disposing our forces in line in such manner as would best promote economy in men and reduce casualties.

On the enemy's side, some little activity continued until the end of the year, and local attacks were made by him both on the Cambrai front and in the Ypres sector; resulting in certain small modifications in the line held by us. In these engagements, the policy followed by me was to avoid involving troops in struggles for non-essential positions, and subordinate commanders were instructed accordingly.

The first of the enemy's minor attacks took place on the 12th December in the neighbourhood of Bullecourt, and after sharp fighting led to the loss of point of the salient held by us east of that village, with a consequent shortening of our line. Other local attacks on the 14th and 22nd December at Polderhoek Château and astride the Ypres-Staden Railway also resulted in small and unimportant withdrawals of portions of our outpost line in these localities.

On the 30th December a somewhat more serious attempt was made by the enemy against our positions on Welsh Ridge, on the Cambrai front. The attack, made in the early morning on a front of over two miles from La Vacquerie northwards towards Marcoing, was delivered in considerable strength and elaborate precautions were taken by the enemy to effect surprise. South of Marcoing, the enemy gained possession of a somewhat isolated trench sited on the northern slopes of Welsh Ridge, compelling our troops to fall back to a sunken road lying across the base of the salient, where they organised a successful resistance.

At the southern end of the ridge near La Vacquerie the enemy's attack succeeded in overrunning not only our forward posts but also the trench line on the crest of the ridge, with all its advantages of observation. During the afternoon, however, an admirably executed counter-attack by two companies of the 63rd Division drove the enemy from the crest of the ridge and regained all the essential parts of our former positions.

On the 5th, and again on the 8th January, the enemy made two other local attacks east of Bullecourt, both of which were unsuccessful.

Early in March there was a recrudescence of hostile activity in the northern sector. Following upon an unsuccessful attack on the Belgian advanced positions north of Dixmude on the 6th March, two local attacks were made by the enemy two days later on the British front, the one south and north of the Menin Road, and the other on a front of over a mile south of Houthulst Forest. Both these attacks were repulsed after sharp fighting and our line maintained or re-established by counter-attacks.

During the whole of this period hostile raiding parties displayed greatly increased activity, but the vigilance of our troops prevented them from achieving any success in more than a small proportion of instances. On our side, during the earlier part of the winter, raiding activity was deliberately cut down to the lowest limits consonant with the maintenance of an adequate knowledge of the enemy's dispositions. In the three and a half months extending from the morning of the 8th December 1917 to the opening of the German offensive, some 225 raids were attempted by the enemy.

Not more than 62 of these were successful in obtaining any identification from our lines, while in 67 cases his raiding parties left prisoners or dead in our hands. During the same period some 125 raids were carried out by us, 77 of which were successful in obtaining prisoners or identifications; while in 31 other cases the enemy's trenches were found to have been evacuated.

Besides raids, considerable patrolling activity took place on both sides. In this form of warfare our troops maintained a marked superiority over the enemy on almost all occasions and secured many prisoners, in addition to inflicting frequent casualties on hostile patrols and working parties.

INDICATIONS OF THE COMING ATTACK.

(8) Towards the middle of February 1918, it became evident that the enemy was preparing for a big offensive on the Western front. It was known from various sources that he had been steadily increasing his forces in the Western theatre since the beginning of November 1917. In three and a half months 28 infantry divisions had been transferred from the Eastern theatre and 6 infantry divisions from the Italian theatre. There were reports that further reinforcements were on their way to the West, and it was also known that the enemy had greatly increased his heavy artillery in the Western theatre during the same period. These reinforcements were more than were necessary for defence, and, as they were moved at a time when the distribution of food and fuel to the civil population in Germany was rendered extremely difficult through lack of rolling stock, I concluded that the enemy intended to attack at an early date.

Constant air reconnaissances over the enemy's lines showed that rail and road communications were being improved and ammunition and supply dumps increased along the whole front from Flanders to the Oise. By the end of February 1918 these preparations had become very marked opposite the front held by the Third and Fifth British Armies, and I considered it probable that the enemy would make his initial effort from the Sensée River southwards. As the 21st March approached it became certain that an attack on this sector was imminent, and counter-preparation was carried out nightly by our artillery on the threatened front. By the 21st March the number of German infantry divisions in the Western theatre had risen to 192, an increase of 46 since the 1st November 1917.

British Dispositions to Meet the Enemy's Offensive.

(9) In making the necessary distribution of the forces under my command to meet the threatened German attack, the enemy's possible objectives and the relative importance of ground in the various sectors had to be taken into consideration. These objectives and their bearing on the distribution of the troops are set forth below:—

(1) In the northern portion of the British area lie the northern Channel ports of Dunkirk, Calais, and Boulogne, the security of which necessitated the maintenance of sufficient troops in the neighbourhood. Little or no ground could be given up on this front, and therefore the necessary reserves must be kept in close proximity.

Although, as a rule, the state of the ground would preclude a general offensive in this sector early in the year, the weather had been exceptionally dry, and preparations for an attack by the enemy astride the Menin Road were known to be in an advanced state.

(2) In the central portion lie the northern collieries of France and certain important tactical features which cover our lateral communications.

Here also little or no ground could be given up, except in the Lys Valley itself.

(3) In the southern portion of the British area southeast of Arras, in contrast to the central and northern portions, ground could be given up under great pressure without serious consequences, the forward area of this sector consisting chiefly of a wide expanse of territory devastated by the enemy last spring in his withdrawal.

As shown in paragraph (8) it was evident that the enemy was about to make a great effort south of Arras. An attack on this front would undoubtedly have as its object the separation of the French and British armies and the capture of the important centre of communications of Amiens. To meet this eventuality more than half my available troops were allocated to the defence of this sector, together with the whole of the cavalry. In addition, as previously stated, arrangements had been made for the movement of a French force to the southern portion of the British area north of the River Oise in case of need.

(4) Arrangements were made in detail for the rapid transport by rail or bus of a force of such British divisions as could be held back in reserve to meet any emergency on any sector of the British front.

THE SITUATION ON THE EVE OF THE ATTACK.

(10) On the 19th March my Intelligence Department reported that the final stages of the enemy's preparations on the Arras-St. Quentin front were approaching completion, and that from information obtained it was probable that the actual attack would be launched on the 20th or 21st March. On our side our dispositions to meet the expected offensive were as complete as the time and troops available could make them.

The front of the Fifth Army, at that date commanded by General Sir H. de la P. Gough, K.C.B., K.C.V.O., extended from our junction with the French just south of Barisis to north of Gouzeaucourt, a distance of about forty-two miles, and was held by the III., XVIII., XIX. and VII. Corps, commanded respectively by Lieut.-General Sir R. H. K. Butler, K.C.M.G., C.B., Lieut.-General Sir I. Maxse, K.C.B., C.V.O., D.S.O., Lieut.-General Sir H. E. Watts, K.C.B., C.M.G., and Lieut.-General Sir W. N. Congreve, V.C., K.C.B., M.V.O.

Over 10 miles of this front between Amigny Rouy and Alaincourt were protected by the marshes of the Oise River and Canal, and were therefore held more lightly than the remainder of the line; but on the whole front of this Army the number of divisions in line only allowed of an average of one division to some 6,750 yards of front.

The Third Army, under the command of General the Hon. Sir J. H. G. Byng, K.C.B., K.C.M.G., M.V.O., held a front of about 27 miles from north of Gouzeaucourt to south of Gavrelle with the V., IV., VI. and XVII. Corps, under the respective commands of Lieut.-General Sir E. A. Fanshawe, K.C.B., Lieut.-General Sir G. M. Harper, K.C.B., D.S.O., Lieut.-General Sir J. A. L. Haldane, K.C.B., D.S.O., and Lieut.-

General Sir C. Fergusson, Bt., K.C.B., K.C.M.G., M.V.O., D.S.O. The average length of front held by each division in line on the Third Army front was about 4,700 yards.

The general principle of our defensive arrangements on the fronts of these Armies was the distribution of our troops in depth. With this object three defensive belts, sited at considerable distances from each other, had been constructed or were approaching completion in the forward area, the most advanced of which was in the nature of a lightly held outpost screen covering our main positions. On the morning of the attack the troops detailed to man these various defences were all in position.

Behind the forward defences of the Fifth Army, and in view of the smaller resources which could be placed at the disposal of that Army, arrangements had been made for the construction of a strong and carefully sited bridgehead position covering Péronne and the crossings of the River Somme south of that town. Considerable progress had been made in the laying out of this position, though at the outbreak of the enemy's offensive its defences were incomplete.

THE ENEMY'S DISPOSITIONS.

(11) From the information at my disposal, it was expected that the enemy's heaviest attack would fall between the Sensée River and the neighbourhood of the Bapaume-Cambrai road, and on this front of some 16,000 yards eighteen German divisions are known to have been employed in line and in immediate reserve on the 21st March. It was correctly anticipated that the Flesquières salient itself would not be directly attacked in strength, but that the attack would be continued in great force from the southern flank of the salient to St. Quentin. On this front of some 48,000 yards, from Gouzeaucourt to the Oise River at Moy, forty German divisions were set in motion on the first day.

An event which, having regard to the nature of the ground, was not considered probable, was that the enemy would be able to extend the flank of his attack in any considerable strength beyond Moy. The rapid drying of the marshes, due to an exceptionally dry spring, in fact enabled the enemy to attack this lightly held front with three fresh divisions, in addition to the three divisions already in line.

COMPARISON OF FORCES ENGAGED.

(12) In all at least sixty-four German divisions took part in the

operations of the first day of the battle, a number considerably exceeding the total forces composing the entire British Army in France. The majority of these divisions had spent many weeks and even months in concentrated training for offensive operations, and had reached a high pitch of technical excellence in the attack.

To meet this assault the Third Army disposed of eight divisions in line on the front of the enemy's initial attack, with seven divisions available in reserve. The Fifth Army disposed of fourteen divisions and three cavalry divisions, of which three infantry divisions and three cavalry divisions were in reserve. The total British force on the original battle front, therefore, on the morning of the 21st March was twenty-nine infantry divisions and three cavalry divisions, of which nineteen infantry divisions were in line.

Launched on a front of about fifty-four miles on the 21st March, the area of the German offensive spread northwards on the 28th March, until from La Fère to beyond Gavrelle some sixty-three miles of our former line were involved. On this front a total of seventy-three German divisions were engaged during March against the Third and Fifth Armies and the right of the First Army, and were opposed in the first place by twenty-two British infantry divisions in line, with twelve infantry divisions and three cavalry divisions in close reserve.

As soon as it became evident that the enemy had thrown practically the whole of his striking force against this one battle front, it became both possible and necessary to collect additional reserves from the remainder of my front, and hurry them to the battlefield. Plans previously drawn up to meet such an eventuality were put into execution at once, and before the end of March, by which date the principal German effort had been broken, a further force of eight British divisions was brought south and sent into the fight. Prior to the 9th April four other British divisions were engaged, making a total of forty-six British infantry divisions and three cavalry divisions employed on the Somme battle front.

The Attack Opened.

(13) Shortly before 5 a.m. on the 21st March a bombardment of great intensity, with gas and high explosive shell from all natures of artillery and trench mortars, was opened against practically the whole fronts of the Fifth and Third Armies from the Oise to the Scarpe River, while road centres and railways as far back as St. Pol were engaged by high velocity guns. Violent bombardments were opened also

on the French front in wide sectors east and north-east of Rheims, and on portions of the British front between the Scarpe River and Lens. Our positions from south of the La Bassée Canal to the River Lys were heavily shelled with gas, and battery areas between Messines and the Ypres-Comines Canal were actively engaged. Dunkirk was bombarded from the sea.

The hour of the enemy's assault varied in different sectors, but by about 9.45 a.m. a general attack had been launched on a battle front of fifty-four miles between the Oise and the Sensée Rivers. Later in the day, as visibility improved, large numbers of low-flying aeroplanes attacked our troops and batteries.

Favoured by a thick white fog, which hid from our artillery and machine gunners the S.O.S. signals sent up by our outpost line, and in numbers which made loss of direction impossible, the attacking German infantry forced their way into our foremost defensive zone. Until 1 p.m. the fog made it impossible to see more than 50 yards in any direction, and the machine guns and forward field guns which had been disposed so as to cover this zone with their fire were robbed almost entirely of their effect. The detachments holding the outpost positions were consequently overwhelmed or surrounded, in many cases before they were able to pass back information concerning the enemy's attack.

The attack being expected, reserves had been brought forward and battle stations manned. On all parts of the battle front garrisons of redoubts and strong points in the forward zone held out with the utmost gallantry for many hours. From some of them wireless messages were received up to a late hour in the day, giving information of much value. The losses which they were able to inflict upon the enemy were undoubtedly very great and materially delayed his advance. The prolonged defence of these different localities, under conditions which left little hope of any relief, deserves to rank among the most heroic actions in the history of the British Army.

So intense was the enemy's bombardment that at an early hour our communications were severed, and so swift was his advance under the covering blanket of the mist that certain of our more advanced batteries found the German infantry close upon them before they had received warning from their own infantry that the expected attack had been launched. Many gallant deeds were performed by the personnel of such batteries, and on numerous occasions heavy losses were inflicted on bodies of hostile troops by guns firing over open sights at point-blank range.

Ronssoy Captured.

(14) During the morning reports were received that the enemy had penetrated our front line opposite La Fère, and had also broken into our forward positions north of the Bapaume-Cambrai road, and opposite Lagnicourt and Bullecourt. The first indication that the progress made by him was developing a serious aspect was the news that at noon German infantry were entering Ronssoy. This meant that in this sector the attack had already reached and penetrated a considerable distance into the second defensive belt which constituted our battle positions.

The enemy's success at this point was followed up vigorously. Templeux-le-Guerard fell into his hands shortly afterwards, while the villages of Hargicourt and Villeret, attacked simultaneously in flank and rear, were practically surrounded, and were entered about midday.

Thereafter the enemy was held up by the resistance of our troops in the rear defences of the battle zone, greatly assisted by the very gallant action of the 24th Division in Le Verguier and the 21st Division at Epéhy, on the two flanks of his advance. Both these divisions, under command respectively of Major-General A. C. Daly, C.B., and Major-General D. G. M. Campbell, C.B., held out throughout the day against repeated attacks delivered in great strength, and killed large numbers of the enemy. In this fighting parties of German troops who had entered Peizière on the northern outskirts of Epéhy were driven out by our infantry, with the assistance of tanks, which on this and many subsequent occasions did valuable and gallant work.

The Situation at Midday.

(15) At midday the enemy's infantry had reached the first line of our battle positions in strength on practically the whole front of his attack, except at the Flesquières salient, where his assaults were not pressed with the same weight as elsewhere. Save in the neighbourhood of Ronssoy, however, and at certain other points in a less serious degree, our battle positions themselves had not been entered, while at numerous localities in front of them fierce fighting was taking place around strong points still occupied by our troops.

Assisted by the long spell of dry weather, hostile infantry had crossed the river and canal north of La Fère, and south of St. Quentin had penetrated into the battle zone between Essigny and Benay. At Maissemy also our battle positions were entered at about noon, but the vigorous resistance of the 61st and 24th Divisions, assisted by troops of the 1st Cavalry Division, prevented the enemy from developing his success.

On the Third Army front also, the attack had succeeded by midday in breaking into the battle zone at certain points, and heavy fighting was taking place all along the line from the Canal du Nord north-westwards to the Sensée River. Astride the canal the enemy was held up by the 17th Division, under command of Major-General P. R. Robertson, C.B., C.M.G., and made no progress. Farther west he had entered Doignies and had taken Louverval. In Lagnicourt and to the south of it the 6th Division, under command of Major-General T. O. Marden, C.M.G., were still maintaining a gallant fight for the possession of the first line of their battle positions; but beyond that village the battle zone had been entered at Noreuil, Longatte, and Ecoust St. Mein, all of which places had fallen into the enemy's hands.

THE STRUGGLE FOR THE BATTLE ZONE.

(16) Fighting in and in front of our battle positions continued with the greatest intensity throughout the afternoon and evening. Except for certain small gains, the enemy was held by our defence, and even driven back in places by our counter-attacks. Reports received from all parts of the front testified to the unusual severity of his losses.

The most serious progress made by the enemy during this part of the struggle was on the right, south of St. Quentin. At Fargnier, having reached the eastern portion of the village by 4 p.m., during the remainder of the day his troops pressed on to the Crozat Canal and captured Quessy. North of this point the 18th Division, under command of Major-General R. P. Lee, C.B., reinforced by troops of the 2nd Cavalry Division, still held their battle positions intact, though threatened on both flanks by the enemy's progress at Quessy and at Benay, and successfully restored the situation in the neighbourhood of Ly-Fontaine by a counter-attack. Many of the strong points in the forward zone on the front of this division were also holding out, though surrounded. Wireless messages from their gallant defenders were received as late as 8.30 p.m., and rifle fire was heard in their vicinity until midnight.

Between the neighbourhood of Benay and the Somme Canal, the enemy by the evening had forced back our troops, after heavy fighting, to the rear line of their battle positions. Parties of our infantry, however, were still holding out east and north-east of Essigny, and certain of our troops in front of this line were still intact.

About Roupy and Savy all hostile attempts, in which tanks were used, to break into the battle positions of the 30th Division, under command of Major-General W. de L. Williams, C.M.G., D.S.O., were repulsed with the heaviest losses, our troops carrying out a number of successful counterattacks. In this sector, the advancing German infantry frequently bunched together and offered good targets to our artillery and machine guns.

On the remainder of the Fifth Army front our battle positions still held, the 9th Division, under command of Major-General H. H. Tudor, C.B., C.M.G., retaining also nearly the whole of their forward positions, having twice retaken by counter-attack the important local feature on their right flank known as Chapel Hill.

On the Third Army front, our line in the Flesquières salient had not been heavily attacked, and was substantially intact. Beyond this sector, fierce fighting took place around Demicourt and Doignies, and north of the village of Beaumetz-les-Cambrai. In this area the 51st Division, under command of Major-General G. T. C. Carter-Campbell, D.S.O., was heavily engaged, but from noon onwards practically no progress was made by the enemy. A counter-attack carried out by two battalions of the 19th Division, Major-General G. D. Jeffreys, C.M.G., commanding the division, with a company of tanks recovered a portion of this ground in the face of strong resistance, and secured a few prisoners, though it proved unable to clear the village of Doignies.

Lagnicourt fell into the enemy's hands during the afternoon, and heavy attacks were made also between Noreuil and Croisilles. At one time, hostile infantry were reported to have broken through the rear line of our battle positions in this sector in the direction of Mory. By nightfall the situation had been restored; but meanwhile the enemy had reached the outskirts of St. Leger and was attacking the 34th Division, under command of Major-General C. L. Nicholson, C.B., C.M.G., about Croisilles heavily from the south-west. A strong attack launched at 5 p.m. against the 3rd Division, under command of Major-General C. J. Deverell, C.B., north of Fontaine-les-Croisilles on the left bank of the Sensée River, was broken up by machine-gun fire.

At the end of the first day, therefore, the enemy had made very considerable progress, but he was still firmly held in the battle zone, in which it had been anticipated that the real struggle would take place. Nowhere had he effected that immediate breakthrough for which his troops had been training for many weeks, and such progress as he had made had been bought at a cost which had already greatly reduced his chances of carrying out his ultimate purpose.

THE FIRST WITHDRAWALS.

(17) In view of the progress made by the enemy south of St. Quentin, the thinness of our line on that front, and the lack of reserves with which to restore the situation in our battle positions, the Fifth Army Commander decided on the evening of the 21st March, after consultation with the G.O.C., III. Corps, to withdraw the Divisions of that Corps behind the Crozat Canal. The movement involved the withdrawal of the 36th Division, on the right of the XVIII. Corps, to the line of the Somme Canal.

The enemy's advance south and north of the Flesquières salient rendered a withdrawal by the V. Corps and by the 9th Division on its right necessary also. Orders were accordingly issued to the Divisions concerned for a line to be taken up, as a first stage, along the high ground known as Highland Ridge, and thence westwards along the Hindenburg Line to Havrincourt and Hermies.

These different withdrawals were carried out successfully during the night. The bridges across the Crozat and Somme Canals were destroyed, though in some cases not with entire success, it being probable that certain of them were still practicable for infantry. Instances of great bravery occurred in the destruction of these bridges. In one case, when the electrical connection for firing the demolition charge had failed, the officer responsible for the destruction of the bridge personally lit the instantaneous fuse and blew up the bridge. Many of the bridges were destroyed in the close presence of the enemy.

As by this time it had become clear that practically the whole of the enemy's striking force had been committed to this one battle, my plans already referred to for collecting reserves from other parts of the British front were put into immediate execution. By drawing away local reserves and thinning out the front not attacked, it was possible, as pointed out above, to reinforce the battle by eight divisions before the end of the month. Steps were taken also to set in operation at once the schemes previously agreed upon with the French for taking over a portion of the battle front.

THE SECOND DAY OF THE BATTLE.

(18) On the morning of the 22nd March the ground was again enveloped in thick mist, under cover of which the enemy renewed his attacks in great strength all along the line. Fighting was again very

heavy, and short-range fire from guns, rifles, and machine guns caused enormous losses to the enemy's troops. The weight of his attack, however, combined with the impossibility of observing beforehand and engaging with artillery the massing of his troops, enabled him to press forward.

THE FIGHT FOR THE CROZAT CANAL.

(19) In the south the enemy advanced during the morning as far as the line of the canal at Jussy, and a fierce struggle commenced for the passage of the canal, his troops bringing up trench mortars and machine guns, and endeavouring to cross on rafts under cover of their fire. At 1 p.m. he succeeded in effecting a crossing at Quessy, and made progress during the afternoon in the direction of Vouel. His further advance in this sector, however, was delayed by the gallant resistance of troops of the 58th Division, under command of Major-General A. B. E. Cator, D.S.O., at Tergnier, and it was not until evening, after many costly attempts and much sanguinary fighting, that the enemy gained possession of this village. During the afternoon hostile infantry crossed the canal also at La Montagne and at Jussy, but in both cases, were counter-attacked and driven back by troops of the 18th Division and 2nd Cavalry Division, Major-General T. T. Pitman, C.B., commanding the 2nd Cavalry Division.

LE VERGUIER AND EPÉHY LOST.

(20) In the centre of the battle front the enemy made a strong and determined effort to develop the success gained at Templeux-le-Guerard on the previous day, and in the early morning captured Ste. Emilie and Hervilly. Hervilly was retaken by troops of the 1st Cavalry Division (under command of Major-General R. L. Mullens, C.B.), assisted by tanks, at 9 a.m. At midday, after heavy fighting in the neighbourhood of Roisel, the 66th Division, under command of Major-General N. Malcolm, D.S.O., still held their positions in this sector, having for the time being definitely stopped the enemy's advance.

To the south and north, however, the progress of the German infantry continued. Constantly attacked from almost every direction, Le Verguier fell into the enemy's hands at about 10 a.m., after a most gallant defence. On the left bank of the Cologne River the capture of Ste. Emilie was followed by the fall of Villers Faucon, and both Roisel and Epéhy were threatened with envelopment from the rear.

Accordingly, our troops about Roisel were withdrawn during the afternoon under orders, the enemy making no attempt to interfere, and were directed to reorganise behind the line of our third defensive belt between Bernes and Boucly, which was already manned by the 50th Division, temporarily commanded by Brig.-General A. F. U. Stockley, C.M.G. Later in the afternoon the troops of the 21st Division in Epéhy also fell back under orders, though with more difficulty, as parties of hostile infantry were west of the village. To the north the 9th Division held their battle positions practically intact until the late afternoon, when they were withdrawn under orders to the rear line of defence between Nurlu and Equancourt. This retirement also was made with great difficulty.

THE BATTLE ON THE THIRD ARMY FRONT.

(21) The divisions holding the Flesquières salient were not seriously involved during the morning of the 22nd March, but in the evening strong attacks were made both at Villers Plouich and at Havrincourt. All these attacks were repulsed with great slaughter.

Farther north fighting was severe and continuous throughout the day. Shortly before noon the enemy attacked Hermies strongly from the north-west, and repeated his attacks at intervals during the remainder of the day. These attacks were completely repulsed by the 17th Division. Heavy losses were inflicted on the German infantry in the fighting in this area, the leading wave of a strong attack launched between Hermies and Beaumetz-les-Cambrai being destroyed by our fire.

In the neighbourhood of Beaumetz the enemy continued his assaults with great determination, but was held by the 51st Division and a brigade of the 25th Division until the evening, Major-General Sir E. G. T. Bainbridge, K.C.B., commanding the 25th Division. Our troops were then withdrawn under orders to positions south of the village. Very severe fighting took place at Vaulx Wood and Vaulx Vraucourt, as well as about St. Leger and north of Croisilles, which latter village our troops had evacuated during the night.

At Vraucourt the enemy broke through the rear fine of the battle zone and penetrated into the village. There he was counter-attacked by infantry and tanks, and driven out. Further west, after heavy fighting, his troops forced their way into our positions along the line of the Croisilles-Henin-sur-Cojeul road. On the left of this attack troops of the 34th Division maintained themselves in St. Leger until the afternoon, when they fell back to a line of trenches just west of the village. To the north the 3rd Division brought back their right flank to a fine facing south-east, and in this position successfully beat off a heavy attack.

THE BREAK THROUGH AT ST. QUENTIN.

(22) With Maissemy already in the enemy's hands, the fall of Le Verguier greatly weakened the defence of the centre of the Fifth Army. The rear fine of our battle positions was held during the morning, in spite of unceasing pressure from large hostile forces, but as the day wore on the great concentration of German divisions attacking west of St. Quentin had its effect. During the early afternoon our troops east of Holnon Wood were forced to withdraw from their battle zone trenches; while after repulsing heavy attacks throughout the morning, the 30th Division were again attacked during the afternoon and evening and compelled to give ground. Our troops, fighting fiercely and continuously, were gradually forced out of the battle zone on the whole of this front, and fell back through the 20th Division, under command of Major-General W. D. Smith, C.B., and the 50th Division holding the third defensive zone between Happencourt, Villeveque and Boucly, in the hope of reorganising behind them.

In this fighting the action of the 1st Battalion Royal Inniskilling Fusiliers, 36th Division, deserves special mention. This battalion held a redoubt in the forward zone near Fontaine-les-Clercs throughout the whole of the first day of the battle, and on the following day, after the troops on their right had withdrawn in accordance with orders, still maintained their position, although surrounded by the enemy. After a magnificent fight, in which all the enemy's attacks were repulsed with great loss, at 3 p.m. the officer commanding the battalion sent back a small party of troops, who succeeded in getting through to our lines. The remainder of the battalion continued the fight to the end.

By 5.30 p.m. the enemy had reached the third zone at different points, and was attacking the 50th Division heavily between Villeveque and Boucly. Though holding an extended front of some 10,500 yards, the division succeeded in checking the enemy's advance, and by a successful counterattack drove him temporarily from the village of Coulaincourt. At the close of the engagement, however, the troops of the 50th Division about Poeuilly had been forced back, and by continued pressure along the south bank of the Omignon River the enemy had opened a gap between their right flank and the troops of the 61st Division, under command of Major-General C. J. Mackenzie,

C.B., and of the 20th Division farther south. At this gap, during the late afternoon and evening, strong bodies of German troops broke through the third defensive zone about Vaux and Beauvois.

All available reserves at the disposal of the Fifth Army had already been thrown into the fight, and except for one French division and some French cavalry in the III. Corps area, no further support was within reach of the fighting line. There remained, therefore, no course open but to fall back on the bridgehead positions east of the Somme.

THE WITHDRAWAL TO THE SOMME.

(23) Accordingly, at 11 p.m. on the 22nd March, orders were issued by the Fifth Army Commander that the troops of the XVIII. Corps should fall back during the night behind the line of the Somme south of Voyennes, in touch with the III. Corps on their right; while the XIX. and VII. Corps endeavoured to secure the main Péronne bridgehead on the line Croix Molignaux—Monchy—Lagache—Vraignes, and thence northwards along the third zone of defence to the junction with the Third Army about Equancourt.

These withdrawals were carried out under constant pressure from the enemy, covered by rear-guards of the 20th, 50th, and 39th Divisions (Major-General E. Feetham, C.B., C.M.G., commanding the last-mentioned division), which were continually in action with the German troops.

On the Third Army front also, certain necessary readjustments of our line were carried out during the night. On the right, the evacuation of the Flesquières salient was continued, our troops withdrawing to a line covering Equancourt and Metz-en-Couture in touch with the Fifth Army about Equancourt. In the centre, the troops still in advance of the third defensive zone, were brought back to that system. On the left, our troops withdrew from the remainder of their forward positions south of the Scarpe, taking up the rear line of their battle positions between Henin-sur-Cojeul and Fampoux.

As on the southern portion of the battle front, the enemy followed up our troops closely, except on the left, where for a time he was unaware of what we had done. Elsewhere, more or less continuous fighting took place throughout the night, and in the early morning parties of the enemy succeeded in finding a gap in our new line about Mory.

THE DECISION TO ABANDON THE PERONNE BRIDGEHEAD.

(24) Reports that the enemy had forced the line of the Crozat Ca-

nal, combined with the loss of the Vaux-Poeuilly positions, and information obtained by the Air Service that the German front as far back as Mont D'Origny was packed with advancing troops, led the Fifth Army Commander to reconsider his decision to offer battle afresh east of the Somme. Considering that if involved in a general engagement his tired troops might be exposed to a decisive defeat before help could arrive, and that the situation might then be exploited by the enemy to a disastrous extent, he decided to continue the withdrawal at once to the west bank of the Somme.

On the morning of the 23rd March, therefore, confirming instructions previously given by telephone, orders were issued by the Fifth Army to the XIX. Corps to carry out a gradual withdrawal to the line of the Somme. The VII. Corps was directed to conform to this movement and to take up a position on the general line Doingt-Nurlu.

This order involved the abandonment of the main Péronne bridgehead position. It greatly shortened the time available for clearing our troops and removable material from the east bank of the river, for completing the necessary final preparations, for the destruction of the river and canal bridges, for reforming west of the river the divisions which had suffered most in the previous fighting, and generally for securing the adequate defence of the river line.

THE CROZAT CANAL CROSSED.

(25) Meanwhile, the enemy had recommenced his attacks. The footing obtained by him on the west bank of the Crozat Canal was gradually increased, in spite of counter-attacks by British and French troops at Tergnier and at other points. During the morning, he forced the passage of the canal at Jussy, where he was reported to have employed tanks east of the canal. Shortly afterwards hostile infantry crossed at Mennessis, though suffering great loss from the fire of a machinegun detachment of the Canadian Cavalry Brigade. By midday our troops had been pressed back from the line of the canal to the wooded ground to the west, where fierce confused fighting continued throughout the afternoon about Noureuil, Faillouel, and Cugny, infantry and cavalry offering a most resolute resistance to the enemy's advance and performing many gallant actions.

THE CROSSING AT HAM.

(26) In the course of the withdrawal to the Somme on the previous night, a gap occurred in our line in the neighbourhood of Ham,

and the enemy, following closely upon our troops, entered the town during the early morning. Before midday bodies of German infantry, though at first only in small numbers, succeeded in crossing the river about Ham and Pithon, where the bridges had not been completely destroyed. In the afternoon these forces increased in strength, gradually pressing back our troops, until a spirited counterattack by troops of the 20th and 61st Divisions about Verlaines restored the situation in this locality. To the east of this point, heavy fighting took place around Ollezy, which the 36th Division, under command of Major-General O. S. W. Nugent, C.B., D.S.O., regained and held until a late hour, and around Aubigny and Brouchy, both of which villages, however, fell into the enemy's hands before night.

Farther north, the withdrawal to the west bank of the Somme was carried out successfully during the morning and early afternoon, effectively covered by troops of the 50th Division. By 3.15 p.m. all troops were across the river, and the bridges for the most part destroyed.

All bridges over the canals and rivers in the Fifth Army area had been carefully listed early in February and reconnoitred for demolition. The necessary explosives were stored in the neighbourhood of each bridge, and a definite party of Royal Engineers detailed for its destruction. As has been seen, however, owing to the effects of the enemy's artillery fire, which blew up some of the charges and cut the leads of others, the destruction of the bridges was in certain cases incomplete.

None the less, the situation on the Somme front north of Ham was for the time being not unsatisfactory. In the course of the afternoon, strong attacks at Offoy and Bethencourt were repulsed with heavy loss by rifle and machine-gun fire. In the evening, the enemy's attempts to come down the open slopes on the east bank of the river were heavily punished by artillery fire, as they were on several subsequent occasions. It is believed that north of Ham none of the enemy succeeded in crossing the river before nightfall.

THE NORTHERN FRONT FIRM.

(27) Meanwhile, very heavy fighting had been taking place on the northern portion of the battle front. The enemy pressed closely upon our troops, as they withdrew to the line of the ridge running from north of Péronne to Nurlu and Equancourt. Heavy attacks developed at an early hour between these two places, and also between Le Bucquière and Beugny, and at Mory.

On the Third Army front, where our resources were greater, the enemy was held in check, though he gained possession of Le Bucquière and Beugny after a prolonged struggle. In this fighting the 9th Battalion Welsh Regiment, 19th Division, greatly distinguished itself in the defence of Beugny, which it held till dusk, thereby enabling the other battalions of its brigade in position to the north of the village to extricate themselves successfully from what would otherwise have been a hopeless situation.

No less than six separate attacks, in two of which the enemy brought up cavalry and guns, were repulsed by the 124th Brigade of the 41st Division, Major-General Sir S. T. B. Lawford, K.C.B., commanding the division, opposite Vaulx Vraucourt. The fighting in this sector of the front was very severe, but here and at all points north of the Bapaume-Cambrai Road our line was maintained. About 3.30 p.m. the enemy again attacked five times from the direction of Vaulx and five times from Beaumetz-lez-Cambrai, and on each occasion, was repulsed. The 40th Division, under command of Major-General J. Ponsonby, C.B., C.M.G., D.S.O., regained Mory during the afternoon by successful counterattacks, and the 31st Division, under command of Major-General R. J. Bridgford, C.B., C.M.G., D.S.O., drove off the attacks of two German divisions about St. Leger with heavy loss.

THE RETREAT TO THE TORTILLE.

(28) At the junction of the Third and Fifth Armies the situation was less satisfactory, and as the day wore on it became critical.

During the morning, the divisions of the V. Corps had proceeded with their withdrawal, and, covered by rear-guards who were heavily engaged, had fallen back from the Metz-en-Couture salient to the defences of the third zone about Ytres. The left of the VII. Corps, however, had been withdrawn under orders during the morning from the Nurlu positions to the line of the Canal du Nord, north of Moislains. As the result of this movement, a gap was formed between the flank divisions of the two corps, and this gap the enemy rapidly exploited.

Though vigorous efforts were made to re-establish touch both by the 47th Division, under command of Major-General Sir G. F. Gorringe, K.C.B., K.C.M.G., D.S.O., and by a brigade of the 2nd Division, Major-General C. E. Pereira, C.B., C.M.G., commanding the division, they were unsuccessful. The right of the V. Corps was forced back by pressure from the southeast first to the neighbourhood of Four Winds Farm, south of Ytres, where troops of the 47th Division made a gallant stand in the open until nightfall, and later to a position east of Rocquigny.

The divisions of the VII Corps, after heavy fighting during the afternoon, were forced back west of Péronne, and across the line of the River Tortille to the high ground about Bouchavesnes and Government Farm, south of Sailly-Saillisel. At dusk, however, the line was still in movement. Small parties of the enemy searched constantly for gaps, and, having found them, bodies of German infantry pressed through in force and compelled our troops to make further withdrawals.

THE EXTENSION OF THE FRENCH FRONT.

(29) From the time when the indications of an offensive on my front first became definite I had been in close touch with the Commander-in-Chief of the French Armies. On different occasions, as the battle developed, I discussed with him the situation and the policy to be followed by the Allied Armies. As the result of a meeting held in the afternoon of the 23rd March, arrangements were made for the French to take over as rapidly as possible the front held by the Fifth Army south of Péronne, and for the concentration of a strong force of French divisions on the southern portion of the battle front.

For my own part, after consultation with the First and Second Army Commanders, General Sir H. S. Home, K.C.B., K.C.M.G., and General Sir H. C. O. Plumer, G.C.B., G.C.M.G., G.C.V.O., concerning the situation on the fronts of their Armies and the possibilities of attacks developing there also, I arranged for the formation from the troops under their command of a special force of reserve divisions for action as occasion might demand. Measures were also taken to permit of the employment of the Canadian Corps for counterattack, in the event of the enemy succeeding in piercing my front.

In this connection I desire to express my deep appreciation of the complete unselfishness with which the needs of their own fronts were at all times subordinated by the Army Commanders to the more pressing demands of the battle. A variety of considerations made it necessary for me at this date to draw particularly heavily upon the resources of the Second Army. All my demands were met by the Second Army Commander in the most helpful and disinterested spirit.

THE RETREAT ACROSS THE SOMME BATTLEFIELD.

(30) During the night of the 23rd-24th March the situation on the battle front remained unchanged as far south as the neighbour-

hood of Ytres. Beyond that point divisions and brigades had lost touch in the course of their frequent withdrawals, and under the constant pressure of the enemy the rearward movement continued. At dawn German infantry had already reached Bus, Lechelle, and Le Mesnil-en-Arrouaise, and during the morning of the 24th March entered Saillisel, Rancourt, and Cléry.

It became necessary to order the evacuation of Bertincourt, and gradually to swing back the right of the Third Army in conformity with the movement farther south. To the north of Bertincourt, though the enemy gained possession of Mory in the early morning after continuous fighting throughout the night, our troops substantially maintained their positions, the Guards Division, under command of Major-General G. P. T. Feilding, C.B., C.M.G., D.S.O., and the 3rd and 31st Divisions in particular, beating off a succession of heavy attacks.

The enemy's advance at the junction of the Third and Fifth Armies was not made without heavy sacrifice. In the retirement of our troops there was no panic of any sort. Units retreated stubbornly from one position to another as they found them turned and threatened with isolation; but at many points fierce engagements were fought, and wherever the enemy attempted a frontal attack he was beaten off with loss.

During the early part of the morning troops of the 17th Division drove off four attacks east of Barastre, and the 47th Division held the village of Rocquigny from sunrise until well into the afternoon, beating off all attacks with rifle and machine-gun fire, until the enemy worked round their flank between Rocquigny and Le Transloy and forced them to withdraw.

South of this point, however, the enemy pressed forward rapidly through the gap which he had made, and succeeded in isolating a part of the South African Brigade, 9th Division, near Marrières Wood, north of Cléry. These troops maintained a most gallant resistance until 4.30 p.m., when they had fired off all their ammunition, and only about 100 men remained unwounded. Early in the afternoon German infantry entered Combles, and having gained the high ground at Marvel, were advancing towards Les Boeufs. Their continued progress threatened to sever the connection between the Fifth and Third Armies, and the situation was serious.

In view of this situation the 5th and 4th Corps were ordered to fall back to the general line, Bazentin—Le Sars—Grevillers—Ervillers. Meanwhile the leading troops of the 35th Division, under command of Major-General G. McK. Franks, C.B., which was arriving at Bray-sur-Somme, and certain composite battalions composed of all available troops in the Albert area, and including tanks personnel with Lewis guns, were hurried forward along the north bank of the river to the support of the 7th Corps. During the afternoon, also, units of the 1st Cavalry Division reached Montauban.

The enemy had already passed Cléry, and was pressing the remaining troops of the 9th and 21st Divisions hard when these various bodies of troops came into action. The 15th Battalion, Cheshire Regiment, and the 15th Battalion, Notts and Derby Regiment, of the 35th Division checked the enemy by a successful counter-attack, and thereafter a line was taken up and held from the river at Hem to Trônes Wood and Longueval. For the moment the danger in this sector was averted.

The withdrawal of the right and centre of the Third Army was carried out during the afternoon and evening in circumstances of great difficulty, as on the right flank bodies of German infantry were already between our troops and the positions to which they were directed to fall back. In this withdrawal valuable service was rendered by twelve machine guns of the 63rd Division, Machine Gun Battalion, in Les Boeufs. These guns held up the enemy's advance from Morval at a critical period, firing 25,000 rounds into the enemy's advancing masses, and by their action enabling their division to reach the position assigned to it.

By nightfall the divisions of the 5th Corps had taken up their line successfully between Bazentin, High Wood, Eaucourt, l'Abbaye, and Ligny-Thilloy. Before midnight the troops of the IV. Corps, who had carried out their withdrawal by stages in the face of constant attacks, were established on the line assigned to them west of Bapaume, between La Barque and Ervillers. Touch between the several divisions of the V. Corps and between the V. and IV. Corps, however, was not properly established.

THE FIGHT FOR THE SOMME CROSSINGS.

(31) South of Péronne the night of the 23rd-24th March passed comparatively quietly; but with the dawn powerful attempts were made by the enemy to force the crossings of the Somme, and these attempts were by no means confined to the recognised points of passage. Owing to the dry weather the river and marshes did not constitute a very formidable obstacle to infantry, while the trees and undergrowth

along the valley afforded good cover to the enemy, and limited the field of fire of the defenders.

In the early morning, hostile forces which had crossed the river at St. Christ and Bethencourt were attacked and driven back by troops of the 8th Division, under command of Major-General W. C. G. Heneker, C.B., D.S.O., and of the 20th Division; but at Pargny the enemy succeeded in maintaining himself on the west bank of the river, and the flanks of the 8th and 20th Divisions were no longer in touch. During the remainder of the day the enemy repeated his attacks at these and other points, and also exercised strong pressure in a westerly and south-westerly direction from Ham. Our troops offered vigorous resistance, and opposite Ham a successful counter-attack by the 1/5th (Pioneer) Battalion, Duke of Cornwall's Light Infantry, 61st Division, materially delayed his advance.

At nightfall the line of the river north of Epenancourt was still held by us, but the gap opposite Pargny had been enlarged, and the enemy had reached Morchain. South of that point the 20th Division, with its left flank in the air and having exhausted all reserves in a series of gallant and successful counter-attacks, fell back during the afternoon to the line of the Libermont Canal, to which position the great weight of the enemy's attacks from Ham had already pressed back the troops on its right.

The Retreat from Chauny.

(32) In the area between the Somme and the Oise the enemy's attacks had recommenced at dawn in thick fog, and were pressed with great energy. Troops of the 20th and 36th Divisions at Eaucourt and Cugny found their retreat endangered by the progress made by the enemy on their flanks, and extricated themselves with difficulty, falling back on Villeselve, and ultimately to the neighbourhood of Guiscard. The withdrawal of the troops at Cugny was made possible by a brilliant mounted charge by a squadron of the 6th Cavalry Brigade, which broke through the German line, taking over 100 prisoners and sabring a large number of the enemy.

Throughout the whole of the fighting in this area very gallant work was done, both mounted and dismounted, by units of the 2nd and 3rd Cavalry Divisions, Major-General A. E. W. Harman, D.S.O., commanding the 3rd Cavalry Division, in support of our own and the French infantry. The work of the mounted troops, in particular, was invaluable, demonstrating in marked fashion the importance of the part which cavalry have still to play in modern war. So urgent was the demand for more mounted men that arrangements were made during the progress of the battle to provide with horses several regiments of Yeomanry who had but recently been dismounted for employment with other arms. In common with the rest of the cavalry, these Yeomanry did excellent service. Without the assistance of mounted troops, skilfully handled and gallantly led, the enemy could scarcely have been prevented from breaking through the long and thinly held front of broken and wooded ground before the French reinforcements had had time to arrive.

Though French troops were coming rapidly to the assistance of the III. Corps, which on this day passed under the command of the Third French Army, the Allied forces were not yet in sufficient strength to hold up the enemy's advance. After heavy fighting throughout the morning to the east and north of Chauny, our line was gradually forced back to the south and west of that town. In the course of the night the French and British troops immediately north of the Oise were withdrawn to the ridge above Crepigny, whence the line ran across the high ground covering Noyon to the neighbourhood of Guiscard and Libermont.

THE ANCRE CROSSED.

(33) During the night of the 24th-25th March constant fighting took place on the northern portion of the battle front about Sapignies and Behagnies, where the enemy made determined but unsuccessful efforts to break through.

On the following day the enemy maintained great pressure on this front from Ervillers to the south. Shortly after dawn a very heavy attack on our positions east of the Arras-Bapaume road between Favreuil and Ervillers was repulsed with great loss, and a counter-attack by the 42nd Division, under command of Major-General A. Solly-Flood, C.M.G., D.S.O., drove the enemy out of Sapignies. Later in the morning the 2nd Division beat off an attack at Ligny-Thilloy, and our positions to the north of this point were maintained practically unchanged until midday.

At noon fresh attacks developed in great force, and under the weight of the assault the right of the IV. Corps, with which the divisions of the V. Corps were not in touch, was gradually pressed back. The enemy gained Grevillers, in which neighbourhood the 19th Division was hotly engaged, and also Bihucourt. North of this point our

179

positions were substantially maintained, and at the end of the day our troops still held Ervillers, where the 1st/10th Battalion, Manchester Regiment, 42nd Division, had repulsed eight attacks.

On the north bank of the Somme also, between the neighbourhood of Hem and Trônes Wood, all the enemy's attacks were held. Though their left flank was constantly in the air, the various forces operating in this sector maintained a gallant and most successful resistance all day, counter-attacking frequently. Prisoners from five German divisions were taken by us in the course of this fighting, and the enemy's casualties were stated by them to have been abnormally heavy.

Between Montauban and the neighbourhood of Grevillers, however, our troops had been unable to establish touch on the line to which they had withdrawn on the 24th March. After heavy fighting throughout the morning and the early part of the afternoon, in which the 63rd Division in particular, under command of Major-General C. E. Lawrie, C.B., D.S.O., beat off a number of strong assaults, divisions commenced to fall back individually towards the Ancre, widening the gap between the V. and IV. Corps.

During the afternoon the enemy reached Courcelette, and was pressing on through the gap in our line in the direction of Pys and Irles, seriously threatening the flank of the IV. Corps. It became clear that the Third Army, which on this day had assumed command of all troops north of the Somme, would have to continue the withdrawal of its centre to the line of the River Ancre, already crossed by certain of our troops near Beaucourt.

All possible steps were taken to secure this line, but by nightfall hostile patrols had reached the right bank of the Ancre north of Miraumont and were pushing forward between the flanks of the V. and IV. Corps in the direction of Serre and Puisieux-au-Mont. In view of this situation, the IV. Corps fell back by stages during the night and morning to the line Bucquoy-Ablainzevelle, in touch with the VI. Corps about Boyelles. On the right the remaining divisions of the Third Army were withdrawn under orders to the line Bray-sur-Somme–Albert, and thence took up positions along the west bank of the Ancre to the neighbourhood of Beaumont Hamel.

In spite of the dangerous gap about Serre the general position on the Third Army front, though still serious, gave less cause for anxiety. Considerable reinforcements had now come into line, and had shown their ability to hold the enemy, whose troops were becoming tired, while the transport difficulties experienced by him in the area of the old Somme battlefield were increasing. Other reinforcements were coming up rapidly, and there seemed every hope that the line of the Ancre would be secured and the enemy stopped north of the Somme.

THE SITUATION SOUTH OF THE SOMME.

(34) South of the Somme the situation was less satisfactory. The greater portion of the defensive line along the river and canal had been lost, and that which was still held by us was endangered by the progress made by the enemy north of the Somme. All local reserves had already been put into the fight, and there was no immediate possibility of sending further British troops to the assistance of the divisions in line.

On the other hand, the French forces engaged were increasing steadily, and on this day our Allies assumed responsibility for the battle front south of the Somme, with general control of the British troops operating in that sector. The situation still remained critical, however, for every mile of the German advance added to the length of front to be held, and, while the exhaustion of my divisions was hourly growing more acute, some days had yet to pass before the French could bring up troops in sufficient strength to arrest the enemy's progress.

THE ENEMY IN NOYON.

(35) During the night the enemy had gained possession of Guiscard, and in the early morning of the 25th March, strongly attacked the Allied positions on the wooded spurs and ridges east and northeast of Noyon. The position of the French and English batteries north of the Oise Canal became hazardous, and they were accordingly withdrawn across the canal at Appilly. Dismounted troops of the Canadian Cavalry Brigade actively assisted in covering this withdrawal, which was successfully completed at 1 p.m. Shortly afterwards another heavy attack developed in this sector and was checked after hard fighting. At the close of this engagement, troops of the 18th Division retook the village of Baboeuf by a brilliant counter-attack, capturing 150 prisoners. Early in the fight French armoured cars rendered valuable service and killed a number of the enemy.

Meanwhile the enemy's progress south and west of Guiscard had continued, and that night his troops entered Noyon. The French and British troops to the east of the town were therefore ordered to withdraw southwards across the Oise, and by the morning of the 26th March this had been successfully accomplished.

After this date, the troops of the III. Corps were gradually relieved by the French reinforcements and sent north to rejoin the Fifth Army.

THE RETREAT FROM THE SOMME.

(36) On the Fifth Army front, also, fighting had recommenced at an early hour. Hostile attacks at Licourt and to the south of it widened the gap between the XVIII. and XIX. Corps and the enemy entered Nesle, forcing the French and British troops back to the high ground on the south bank of the Ingon River, south-west of the town. To the south of this point his troops crossed the Libermont Canal, while to the north the right of the XIX. Corps was slowly pushed back in the direction of Chaulnes. Marchelepot was burning, but our troops at midday were reported to be still holding the line of the canal east of Villers Carbonnel and Barleux.

In view, however, of the situation to the south, and the progress made by the enemy on the right bank of the Somme west of Péronne, it was impossible for this position to be maintained. Accordingly, our troops were gradually withdrawn during the evening to the general line Hattencourt-Estrées-Frise, the 39th Division delivering a counter-attack south of Biaches to cover the withdrawal in that area.

A gap still existed between the XVIII. and XIX. Corps west of Nesle, and the Germans had already reached Liancourt Wood, when the 61st Brigade of the 20th Division, which had hitherto been engaged with the 36th Division farther south, was brought up in busses to the neighbourhood of Liancourt. Though reduced to some 450 rifles in its previous fighting, the brigade successfully held up the enemy's advance and made it possible for the remainder of its division to withdraw unmolested through Roye on the morning of the 26th March.

CAREY'S FORCE.

(37) The whole of the troops holding the British line south of the Somme were now greatly exhausted, and the absence of reserves behind them gave ground for considerable anxiety. As the result of a conference held by the Fifth Army Commander on the 25th March, a mixed force, including details, stragglers, schools personnel, tunnelling companies, Army troops companies, field survey companies, and Canadian and American engineers, had been got together and organised by General Grant, the Chief Engineer to the Fifth Army. On the 26th March these were posted by General Grant, in accordance with orders given by the Fifth Army Commander, on the line of the old Amiens

defences between Mézières, Marcelcave, and Hamel. Subsequently, as General Grant could ill be spared from his proper duties, he was directed to hand over command of his force to General Carey.

Except for General Carey's force there were no reinforcements of any kind behind the divisions which had been fighting for the most part continuously since the opening of the battle. In consideration of this fact, and the thinness of our fighting line, the Fifth Army Commander did not deem it practicable for our troops to attempt to maintain the Hattencourt-Frise positions if seriously attacked. Accordingly, orders had been given on the night of the 25th March that, in the event of the enemy continuing his assaults in strength, divisions should fall back, fighting rear-guard actions, to the approximate line Le Quesnoy-Rosières-Proyart. This line was intended to link up with the right of the Third Army at Bray.

The Attempt to Sever the Allied Armies.

(38) On the morning of the 26th March the enemy recommenced his attack in strength south-westwards and westwards from Nesle, in the double hope of separating the French and British Armies and interfering with the detraining arrangements of our Allies by the capture of Montdidier.

Heavy attacks developed also about Hattencourt, in the neighbourhood of the St. Quentin-Amiens road, and at Herbecourt. Under the pressure of these assaults our divisions commenced to withdraw slowly in accordance with orders to the line indicated above. This was taken up successfully and maintained, a number of hostile attacks during the afternoon and evening being beaten off by counter-attacks in which local commanders displayed great energy and initiative.

As the British forces retired westwards, however, the French troops on their right were gradually forced back in a south-westerly direction beyond Roye, leaving a gap between the French and British Armies of which the enemy took immediate advantage. To fill this gap, the 36th and 30th Divisions, which on the previous day had been withdrawn to rest, were put once more into the battle and speedily became involved in heavy fighting about Andechy and to the north of that place. Though the enemy had penetrated behind them and had taken Erches, the troops of the 36th Division at Andechy maintained a most gallant resistance until the afternoon of the 27th March, thereby playing no small part in preventing the enemy from breaking through between the Allied Armies.

On this part of the battle front a very gallant feat of arms was performed on this day by a detachment of about 100 officers and men of the 61st Brigade, 20th Division, at Le Quesnoy. The detachment was detailed to cover the withdrawal of their Division, and under the command of their Brigade Major, Captain E. P. Combe, M.C., successfully held the enemy at bay from early morning until 6 p.m. at night, when the eleven survivors withdrew under orders, having accomplished their task.

At the end of the day, although the enemy's thrust west of Roye had pressed back our right somewhat beyond the positions to which it had been intended to withdraw, the British forces south of the Somme were in touch with the French, and the general line, Guerbigny—Rouvroy-en-Santerre—Proyart, had been taken up successfully.

THE NORTHERN ADVANCE STOPPED.

(39) Meanwhile, north of the Somme the battle was entering upon its final stages; though the enemy's effort was not yet fully spent and his troops were still capable of powerful attacks.

During the morning of the 26th March our troops continued the taking up of the Ancre line without much interference from the enemy, but between Hamel and Puisieux the situation was not yet clear. A gap still existed in this area between the V. and IV. Corps, through which bodies of German infantry worked their way forward and occupied Colincamps with machine guns. These machine guns were silenced by a section of field artillery of the 2nd Division, which gallantly galloped into action and engaged them over open sights.

Early in the afternoon troops of the New Zealand Division, under command of Major-General Sir A. H. Russell, K.C.B., K.C.M.G., retook Colincamps, while a brigade of the 4th Australian Division, Major-General E. G. Sinclair-Maclagan, C.B., D.S.O., commanding the division, filled the gap between Hebuterne and Bucquoy. In the fighting in this area our fight tanks came into action for the first time and did valuable service.

With the arrival of fresh troops our fine on this part of the front became stable, and all attempts made by the enemy during the day to drive in our positions about Bucquoy and to the north were repulsed with great loss.

THE WITHDRAWAL FROM BRAY-SUR-SOMME.

(40) Farther south, the Bray-sur-Somme—Albert line had been

taken up successfully on the night of the 25th-26th March, and fighting of a minor character occurred during the morning, particularly at Meaulte, where troops of the 9th Division beat off a strong attack. Owing, however, to a misunderstanding, the Bray-sur-Somme—Albert line was regarded by the local commander as being merely a stage in a further retirement to the line of the Ancre, south of Albert. Accordingly, on the afternoon and evening of 26th March, the withdrawal was continued, and when the higher command became aware of the situation the movement had already proceeded too far for our former positions to be re-established.

By the time the withdrawal had been stopped the right of the Third Army rested on the Somme about Sailly-le-Sac; while the Fifth Army still held the south bank of the Somme north of Proyart, about five miles farther east. The left flank of the Fifth Army, therefore, was dangerously uncovered, being protected merely by the natural obstacle of the river and an improvised force of 350 men with Lewis guns and armoured cars which had been sent up to hold the crossings.

GENERAL FOCH APPOINTED TO TAKE COMMAND OF THE ALLIED FORCES.

(41) On this day, the 26th March, the Governments of France and Great Britain decided to place the supreme control of the operations of the French and British forces in France and Belgium in the hands of General Foch, who accordingly assumed control.

THE ENEMY IN ALBERT.

(42) During the night of the 26th-27th March, the enemy had gained possession of Albert after some fighting with our rear-guards in the town, and obtained a footing in Aveluy Wood. His efforts to force our positions on the high ground west of the Ancre, however, met with no success, and several attempts made by him on the 27th March to debouch from Albert were driven back with heavy loss to his troops.

About midday, a series of strong attacks commenced all along our front from about Bucquoy to the neighbourhood of Hamelincourt, in the course of which the enemy gained possession of Ablainzevelle and Ayette. Elsewhere, all his assaults were heavily repulsed by troops of the 62nd Division, under command of Major-General W. P. Braithwaite, C.B., and of the 42nd and Guards Divisions. On the remainder of our front north of the Somme, save for minor readjustments of our line at certain points, in the course of which we captured a number of prisoners and machine guns, our positions remained unchanged.

THE FIGHT FOR THE ROSIÈRES LINE.

(43) South of the Somme, meanwhile, the enemy had recommenced his attacks at about 8.30 a.m. on the greater part of the Fifth Army front and against the French. The line occupied by our troops at this time, had it been maintained, would have preserved Amiens from serious bombardment, and orders were issued that every effort was to be made to hold our positions. In the fighting which followed troops of all divisions, despite the weakness of their numbers, and the tremendous strain through which they had already gone, displayed a courage and determination in their defence for which no praise can be too high.

At 10 a.m. the 8th Division at Rosières had already repulsed a heavy attack, and the enemy was pressing hard against our positions in the neighbourhood of Proyart. The results of the unfortunate withdrawal from Bray now became apparent. The enemy was not slow to take advantage of the position held by him along the north bank of the Somme in the rear of our troops, and in spite of our efforts to destroy or hold the river crossings, began to pass strong parties of infantry to the south bank at Cerisy.

Being heavily attacked in front and with bodies of the enemy established south of the river in their immediate rear, our troops at Proyart and to the north were compelled to fall back. The enemy gained Framerville, Proyart, and Morcourt, and endeavoured to advance southwards behind our line.

In view of the absence of reserves behind this front other than the composite force already referred to, the situation was serious. Troops of the 1st Cavalry Division were hurried across the river and occupied Bouzencourt, in which neighbourhood they had sharp fighting. A very gallant and successful counter-attack carried out with great dash by the 2nd Battalion Devon Regiment and the 22nd (Pioneer) Battalion Durham Light Infantry, both of the 8th Division (which was itself heavily engaged at the time at Rosières), supported by troops of the 50th Division, at this date under command of Major-General H. C. Jackson, D.S.O., held up the enemy a short distance south-west of Proyart. A counter-attack by the 66th Division restored the situation about Framerville, and at nightfall our troops were still east and north of Harbonnières, whence our line ran north-westwards to Bouzencourt.

South of Harbonnières, the 8th Division held the village of Rosières against all attacks and killed great numbers of the enemy. South of this point, as far as Arvillers, troops of the 24th, 30th, and 20th Divisions maintained their positions substantially unchanged throughout the day, though beyond their right flank the enemy passed Davenscourt and captured Montdidier.

The Amiens Defences.

(44) During the night of the 27th-28th March, parties of the enemy worked their way southwards from Morcourt and Cerisy and entered Bayonvillers and Warfusée-Abancourt, astride the main Amiens road. Our troops east of these places were seriously endangered, and in the early morning of 28th March were directed to withdraw to the line Vrely-Marcelcave. Our line from Marcelcave to the Somme was manned by Carey's Force, with the 1st Cavalry Division in close support. During the evening the enemy concentrated heavy artillery fire on Marcelcave, and forced these troops to withdraw a short distance to the west of the village.

The position of our troops at Arvillers and Vrely, however, in the deep and narrow salient between the Avre and Luce Rivers, was rapidly becoming untenable. The enemy was pushing southwards from Guillaucourt, and beyond our right flank had entered Contoire and was pressing the French troops back upon Hangest-en-Santerre. A gallant attempt by troops of the 61st Division to regain Warfusée-Abancourt and lighten the pressure from the north proved unsuccessful, and in the course of the afternoon and evening our troops fell back through the 20th Division, which during the evening was disposed on the line Mézières-Démuin. At nightfall we held approximately the Amiens defence line on the whole front south of the Somme from Mézières to Ignaucourt and Hamel.

The nature of the fighting on the southern portion of the battle front where our troops had been engaged for a full week with an almost overwhelming superiority of hostile forces had thrown an exceptional strain upon the Fifth Army Commander and his Staff. In order to avoid the loss of efficiency which a continuance of such a strain might have entailed, I decided to avail myself of the services of the Staff of the Fourth Army, which was at this time in reserve.

General Sir H. S. Rawlinson, Bart., G.C.V.O., K.C.B., K.C.M.G., who had but recently given up the command on appointment to Versailles, accordingly returned to his old army, and at 4.30 p.m. on this day assumed command of the British forces south of the Somme. At the same time the construction of new defence lines made necessary by the enemy's advance called for the appointment of an able and experienced Commander and Staff to direct this work and extemporise garrisons for their defence. I accordingly ordered General Gough to undertake this important task.

THE ATTACK ON ARRAS.

(45) Meanwhile between 7 and 8 a.m. on the morning of the 28th March fighting of the utmost intensity had broken out north of the Somme from Puisieux to north-east of Arras. Finding himself checked on the northern flank of his attack, the enemy on this day made a determined effort to obtain greater freedom for the development of his offensive, and struck in great force along the valley of the Scarpe at Arras.

This development of the battle, which had been foreseen as early as the 23rd March, involved the right of the XIII. Corps, under command of Lieut.-General Sir H. de B. de Lisle, K.C.B., D.S.O., on the right of the First Army, and represented a considerable extension of the original front of attack. A German success in this sector might well have had far-reaching effects. There is little doubt that the enemy hoped to achieve great results by this new stroke, and that its failure was a serious set-back to his plans.

After a bombardment of great violence three fresh German divisions advanced to the assault along the north bank of the Scarpe River against the positions held by the 4th and 56th British Divisions, under the command respectively of Major-General T. G. Matheson, C.B., and Major-General F. A. Dudgeon, C.B., and were supported in their attack by the two German divisions already in line. According to captured documents, the enemy's immediate object was to gain the general line Vimy—Bailleul—St. Laurent—Blangy, when three special assault divisions were to carry the Vimy Ridge on the following day. Immediately south of the Scarpe four German divisions were engaged, to two of which were assigned the tasks of capturing Arras, and the heights overlooking the town.

This assault, the weight of which fell on the 3rd and 15th British Divisions, Major-General H. L. Reed, V.C., C.B., C.M.G., commanding the latter division, was supported by powerful attacks, in which eleven hostile divisions were engaged, along our whole front southwards to beyond Bucquoy. Still farther south, as far as Dernancourt, strong local attacks were delivered at different points. The methods followed by the enemy on this occasion were the same as those employed by him on the 21st March, but in this instance the thick fog which had played so decisive a part on that day was absent. In consequence, our artillery and machine guns were given every opportunity to engage the German infantry both when assembling and while advancing to the attack, and the heaviest losses were inflicted on them by our fire.

Immediately prior to the assault, masses of German infantry with artillery in rear of them were observed drawn up in close formation on Greenland Hill, and were shelled by our artillery. North of the Scarpe, about Roeux, great execution was done at point-blank range by single guns which we had placed in forward positions close up to our front line. The enemy's infantry in this sector are reported to have advanced almost shoulder to shoulder in six lines, and on the whole front our machine gunners obtained most favourable targets.

The weight and momentum of his assault and the courage of his infantry, who sought to cut their way through our wire by hand under the fire of our machine guns, sufficed to carry the enemy through the gaps which his bombardment had made in our outpost line. Thereafter, raked by the fire of our outposts, whose garrisons turned their machine guns and shot at the enemy's advancing lines from flank and rear, and met by an accurate and intense fire from all arms, his troops were everywhere stopped and thrown back with the heaviest loss before our battle positions.

A second attack launched late in the afternoon north of the Scarpe, after a further period of bombardment, was also repulsed at all points. At the end of the day our battle positions astride the Scarpe were intact on the whole front of the attack, and in the evening successful counter-attacks enabled us to push out a new outpost line in front of them. Meanwhile, the surviving garrisons of our original outpost line, whose most gallant resistance had played so large a part in breaking up the enemy's attack, had fought their way back through the enemy, though a party of the 2nd Battalion, Seaforth Highlanders, 4th Division, remained cut off at Roeux until successfully withdrawn during the night.

On the southern portion of his attack, the enemy's repulse was, if possible, even more complete than on the new front east of Arras. Attacks on the Guards Division and on the 31st Division were defeated after all-day fighting. The 42nd Division drove off two attacks from the direction of Ablainzevelle, and the 62nd Division with an attached brigade of the 4th Australian Division also beat off a succession of heavy attacks about Bucquoy with great loss to the enemy.

Less important attacks at different points between Hebuterne and Dernancourt were in each case repulsed, and led to the capture of a number of prisoners by our troops.

The End of the First Stage.

(46) With this day's battle, which ended in the complete defeat of the enemy on the whole front of his attack, the first stage of the enemy's offensive weakened and eventually closed on the 5th April. During these days hostile pressure continued south of the Somme, and after much fierce and fluctuating fighting in this area, accompanied by a number of strong local attacks also on the northern portion of the battle front, the enemy on the 4th and 5th April made final unsuccessful efforts to overcome the resistance of the Allies. These attacks, however, though formidable, lacked the weight that had made his earlier successes possible, while the strength of the Allied positions increased from day to day.

During the night of the 28th-29th March, our outpost line between Arleux-en-Gohelle and Avion was withdrawn to conform to our positions farther south. Except at minor points, no further ground was gained by the enemy north of the Somme; while by successful local operations on the 30th March and the night of the 2nd-3rd April, the New Zealand Division advanced their line at Hebuterne, capturing 250 prisoners and over 100 machine guns, and the 32nd Division, under command of Major-General C. B. Shute, C.B., C.M.G., retook Ayette with 192 prisoners. A number of prisoners were taken by us also in local fighting at other points.

The Fighting in the Avre and Luce Valleys.

(47) During these latter days the problem south of the Somme was to disengage the divisions which had been fighting since the 21st March, and give them an opportunity to reorganise. Profiting by the great weariness of our troops, the enemy was making progress by local attacks rather than by general attacks in force, and there is little doubt that, had it been possible to put in fresh troops a few days earlier, the enemy's advance could have been stopped and even turned back without much difficulty.

The divisions of the III. Corps, which had already been heavily engaged, were on their way to reinforce our line. These troops, however, had not yet arrived, and on the 29th March the greater part of the British front south of the Somme was held by Carey's Force, assisted by the 1st Cavalry Division and such troops of the divisions originally engaged as it had not yet been found possible to withdraw. In rear of these troops, a few of the divisions of the Fifth Army were given a brief opportunity to reassemble.

Hostile pressure recommenced during the morning of 29th March from Démuin southwards, and in spite of vigorous counter-attacks our troops and the French were forced back from Mézières.

During the night the enemy established a footing in Moreuil Wood, and on the following morning attacked on both sides of the River Luce. Our line in Moreuil Wood was restored by a brilliant counter-attack carried out by the Canadian Cavalry Brigade, supported by the 3rd Cavalry Brigade, but the enemy gained possession of Démuin. North of the Luce also the enemy made some progress, but in the afternoon, was held up and finally driven back into Aubercourt by counter-attacks carried out by troops of the 66th Division and the 3rd Australian Division, Major-General Sir J. Monash, K.C.B., commanding the latter division.

In this operation a squadron of the 2nd Cavalry Division co-operated very finely. In the evening, a most successful counter-attack by troops of the 20th and 50th Divisions re-established our line south of the Luce and captured a number of prisoners.

Other hostile attacks on both banks of the Somme were repulsed with heavy loss to the enemy by the 1st Cavalry Division and the 3rd Australian Division, a battalion of United States Engineers rendering gallant service south of the river.

The fighting between the Avre and the Luce continued during the evening of this day, and in the afternoon of the 31st March developed into strong attacks between Moreuil and Démuin. Powerful assaults were delivered also on the French front as far south as Montdidier. In both cases the enemy made progress after heavy fighting, at the close of which troops of the 8th Division carried out a successful counter-attack, thereby considerably improving the situation West of Moreuil Wood. At the end of the day our line ran from Moreuil Station to Hangard, and thence to our old line west of Warfusée-Abancourt.

On the following morning troops of the 2nd Cavalry Division and of the 8th Division again attacked, and as the result of a very gallant action effected a further improvement in our positions in this neighbourhood. On the 2nd April, for the first time since the opening of the enemy's offensive, no attack took place on the British front south of the Somme.

THE FINAL EFFORT.

(48) On the 4th and 5th April the enemy made a final effort to prevent the French and British line from becoming stable.

The principal attack on the 4th April was made south of the Somme, and involved the whole of the British front between the river and Hangard, where we joined the French, and also the French Army on our right. The first assault delivered at 7 a.m., after a comparatively short bombardment, was completely repulsed on the right of our line, but on the left obliged our troops to fall back to the west of Hamel and Vaire Wood. During the afternoon the enemy again attacked heavily on the right, and caused our line to be withdrawn a short distance in the neighbourhood of Hangard Wood.

The enemy attacked in dense formation, and his infantry afforded excellent targets for our artillery and machine guns. Particularly heavy losses were inflicted on the enemy by the artillery of the 3rd Australian Division, on the north bank of the Somme, which engaged his troops across the river over open sights with excellent effect.

The attack on the French front succeeded in making some progress on both sides of the Avre River.

On the 5th April the principal German effort was made north of the Somme, the enemy attacking heavily on practically the whole front from Dernancourt to beyond Bucquoy. Strong local attacks were made also south of the Somme about Hangard, where the French and British troops had severe fighting until late in the day, and in the sector immediately south of the river, where the attacking German infantry were stopped by our artillery and machine-gun fire.

North of the river, except for minor readjustments of our line at certain points, particularly in the neighbourhood of Bucquoy, where he gained the eastern portion of the village, the enemy's efforts were entirely without result. His troops, held or driven back at all points, lost heavily, and any hope that he may have entertained of opening the road to Amiens at the eleventh hour ended in an exceedingly costly repulse.

In the neighbourhood of Rossignol Wood, the enemy's attack was entirely disorganised by a local attack carried out at a somewhat earlier hour by the 37th Division, under command of Major-General H.

B. Williams, C.B., D.S.O., as the result of which our positions were improved and over 130 prisoners captured by us.

With the failure of his attacks on the 4th and 5th April the enemy's offensive on the Somme battle front ceased for the time being, and conditions rapidly began to approximate to the normal type of trench warfare, broken only by occasional local attacks on either side.

Reason for Retirement on the Right of the Battle Front.

(49) Though the enemy's progress had been stopped, this result had been obtained only by the sacrifice of a very considerable area of ground and by a great expenditure of reserves.

This latter factor was to have a material influence upon the course of the subsequent fighting on the northern portion of the British front. Before passing, therefore, to the operations on the Lys, it will be convenient to give some account of the causes to which the retirement on the Fifth Army front and the right of the Third Army can be attributed:—

(1) In the first place, the forces at the disposal of the Fifth Army were inadequate to meet and hold an attack in such strength as that actually delivered by the enemy on its front.

The reason for this state of affairs has already been pointed out in paragraph 9 of this report, in which the relative importance of the various portions of the line held by the British Army was explained. The extent of our front made it impossible, with the forces under my command, to have adequate reserves at all points threatened. It was therefore necessary to ensure the safety of certain sectors which were vital, and to accept risks at others.

In certain sectors, particularly in the northern and central portions of my front, it was of vital importance that no ground should be given up to the enemy. In the southern sector alone, it was possible under extreme pressure to give ground to some extent without serious consequences, over the area devastated by the enemy in his retreat in the spring of 1917. The troops holding this latter part of the front could fall back to meet their reinforcements, which need not necessarily be pushed forward so far or so rapidly as elsewhere. Moreover, the southern sector could be reinforced with French troops more easily than any other portion of the British line. I therefore considered it unsound to maintain a considerable force of reserves south of the River Somme, while it was yet unknown where and to what extent the enemy would commit his reserves.

The Fifth Army was instructed early in February to act accordingly, both in regard to defensive preparations on the ground and in the actual conduct of the defence.

(2) The front south of the River Omignon was only taken over by the British some seven weeks before the enemy's attack, a period insufficient to ensure that the scheme of defence would be in an efficient state of preparation. During the winter it had been possible to hold the defences in this sector very lightly, and they were consequently in themselves inadequate to meet any serious form of attack.

Much work, therefore, had to be carried out by the Fifth Army, and strenuous efforts were made with such resources as were available to improve the defences as rapidly as possible. Great difficulties, however, were met with in the devastated area. The roads were in a bad condition, there was no light railway system, the broad-gauge system was deficient, and there was a serious lack of accommodation for the troops. The amount of labour at our disposal being limited, all available labour units in rear of the forward defensive zones were allotted to the construction of the Péronne Bridgehead defences, which were considered of primary importance, with the result that practically no work had been carried out with the object of securing the line of the River Somme itself.

(3) The thick fog which enveloped the battlefield on the mornings of the 21st and 22nd March undoubtedly masked the fire of artillery, rifles, and machine guns. Where the troops on the ground were more numerous, this was not of such extreme importance; but where the defences were more lightly held, as in the southern sector of the Fifth Army front, and depended for their maintenance on the cross fire of artillery and machine guns, the masking of our fire enabled the enemy to penetrate and turn the flanks of certain important localities.

(4) On the extreme right, the valley of the River Oise, normally marshy and almost impassable during the early spring, was, owing to the exceptionally dry weather, passable for infantry almost everywhere, and formed no serious obstacle. This applies

equally to the valley of the River Somme, which in the latter stage of the battle was easily negotiated by the hostile infantry between the recognised points of passage. A much larger number of troops would therefore have been required to render the defence of these rivers secure. These forces, however, were not available except at the expense of other and more vital portions of my front, and as the exceptional weather conditions could not have been foreseen by the enemy at the time when the preparations for his offensive were undertaken, there was a strong possibility that he would not be able to take advantage of them.

(5) For some time prior to the 21st March it was known that the enemy had been making extensive preparations for an offensive on the Rheims front, and that these preparations were already far advanced. As pointed out above, the bombardment on the battle front had been accompanied by great artillery activity on both sides of Reims. It could not be determined with certainty that this was a feint until the attack upon the British had been in progress for some days. The enemy might have employed a portion of his reserves in this sector, and the knowledge of this possibility necessarily influenced the distribution and utilisation of the French reserves.

THE SITUATION ON THE NORTHERN FRONT.

(50) The possibility of a German attack north of the La Bassée Canal, for which certain preparations appeared to have been carried out, had been brought to my notice prior to the 21st March. Indications that preparations for a hostile attack in this sector were nearing completion had been observed in the first days of April, but its extent and force could not be accurately gauged.

There were obvious advantages for the enemy in such a course of action. In the first place, the depth of his advance on the southern portion of the battle front had left him with a long and dangerously exposed flank between Noyon and Montdidier. The absence of properly organised communications in the battle area made this flank peculiarly vulnerable to a counter-stroke by the French. To prevent this, and preserve the initiative in his hands, it was essential that he should renew his attack without delay.

In the second place, the heavy and prolonged struggle on the Somme had placed a severe strain on the forces under my command

and had absorbed the whole of my reserves. Further, to meet the urgent demands of the battle, I had been forced to withdraw ten divisions from the northern portion of my line, and to replace them by divisions exhausted in the Somme fighting, which had only just been made up with reinforcements recently sent out from home. The divisions thus withdrawn had been taken chiefly from the Flanders front, where, in a normal year, the condition of the ground could be relied upon to make offensive operations on a large scale impossible before May at the earliest.

A strong additional reason for drawing these divisions principally from the north was furnished by conditions on the central portion of my front between the Scarpe and the La Bassée Canal. Should urgent necessity arise it would be possible to give ground to a limited extent in the north, while still preserving strong lines of defence, which could in part be covered by inundations. On the other hand, a breakthrough on our centre, about Vimy, would mean the realisation of the enemy's plan which had been foiled by our defence at Arras on the 28th March, namely, the capture of Amiens and the separation of the bulk of the British armies from the French and from those British forces acting under the direction of the latter.

The enemy's preparations for an offensive in this central sector, the extreme importance of which will readily be understood, had been complete for some time. The admirable and extensive railway system serving it made it possible for him to effect with great rapidity at any moment the concentration of troops necessary for an attack. My own forces in this sector, therefore, could not greatly be reduced.

In consequence of these different factors, the bulk of the divisions in front line in the northern battle, and in particular the 40th, 34th, 25th, 19th, and 9th Divisions which on the 9th April held the portion of my front between the Portuguese sector and the Ypres-Comines Canal, had already taken part in the southern battle. It must be remembered that before the northern battle commenced forty-six out of my total force of fifty-eight divisions had been engaged in the southern area.

At the end of March, however, the northern front was rapidly drying up under the influence of the exceptionally rainless spring, and, in view of the indications referred to, the possibility of an early attack in this sector became a matter for immediate consideration. Arrangements for the relief of the Portuguese divisions, which had been continuously in line for a long period and needed rest, were therefore undertaken during the first week of April, and were to have been completed by the morning of the 10th April. Meanwhile, other divisions winch had been engaged in the Somme fighting, and had been withdrawn to rest and reorganise, were moved up behind the Lys front. Arrangements had already been made for the evacuation of the salient at Passchendaele should circumstances require it, a measure which would both upset any preparations which the enemy might have made for an offensive there and economize a few troops for use elsewhere.

The steps which I could take, however, to meet a danger which I could foresee were limited by the fact that, though the enemy's progress on the Somme had for the time being been stayed, the great mass of hostile divisions still concentrated on that front constituted a threat to the safety of the British Armies of an imperative character. The enemy was in a position to take immediate advantage of any weakening of my forces in that area.

THE LYS BATTLE OPENED.

(51) The persistence of unseasonably fine weather and the rapid drying up of the low-lying ground in the Lys Valley enabled the enemy to anticipate the relief of the 2nd Portuguese Division.

On the night of the 7th April, an unusually heavy and prolonged bombardment with gas shell was opened along practically the whole front from Lens to Armentières. At about 4 a.m. on the 9th April the bombardment recommenced with the greatest intensity with both gas and high explosive shell.

The enemy's attack in the first instance was launched on the northern portion of the front of General Sir H. S. Horne's First Army, held by the XI. and XV. Corps, under command respectively of Lt.-General Sir R. C. R. Haking, K.C.B., K.C.M.G., and Lt.-General Sir J. P. Du Cane, K.C.B. On the 10th April the right of General Sir H. C. O. Plumer's Second Army, held by the IX. Corps, under command of Lt.-General Sir A. Hamilton Gordon, K.C.B., was also involved. In the early stages of the battle the XV. Corps was transferred to the Second Army, and at later dates the extension of the battle front led to the intervention of the I. Corps, under command of Lt.-General Sir Arthur Holland, K.C.B., M.V.O., D.S.O., on the First Army front, and of the XXII. Corps, under command of Lt.-General Sir A. J. Godley, K.C.B., K.C.M.G., on the Second Army front. Subsequently the II. Corps of the Second Army, under command of Lt.-General Sir C. W.

Jacob, K.C.B., became involved in the withdrawal from the Passchen-daele salient.

At about 7 a.m. on the 9th April, in thick fog which again made observation impossible, the enemy appears to have attacked the left brigade of the 2nd Portuguese Division in strength and to have broken into their trenches. A few minutes afterwards, the area of attack spread south and north. Shortly after 7 a.m. the right brigade of the 40th Division reported that an attack had developed on their front, and was being held, but that machine gunners near their right-hand post could see the enemy moving rapidly through the sector to the south of them.

Communication with the divisions in line was difficult, but during the morning the situation cleared up, and it became apparent that a serious attack was in progress on the front of the 55th Division, under command of Major-General H. S. Jeudwine, C.B., and of the 2nd Portuguese and 40th Divisions from the La Bassée Canal to Bois Grenier. Meanwhile, shortly after the opening of the bombardment, orders had been given to the 51st and 50th Divisions to move up behind Richebourg-St.Vaast and Laventie and take up their positions in accordance with the prearranged defence scheme. Both these divisions had also been heavily engaged in the Somme battle, and had but recently arrived in the neighbourhood. The 1st King Edward's Horse and the 11th Cyclist Battalion had been sent forward at once to cover their deployment.

Between 8 a.m. and 9 a.m. the enemy succeeded in occupying the forward posts of the right battalion of the 40th Division, and attacked northwards along the Rue Petillon and Rue de Bois. Our machine-gun posts in this area continued to fight until all but one of their machine guns were destroyed, and by their fire greatly delayed his progress. At 10.15 a.m.; however, his troops were already in Rouge de Bout, more than 2,000 yards in rear of the headquarters of the 40th Division's right battalion, which, at this hour, were still holding out at Petillon. Later in the morning, the 40th Division was pushed back by pressure on its front and flank to a position facing south between Bois Grenier, Fleurbaix, and Sailly-sur-la-Lys, its right brigade in particular having lost heavily.

South of the Portuguese sector, the 55th Division was heavily attacked on its whole front, and by 10.30 a.m. its left brigade had been forced back from its outpost line. The main line of resistance was intact and a defensive flank was formed facing north between Festubert and a strong point just south of Le Touret, where touch was established later with troops of the 51st Division.

Throughout the remainder of the day, the 55th Division maintained its positions against all assaults and by successful counter-attacks captured over 750 prisoners. The success of this most gallant defence, the importance of which it would be hard to overestimate, was due in great measure to the courage and determination displayed by our advanced posts. These held out with the utmost resolution, though surrounded, pinning to the ground those parties of the enemy who had penetrated our defences, and preventing them from developing their attack. Among the many gallant deeds recorded of them, one instance is known of a machine gun which was kept in action although the German infantry had entered the rear compartment of the "pillbox" from which it was firing, the gun team holding up the enemy by revolver fire from the inner compartment.

To the north of the positions held by the 55th Division the weight and impetus of the German attack overwhelmed the Portuguese troops, and the enemy's progress was so rapid that the arrangements for manning the rear defences of this sector with British troops could scarcely be completed in time.

The 1st King Edward's Horse and the 11th Cyclist Battalion, indeed, occupied Lacouture, Vieille Chapelle, and Huit Maisons, and by their splendid defence of those places enabled troops of the 51st and 50th Divisions to come into action east of the Lawe River between Le Touret and Estaires. East of Estaires our troops found the enemy already in possession of the right bank of the river, and touch between the 50th and 40th Divisions could not be established. After heavy fighting the right of the 40th Division was forced back upon the Lys, and early in the afternoon withdrew across the river at Bac St. Maur.

The remainder of the 40th Division, reinforced by troops of the 34th Division, established themselves in a position covering the approaches to Erquinghem and Armentières, between Fort Rompu on the Lys and our old front line northeast of Bois Grenier. Here they successfully maintained themselves, although the line was not readily defensible and was constantly attacked. In this fighting very gallant service was rendered by the 12th Battalion, Suffolk Regiment, 40th Division, who held out in Fleurbaix until the evening, though heavily attacked on three sides.

During the afternoon troops of the 51st and 50th Divisions (chiefly composed of drafts hurriedly sent up to join their regiments) were heavily engaged east of the Lawe River and were gradually pressed back upon the river crossings. The enemy brought up guns to close range and in the evening crossed at Estaires and Pont Riqueul, but in both cases, was driven back by counter-attacks. At the end of the day the bridgeheads were still held by us as far east as Sailly-sar-la-Lys.

In the course of the night our troops at Estaires and in the sector to the south were withdrawn to the left bank of the Lawe and Lys Rivers, after sharp fighting about Pont Riqueul. The bridges across both rivers were blown up, though, as had been the case in the Somme battle, in some instances their destruction was incomplete.

The Crossing at Bac St. Maur.

(52) East of Sailly-sur-la-Lys the enemy had followed closely the troops of the 40th Division, who had crossed at Bac St. Maur, and, though here also the bridge had been blown up, at about 3 p.m., succeeded in passing small parties across the river by an emergency bridge under cover of machinegun fire. During the remainder of the afternoon and evening the strength of his forces north of the river steadily increased, and pushing northwards they reached Croix du Bac. At this point they were counter-attacked early in the night by a brigade of the 25th Division, and pressed back. Our troops were unable, however, to clear the German infantry completely from the village, and during the night the enemy established himself firmly on the north bank of the river.

The Struggle for Estaires.

(53) Early in the morning of the 10th April, the enemy launched heavy attacks covered by artillery fire about the river crossings at Lestrem and Estaires, and succeeded in reaching the left bank at both places; but in each case, he was driven back again by determined counter-attacks by the 50th Division.

The enemy continued to exercise great pressure at Estaires, and fierce street fighting took place, in which both sides lost heavily. Machine guns, mounted by our troops in the upper rooms of houses, did great execution on his troops as they moved up to the attack until the machine guns were knocked out by artillery fire. In the evening the German infantry once more forced their way into Estaires, and after a most gallant resistance the 50th Division withdrew at nightfall to a prepared position to the north and west of the town.

East of Estaires the enemy had already crossed the Lys in strength, with artillery in close support of his infantry, and by the evening had pressed back our troops to a position north of Steenwerck. Thereafter, the arrival of British reinforcements for the time being held up his advance.

THE ATTACK AT MESSINES.

(54) Meanwhile, after an intense bombardment of our front and support lines and battery areas between Frelinghien and Hill 60, strong hostile attacks had developed at about 5.30 a.m. in this sector also.

The outpost positions of the 25th and 19th Divisions in line north of Armentières and east of Messines were driven in, and during the morning the enemy worked his way forward under cover of mist along the valleys of the Warnave and Douve Rivers, on the flanks of our positions in Ploegsteert Wood and Messines. By midday he had gained Ploegsteert Village, together with the south-eastern portions of Ploegsteert Wood, and had captured Messines. North of that village the area of attack extended during the afternoon as far as the north bank of the Ypres-Comines Canal. In this new sector the enemy carried our forward positions as far as Hollebeke, pushing back our line to the crest of the Wytschaete Ridge.

Messines was retaken early in the afternoon by the South African Brigade, 9th Division. During the night this division cleared Wytschaete of parties of German troops. North of Hollebeke our positions astride the Ypres-Comines Canal were substantially unchanged, and on this front the 9th Division killed great numbers of the enemy.

THE WITHDRAWAL FROM ARMENTIERES.

(55) The enemy's advance north of Armentières made the position of the 34th Division in that town very dangerous. Though it had not yet been attacked on its own front, its available reserves had already been heavily engaged in protecting its southern flank. As the northern flank also had now become exposed, it was decided to withdraw the division to the left bank of the Lys. The early stages of the movement were commenced shortly after midday. Though the operation was closely followed up by the enemy and pressed by him on all sides, it was carried out with great steadiness and in good order, and by 9.30 p.m. had been completed successfully. All the bridges across the river were destroyed.

THE FALL OF MERVILLE.

(56) On the morning of the 11th April the enemy recommenced

his attacks on the whole front, and again made progress. Between Givenchy and the Lawe River the successful resistance of the past two days was maintained against repeated assaults. Between Locon and Estaires the enemy, on the previous evening, had established a footing on the west bank of the river in the neighbourhood of Fosse. In this area and northwards to Lestrem he continued to push westwards, despite the vigorous resistance of our troops.

At Estaires, the troops of the 50th Division, tired and reduced in numbers by the exceptionally heavy fighting of the previous three weeks, and threatened on their right flank by the enemy's advance south of the Lys, were heavily engaged. After holding their positions with great gallantry during the morning, they were slowly pressed back in the direction of Merville.

The enemy employed large forces on this front in close formation, and the losses inflicted by our rifle and machinegun fire were unusually heavy. Our own troops, however, were not in sufficient numbers to hold up his advance, and as they fell back and their front gradually extended, gaps formed in the line. Through these gaps bodies of German infantry worked their way forward, and at 6 p.m. had reached Neuf Berquin. Other parties of the enemy pushed on along the north bank of the Lys Canal and entered Merville. As it did not appear possible to clear the town without fresh forces, which were not yet available, it was decided to withdraw behind the small stream which runs just west of the town. This withdrawal was successfully carried out during the evening.

THE WITHDRAWAL FROM NIEPPE AND HILL 63.

(57) Heavy fighting took place on the remainder of the front south of Armentières, and the enemy made some progress. In this sector, however, certain reinforcements had come into action, and in the evening a counter-attack carried out by troops of the 31st Division, recently arrived from the southern battlefield, regained the hamlets of Le Verrier and La Becque.

Meanwhile, north of Armentières strong hostile attacks had developed towards midday, and were pressed vigorously in the direction of Nieppe and Neuve Eglise. In the afternoon, fierce fighting took place about Messines, which the enemy had regained. Beyond this, his troops were not able to push their advance, being checked and driven back by a counter-attack by the South African Brigade. South of Hollebeke the 9th Division had again been heavily attacked during the morning, but had held their positions.

Owing to the progress made by the enemy in the Ploegsteert sector, the position of the 34th Division at Nieppe, where they had beaten off a determined attack during the morning, became untenable. Accordingly, in the early part of the night our troops at Nieppe fell back under orders to the neighbourhood of Pont d'Achelles. Still further to shorten our line and economise men, our troops between Pont d'Achelles and Wytschaete were withdrawn to positions about 1,000 yards east of Neuve Eglise and Wulverghen. This withdrawal involved the abandonment of Hill 63 and of the positions still held by us about Messines.

THE SOUTHERN FLANK STEADY.

(58) Though our troops had not been able to prevent the enemy's entry into Merville, their vigorous resistance, combined with the maintenance of our positions at Givenchy and Festubert, had given an opportunity for reinforcements to build up our line in this sector. As troops of the 3rd, 4th, 5th, 31st, 61st, and 1st Australian Divisions began to arrive the southern portion of the battle front gradually became steady. Time was still required, however, to complete our dispositions, and for the next two days the situation in this area remained critical.

A sudden attack just before dawn on the 12th April broke through the left centre of the 51st Division about Pacaut and Riez du Vinage, and but for the gallantry and resource of two batteries of the 255th Brigade, R.F.A., commanded respectively by Major L. N. Davidson, D.S.O., and Major F. C. Jack, M.C., might have enabled the enemy to cross the La Bassée Canal. Each of these batteries as it retired left a gun within 500 yards of the canal, and, assisted by a party of gunners who held the drawbridge with rifles, worked with them to such good purpose that the enemy's advance was stopped. The 3rd Division was already in action on the right of the 51st Division about Locon, where, though forced to fall back a short distance, our troops inflicted very heavy casualties upon an enemy greatly superior in numbers. On the left of the 51st Division, the 61st Division was coming into action about the Clarence River. Both the 3rd and the 61st Divisions had been engaged in many clays of continuous fighting south of Arras; but with the arrival of these troops, battle-weary though they were, the enemy's progress in this sector of the front was definitely checked.

At Merville also our troops, though compelled to give ground somewhat during the morning, thereafter maintained themselves successfully.

THE THRUST TOWARDS HAZEBROUCK.

(59) Meanwhile, a situation which threatened to become serious had arisen north of Merville. At about 8 a.m. the enemy attacked in great strength on a front extending from south of the Estaires-Vieux Berquin Road to the neighbourhood of Steenwerck. After very heavy fighting, in the course of which the 1st Battalion Royal Guernsey Light Infantry, 29th Division, Major-General D. E. Cayley, C.M.G., commanding the division, did gallant service, he succeeded in the afternoon in overcoming the resistance of our troops about Doulieu and La Becque, forcing them back in a north-westerly direction. As the result of this movement, a gap was formed in our line south-west of Bailleul, and bodies of the enemy who had forced their way through seized Outtersteene and Merris.

In the evening a brigade of the 33rd Division, Major-General R. J. Pinney, C.B., commanding the division, with a body of Cyclists, a Pioneer battalion, and every available man from schools and reinforcement camps, came into action in this sector. On their left, troops of the 25th, 34th, and 49th Divisions, Major-General N. J. G. Cameron, C.B., C.M.G., commanding the last-mentioned division, though heavily attacked, maintained their positions to the south and southeast of Bailleul, and before midnight our line had been reformed.

Next day, the enemy followed up his attacks with great vigour, and the troops of the 29th and 31st Divisions, now greatly reduced in strength by the severe fighting already experienced, and strung out over a front of nearly 10,000 yards east of the Forêt de Nieppe, were once more tried to the utmost. Behind them the 1st Australian Division, under command of Major-General Sir H. B. Walker, K.C.B., D.S.O., was in process of detraining, and the troops were told that the line was to be held at all costs, until the detrainment could be completed.

During the morning, which was very foggy, several determined attacks, in which a German armoured car came into action against the 4th Guards Brigade on the southern portion of our line, were repulsed with great loss to the enemy. After the failure of these assaults, he brought up field guns to point-blank range, and in the northern sector with their aid gained Vieux Berquin. Everywhere, except at Vieux Berquin, the enemy's advance was held up all day by desperate fighting, in which our advanced posts displayed the greatest gallantry, maintaining their ground when entirely surrounded, men standing back to back in the trenches and shooting to front and rear.

In the afternoon the enemy made a further determined effort, and by sheer weight of numbers forced his way through the gaps in our depleted line, the surviving garrisons of our posts fighting where they stood to the last with bullet and bayonet. The heroic resistance of these troops, however, had given the leading brigades of the 1st Australian Division time to reach and organise their appointed line east of the Forêt de Nieppe. These now took up the fight, and the way to Hazebrouck was definitely closed.

The performance of all the troops engaged in this most gallant stand, and especially that of the 4th Guards Brigade, on whose front of some 4,000 yards the heaviest attacks fell, is worthy of the highest praise. No more brilliant exploit has taken place since the opening of the enemy's offensive, though gallant actions have been without number.

The action of these troops, and indeed of all the divisions engaged in the fighting in the Lys Valley, is the more noteworthy because, as already pointed out, practically the whole of them had been brought straight out of the Somme battlefield, where they had suffered severely, and had been subjected to a great strain. All these divisions, without adequate rest and filled with young reinforcements which they had had no time to assimilate, were again hurriedly thrown into the fight, and, in spite of the great disadvantages under which they laboured, succeeded in holding up the advance of greatly superior forces of fresh troops. Such an accomplishment reflects the greatest credit on the youth of Great Britain, as well as upon those responsible for the training of the young soldiers sent out from home at this time.

THE STRUGGLE FOR NEUVE EGLISE.

(60) On the afternoon of the 12th April sharp fighting had taken place in the neighbourhood of Neuve Eglise, and during the night the enemy's pressure in this sector had been maintained and extended. By the morning of the 13th April his troops had forced their way into the village, but before noon were driven out by troops of the 33rd and 49th Divisions by a most successful counter-attack in which a number of prisoners were taken.

In the course of this day, also, a succession of heavy attacks were driven off with great loss to the enemy by the 33rd and 34th Divisions about Méteren and La Crèche. In the evening further attacks developed on this front and at Neuve Eglise. The pressure exercised by the enemy was very great, and bodies of German infantry, having forced their way in between La Creche and Neuve Eglise, began a strong encircling movement against the left of the 34th Division north and east of the former village. During the early part of the night our troops maintained their positions, but before dawn on the 14th April withdrew under orders to a line in front of the high ground known as the Ravelsburg Heights between Bailleul and Neuve Eglise, the enemy having been too severely handled to interfere.

At Neuve Eglise the enemy again forced his way into the village, and heavy and confused fighting took place throughout the night. A party of the 2nd Battalion Worcestershire Regiment, 33rd Division, maintained themselves in the *Mairie* until 2 p.m. on the 14th April, and during the morning of this day other troops of the same division were reported to have cleared the village with bombs. The enemy persisted in his attacks, however, and by midnight Neuve Eglise was definitely in his possession. Other attacks delivered on the 14th April between Neuve Eglise and Bailleul and south-east of Méteren were repulsed.

Farther south, local fighting had taken place meanwhile both on the 13th and 14th April at a number of points between Givenchy and the Forêt de Nieppe. In these encounters the enemy had met with no success. On the other hand, a local operation carried out by the 4th Division on the evening of the 14th April resulted in the recapture of Riez du Vinage with 150 prisoners.

The Capture of Bailleul.

(61) On the morning of the 15th April the 19th Division repulsed hostile attacks about Wytschaete. Late in the afternoon fresh assaults in great strength, in which the Alpine Corps and two other fresh German divisions were engaged, developed against Bailleul and the Ravelsburg Heights. After heavy fighting the enemy gained a footing on the eastern end of the high ground, and, though driven back by a counterattack, re-established his position there and worked west along the ridge. By 7 p.m. the whole of it was in his possession, and the retention of Bailleul itself became very difficult. Two hours later, hostile infantry forced their way into the town, and our troops, who were being heavily attacked from the east and south, were compelled to fall back to positions between Méteren and Dranoutre.

The Withdrawal at Passchendaele.

(62) In order to set free additional British troops for the battle and to delay the execution of any plans which the enemy might be entertaining for extending the flank of his attack to the north, I approved of putting into execution the scheme for the gradual evacuation of the Ypres salient. The first stage in this withdrawal had been carried out on the night of the 12th-13th April, since which date our positions on the Passchendaele Ridge had been held by outposts only.

On the night of the 15th-16th April the withdrawal was carried a stage further, our troops taking up positions along the line of the Steenbeek River and the Westhoek and Wytschaete Ridges.

The Arrival of French Troops.

(63) The constant and severe fighting on the Lys battle front, following so closely upon the tremendous struggle south of Arras, had placed a very serious strain upon the British forces. Many British divisions had taken part both in the northern and southern battles, while others had been engaged almost continuously from the outset of the German offensive. I had represented the state of affairs to General Foch, Commanding-in-Chief the Allied Forces, and had pointed out to him the necessity of relief for the British troops and their need of an opportunity to rest and refit. General Foch had complied with my request without delay. Certain French forces were moved to the north, and by this date were already in position close behind the British front in Flanders.

The First Attacks on Kemmel.

(64) At different times on the 16th April a number of strong local attacks were made by the enemy on the Méteren-Wytschaete front, which were for the most part repulsed with heavy loss to him by the 25th, 34th, and 49th Divisions. At Méteren and Wytschaete, however, he succeeded in penetrating our positions, and after much rather confused fighting established himself in both villages. Counter-attacks delivered during the evening by British and French troops failed to eject him, though at Wytschaete a battalion of the 9th Division reached the eastern edge of the village, and our line was ultimately established close up to its western and northern outskirts.

These attacks were followed on the morning of the 17th April by a determined attempt on the part of the enemy to capture the commanding feature known as Kemmel Hill. The assault was launched after a preliminary bombardment of great intensity, and was accompanied by strong attacks in the Méteren and Merris sectors.

The enemy's attacks in the Kemmel sector were pressed with great determination, but ended in his complete repulse at all points by troops of the 34th, 49th, and 19th Divisions, his infantry being driven out by counter-attacks wherever they had gained a temporary footing in our line. The attacks at Méteren and Merris were also beaten off with heavy loss by the 33rd Division and the 1st Australian Division.

On this day also, the enemy launched a strong assault upon the right of the Belgian Army about the Ypres-Staden Railway. This attack, the object of which was to capture Bixschoote and advance beyond the Yser Canal, ended in complete failure, and left over 700 prisoners in the hands of our Allies.

Operations North of Béthune.

(65) On the 18th April the enemy made a fresh effort to overcome our resistance on the southern flank of his attack.

After a heavy bombardment which at Givenchy is reported to have exceeded in intensity even the bombardment of 9th April, his infantry attacked on nearly the whole front from Givenchy to west of Merville. At Givenchy and Festubert they succeeded at certain points in entering our positions, but after severe and continuous fighting, lasting throughout the day, the troops of the 1st Division, under command of Major-General E. P. Strickland, C.B., C.M.G., D.S.O., regained by counter-attacks practically the whole of their original positions. Elsewhere the enemy failed to obtain even an initial success, being repulsed with exceedingly heavy loss at all points by the 4th and 61st Divisions.

For nearly a week following the failure of these attacks the battle on the Lys front died down, though sharp fighting of a minor character took place from time to time at different points, particularly in the neighbourhood of Festubert, where a strong point known as Route "A" keep changed hands more than once before remaining finally in our possession. Further west, the 4th Division, in co-operation with the 61st Division, carried out a series of successful local operations north of the La Bassée Canal, resulting in the capture of some hundreds of prisoners and a considerable improvement of our positions between the Lawe and the Clarence Rivers.

During this period, also, the French troops which had already come into line in the neighbourhood of Méteren and opposite Spanbroekmolen, gradually relieved the British troops between these two points, and by the morning of the 21st April had taken over the whole of the Kemmel sector.

THE ATTACK ON VILLERS BRETONNEUX.

(66) Local attacks, meanwhile, had taken place from time to time on both sides of the Somme battle front, particularly in the vicinity of Hangard, where our line linked up with the French, and about Aveluy Wood. On the 23rd April a more serious attack, in which four German divisions were employed against the British forces alone and German and British tanks came into conflict for the first time, took place on the Allied front between the Somme and the Avre Valleys.

At about 6.30 a.m., after a heavy bombardment lasting about three hours, the enemy advanced to the assault on the whole British front south of the Somme, under cover of fog. In the ensuing struggle German tanks broke through our line south-east of Villers Bretonneux, and turning to north and south, opened the way for their infantry. After heavy fighting, in which great losses were inflicted on his troops both by our infantry fire and by our light tanks, the enemy gained possession of Villers Bretonneux; but was held up on the edge of the wood just west of that place by a counterattack by the 8th Division. South of Villers Bretonneux, some of our heavy tanks came into action and drove back the German tanks, with the result that the enemy's infantry were stopped some distance to the east of Cachy Village, which formed their objective. North of Villers Bretonneux all attacks were repulsed.

At 10 p.m., on the night of the 23rd-24th April, a counterattack was launched by a brigade of the 18th Division and the 13th and 15th Brigades of the 4th and 5th Australian Divisions, Major-General Sir J. J. T. Hobbs, K.C.B., commanding the latter division, and met with remarkable success. A night operation of this character, undertaken at such short notice, was an enterprise of great daring. The instant decision to seize the opportunity offered, and the rapid and thorough working out of the general plan and details of the attack on the part of the III. Corps Commander and divisional and subordinate commanders concerned, are most worthy of commendation, while the unusual nature of the operation called for the highest qualities on the part of the troops employed. It was carried out in the most spirited and gallant manner by all ranks. The 13th Australian Brigade, in particular, showed great skill and resolution in their attack, making their way through belts of wire running diagonally to the line of their advance, across very difficult country which they had had no opportunity to reconnoitre beforehand.

At daybreak Villers Bretonneux was practically surrounded by our troops. During the morning two battalions of the 8th Division worked their way through the streets and houses, overcoming the resistance of such parties of the enemy as were still holding out. That afternoon Villers Bretonneux was again completely in our possession. In this well-conceived and brilliantly-executed operation nearly 1,000 prisoners were captured by our troops. A German tank was left derelict in our lines, and was salved subsequently.

The Capture of Kemmel Hill.

(67) These operations on the southern front were followed on the 25th April by a renewal of the enemy's attacks in great strength north of the Lys.

Following upon a very violent bombardment, at about 5 a.m. the enemy attacked the French and British positions from Bailleul to the Ypres-Comines Canal with nine divisions, of which five were fresh divisions and one other had been but lightly engaged. The main object of the attack was the capture of Kemmel Hill by a direct assault upon the French, combined with an attack upon the British right south of Wytschaete, aimed at turning the British right flank and separating it from the French. At that date the British right flank lay on the Messines-Kemmel road, at a point about halfway between Kemmel and Wytschaete.

After very heavy fighting, the German infantry worked their way round the lower slopes of the high ground, and at 10 a.m. had succeeded in capturing Kemmel Village and Hill; though elements of French troops held out until a late hour on the hill and in the village.

The weight of the attack in the British sector fell on the 9th Division and attached troops of the 49th Division, who at 7 a.m. were still holding their positions about Wytschaete intact, though heavily engaged. Fierce fighting continued in this neighbourhood for some hours later, and great numbers of Germans were killed by rifle and machine-gun fire at short range. Later in the morning the right of the 9th Division was forced to fall back fighting stubbornly to Vierstraat, but at 1 p.m. our troops still held the Grand Bois north of Wytschaete.

In the afternoon the attack spread northwards along the front held by the 21st Division. By the evening our troops had been gradually pushed back from their forward positions, and held a line running from Hill 60 to Voormezeele, when it passed north of Vierstraat to our junction with the French about La Clytte. The Allied line had not been broken, and reinforcements were hurrying up.

Next day fighting continued fiercely. In the early morning a very gallant counter-attack by the 25th Division, with attached troops of the 21st and 49th Divisions, undertaken in conjunction with the French, penetrated into Kemmel Village, taking over 300 prisoners. Our troops then found themselves exposed to heavy machine-gun fire from the flanks, and were unable to maintain their positions.

Later in the morning the enemy renewed his attacks in strength, but, in spite of repeated efforts, was only able to make small progress at certain points. Troops of the 2ist, 30th, 39th, and 49th Divisions (Major-General C. A. Blacklock, C.M.G., D.S.O., commanding the 39th Division), and the South African Brigade of the 9th Division, had heavy fighting, and made several gallant counter-attacks. It will not have been forgotten that each of the 21st, 30th, and 39th Divisions had experienced severe and prolonged fighting in the Battle of the Somme.

Successful counter-attacks were carried out also by the French, in the course of which the village of Locre was recaptured in a very gallant action.

The capture of Kemmel Hill seriously threatened our position in the Ypres salient, the communications and southern defences of which were now under direct observation by the enemy, while his continued progress to the north-west in the Voormezeele sector would make the extrication of troops east of Ypres most hazardous. A further readjustment of our lines in the salient was accordingly carried out on the night of the 26th-27th April, our troops withdrawing to the general line Pilckem-Wieltje west end of Zillebeke Lake-Voormezeele.

THE ENEMY'S ADVANCE STAYED.

(68) On the 28th April local fighting took place in the neighbourhood of Locre and Voormezeele without material change in the situation; but on the following day, encouraged by the capture of Kemmel Hill, the enemy made a determined effort to improve his success.

After a bombardment of exceptional intensity, which started at 3.10 a.m., a series of strong attacks were launched about 5 a.m. against the French and British positions from west of Dranoutre to Voormezeele. Very heavy fighting rapidly developed on the whole of this front, and ended in the complete repulse of the enemy with the heaviest losses to his troops.

At Locre and to the north of that village the enemy made desperate attempts to overcome the resistance of our Allies and gain possession of the high ground known as the Scherpenberg. At one time, parties of his troops entered Locre, and penetrated to the cross-roads between the Scherpenberg and Mont Rouge; but in both localities successful French counter-attacks drove him out after bitter fighting.

On the British front the positions held by the 21st, 49th, and 25th Divisions were strongly attacked between 5 a.m. and 5.30 a.m. On the failure of these attacks bodies of German infantry advanced at 6 a.m. in mass formation, with bayonets fixed, against the 49th Division, and were repulsed with the heaviest losses. The 25th Division was again attacked at 8.35 a.m., and during the morning repeated attacks were made without result on this division and the 49th Division, as well as on the 21st Division and attached troops of the 30th and 39th Divisions. At all points the attack was pressed vigorously with massed bodies of troops, and the losses suffered by the German infantry were very great. Throughout the whole of the fighting our infantry and artillery fought magnificently, and in more than one instance our troops went out to meet the German attack and drove back the enemy with the bayonet.

At the end of the day, except for a small loss of ground about Voormezeele, our line was intact, and the enemy had undergone a severe and decided check.

In concert with this operation, the Belgian positions astride the Ypres-Staden Railway were again attacked, and once more vigorous counterstrokes by Belgian troops promptly ejected the German infantry from such ground as had been gained by them in their first assault. Here also the enemy's failure was complete.

On the 30th April the French retook Locre early in the morning, but beyond this no infantry action of importance took place, and the month closed with the enemy definitely held on both the southern and the northern battle fronts.

THE TASK OF THE BRITISH ARMIES.

(69) It has been seen that in the Somme battle, by the end of March, in addition to some 10 German divisions engaged against the French, a total of 73 German divisions were engaged and fought to a standstill by 42 British infantry divisions and three cavalry divisions. In

order to complete the comparison between the forces engaged and to enable the nature of the task accomplished by our troops to be realised, it will be of value to give similar figures for the battle of the Lys.

In the Lys battle, prior to the 30th April the enemy engaged against the British forces a total of 42 divisions, of which 33 were fresh and nine had fought previously on the Somme. Against these 42 German divisions 25 British divisions were employed, of which eight were fresh and 17 had taken a prominent part in the Somme battle.

In the six weeks of almost constant fighting, from the 21st March to the 30th April, a total of 55 British infantry divisions and three cavalry divisions was employed on the battle fronts against a force of 109 different German divisions. During this period a total of 141 different German divisions were engaged against the combined British and French forces.

OUR TROOPS.

(70) The splendid qualities displayed by all ranks and services throughout the Somme and Lys battles make it possible to view with confidence whatever further tests the future may bring.

On the 21st March the troops of the Fifth and Third Armies had the glory of sustaining the first and heaviest blow of the German offensive. Though assailed by a concentration of hostile forces which the enemy might well have considered overwhelming, they held up the German attack at all points for the greater part of two days, thereby rendering a service to their country and to the Allied cause the value of which cannot be overestimated. Thereafter, through many days of heavy and continuous rear-guard fighting, they succeeded in presenting a barrier to the enemy's advance until such time as the arrival of British and French reinforcements enabled his progress to be checked.

In the Battle of the Lys, as has been pointed out above, many of the same divisions which had just passed through the furnace of the Somme found themselves exposed to the full fury of a second great offensive by fresh German forces. Despite this disadvantage they gave evidence, in many days of close and obstinate fighting, that their spirit was as high as ever and their courage and determination unabated. Both by them and by the divisions freshly engaged every yard of ground was fiercely disputed, until troops were overwhelmed or ordered to withdraw. Such withdrawals as were deemed necessary in the course of the battle were carried out successfully and in good order.

At no time, either on the Somme or on the Lys, was there anything approaching a breakdown of command or a failure of morale. Under conditions that made rest and sleep impossible for days together, and called incessantly for the greatest physical exertion and quickness of thought, officers and men remained undismayed, realising that for the time being they must play a waiting game, and determined to make the enemy pay the full price for the success which for the moment was his.

In the course of this report it has been possible to refer to a very few of the many instances in which officers and men of all arms and services have shown courage and skill of the highest order. On countless other occasions officers and men, of whose names there is no record, have accomplished actions of the greatest valour, while the very nature of the fighting shows that on all parts of the wide battle fronts unknown deeds of heroism were performed without number.

The British infantryman has always had the reputation of fighting his best in an uphill battle, and time and again in the history of our country, by sheer tenacity and determination of purpose, has won victory from a numerically superior foe. Thrown once more upon the defensive by circumstances over which he had no control, but which will not persist, he has shown himself to possess in full measure the traditional qualities of his race.

The part of the artillery in a defensive battle is at once a most important and a most difficult one. The conditions under which guns are fought in trench warfare make a certain loss of material unavoidable when, in a defensive battle, a sudden change takes place to a war of movement. Yet, even in such circumstances, on which, moreover, the affording of artillery support to our infantry till the last moment is of paramount importance, much can be done, and on countless occasions much was done, by swift and resolute action, to prevent guns falling into the hands of the enemy. The loss of artillery in the series of battles, though considerable, might well have been much greater but for the courage, skill, and resource displayed by all the ranks of the artillery, both heavy and field, and but for the constant efforts made to maintain close co operation between artillery and infantry.

Of the courage and devotion of the artillery numerous instances could be given, but one example must suffice. On the occasion of the attack east of Arras on the 28th March, a six-inch howitzer battery was heavily engaged by the enemy's artillery. After all the gun detachments had been either killed or wounded and all the guns but one had been destroyed, the remaining four officers of the battery continued to serve their last gun, until two of them were killed and the other two wounded.

On the southern battle front, and particularly in the fighting about Noyon, cavalry were once more employed with great effect, and proved their extreme value in warfare of a more open nature. On more than one occasion they were able by rapid and successful action to restore a doubtful situation, while their appearance in the battle gave great encouragement to the infantry.

The work of the Royal Air Force, under command of Major-General J. M. Salmond, C.M.G., D.S.O., in co-operation with the other arms, has been brilliant. Throughout the period of active operations our airmen have established and maintained a superiority over the enemy's air forces without parallel since the days of the first Somme battle. Not content with destroying the enemy in the air, they have vigorously attacked his infantry, guns, and transport with bombs and machine-gun fire, and in the fighting south of the Somme in particular gave invaluable assistance to the infantry by these means on numerous occasions. In addition, the usual work of reconnaissance, photography, artillery co-operation, and bombing has been carried out vigorously and with remarkable results.

Reference has been made more than once in the body of this report to the very valuable work accomplished by tanks and tank personnel in the course of the Somme battle. Throughout the whole of this fighting tanks took part in numerous successful counter-attacks, many of which were instrumental in checking the enemy's progress at critical points. On these occasions tanks have shown that they possess capabilities in defence little, if at all, less than those which they have already proved in attack. In their first encounter with German tanks officers and men of the Tank Corps displayed with success, under conditions new in warfare, the same energy and resource which have always characterised their action.

The experience of the Somme and Lys battles has emphasized once more the great value of the machine gun in defensive warfare, when handled by brave, skilful, and resolute men. In the course of the recent fighting officers and men of the Machine-Gun Corps have furnished innumerable examples of the utmost resolution, courage, and skill in the use of their weapons. They have been largely instrumental in defeating the enemy's determined efforts to break through, and have inflicted on him very severe losses.

The same conditions of warfare on the battle fronts which handicapped the work of the artillery affected trench mortars in an even greater degree. Despite the disadvantages under which they suffered, the personnel of trench-mortar batteries of all natures have performed on numberless occasions the most valuable service in the defence of strong points and defended localities, serving their weapons with effect though surrounded by the enemy, and giving the greatest possible assistance to the infantry and machine-gunners.

The work of the Royal Engineers, both during and subsequent to the retreat on the Somme and on the northern battle front, has been particularly arduous. In addition to the heavy demands made upon them in the destruction of roads and bridges and such-like matters during retreat, and the labour entailed in the construction of new positions, they have frequently been called upon to take their place in the firing line. On such occasions their various units have behaved with the greatest steadfastness and courage, and, in circumstances such as those in which the 251st Tunnelling Company greatly distinguished itself at Givenchy, have added to the high reputation of their service.

In this connection a generous recognition is due to the gallant conduct of the various composite battalions which on different occasions took their place in the firing line.

During the long periods of active fighting the strain placed upon the Signal Service was immense. The frequent changes of headquarters and the shifting of the line entailed constant labour, frequently attended with great danger, in the maintenance of communications; while the exigencies of the battle on more than one occasion brought the personnel of the signal units into the firing line. The Signal Service met the calls made upon it in a manner wholly admirable, and the efficient performance of its duties was of incalculable value.

On different occasions, and particularly on the Third Army front at the commencement of the German offensive, personnel of the Special Brigade (Gas Services) became involved in the infantry battle, and behaved with a like gallantry to that which they have always displayed in the performance of their special duties.

The enormous amount of additional work thrown upon the different branches of my staff and upon the administrative Services and Departments by such fighting as that of March and April can readily be imagined. The evacuation of great masses of stores, hospitals, rolling-stock, agricultural implements, non-combatants, labour units and civilians from the battle area, and the supplying of the troops in constantly changing places with food and ammunition, called for the highest powers of organisation, the most constant forethought and supervision, and the most devoted labour. That all this work was carried out so smoothly and successfully under circumstances of extraordinary difficulty, and that there was never any lack of food or ammunition for the troops, reflects the very highest credit on all concerned.

Upon the Transportation Services, moreover, and particularly upon the omnibus parks, the rapid movement of reserves placed a peculiarly heavy strain, which the different units concerned never failed to meet successfully.

Much additional work, also under circumstances of unusual difficulty and danger, has necessarily been thrown upon the medical and nursing services. The conduct of the Royal Army Medical Corps and Medical Corps of the Overseas Dominions has again been beyond all praise, while the efficient organisation of the medical services as a whole proved itself fully equal to the occasion. I take this opportunity to acknowledge the lasting debt due in this connection to Lt.-General Sir A. T. Sloggett, K.C.B., K.C.M.G., K.C.V.O., K.H.S., until recently Director-General of Medical Services, with whom the work of the medical services has so long been identified.

I desire to express my deep appreciation of the loyal and devoted work of the commanders and staffs of all formations of the British Army serving under me in a period of exceptional stress. In defensive battles of such magnitude as those which have just been fought to a successful conclusion the part played by subordinate commanders and staffs is frequently of decisive importance, demanding great strength of character and a high standard of ability, while the physical and mental strain is correspondingly great. That mistakes should occur in such circumstances is almost inevitable. That they should have been so few as they were, and that control should at all times have been so well maintained, reflects the greatest credit upon the individuals concerned, upon the staff arrangements of all formations, and the Army as a whole.

The part played by the various branches of the staff of an army in the organisation and control of battles such as those referred to in this dispatch is one of the utmost importance, and the strain thrown upon the individual officers composing them is very great.

I wish to thank the heads of the various branches of the staff and of departments and services for the essential share that they and their subordinates have taken in preventing the realisation of the enemy's plans.

I am glad to acknowledge the great assistance given me at all times by my Chief of the General Staff, Lieut.-General the Hon. Sir H. A. Lawrence, K.C.B., whose cool judgment, equable temperament, and unfailing military insight were of the utmost value in circumstances demanding the exercise of such qualities in a peculiarly high degree.

The rapid incorporation of reinforcements and reorganisation of exhausted units without which the battle could scarcely have been maintained was most ably carried out by the Adjutant-General, Lieut. -General Sir G. H. Fowke, K.C.B., K.C.M.G., and his branch.

The work of my Quartermaster-General's Branch under Lieutenant-General Travers Clarke, C.B., in the provision and replacement of munitions and supplies of all kinds, was of the highest importance, and was performed with the greatest ability and success.

The large and incessant demands made upon the Transportation Services in the course of the battle were met in the most admirable manner by my Director-General, Brigadier-General S. D'A. Crookshank, C.I.E., M.V.O., D.S.O., and those working under him.

My thanks are due also to the subordinate members of my Staff at General Headquarters, whose heavy and responsible duties were discharged throughout the period under review with most commendable smoothness and efficiency. In particular I desire to mention the services of my Artillery Adviser, Major-General Sir J. F. N. Birch, K.C.M.G., C.B.; my Engineer-in-Chief, Major-General G. M. Heath, C.B., D.S.O.; the Head of the Operations Section, Major-General J. H. Davidson, C.B., D.S.O.; the Head of the Staff Duties Section, Major-General G. P. Dawnay, C.M.G., D.S.O.; the Head of my Intelligence Section, Brigadier-General E. W. Cox, D.S.O.; and my Director of Army Signals, Major-General Sir J. S. Fowler, K.C.M.G., C.B., D.S.O.

My thanks, and those of all ranks of the British Armies in France, are due also to the different authorities at home, whose prompt and energetic action enabled the unavoidable losses of personnel and material incurred during the battle to be replaced with such rapidity. We are glad also to place on record once again our deep appreciation of the work of the Royal Navy, upon whose unceasing efforts depends the maintenance of the British Forces in France.

OUR ALLIES.

(71) I cannot close this report without paying my personal tribute to the ready and effective assistance given me by the French and Belgian Higher Command in the course of the Somme and Lys battles.

Reference has already been made to the schemes for mutual co-operation and assistance between the French and British Armies which formed so important a part of the Allied plan for the year's campaign. These schemes have been carried out with absolute loyalty. The support rendered by French troops south of the Somme and north of the Lys, and by Belgian troops in taking over the responsibility for the greater part of the line previously held by British troops north of Ypres, has been of incalculable value.

I desire also to express my appreciation of the services rendered by the Portuguese troops who had held a sector of my front continuously throughout the winter months, and on the 9th April, were called upon to withstand the assault of greatly superior forces.

Finally, I am glad to acknowledge the ready manner in which American Engineer Units have been placed at my disposal from time to time, and the great value of the assistance they have rendered. In the battles referred to in this Dispatch, American and British troops have fought shoulder to shoulder in the same trenches, and have shared together in the satisfaction of beating off German attacks. All ranks of the British Army look forward to the day when the rapidly growing strength of the American Army will allow American and British soldiers to co-operate in offensive action.

I have the honour to be,

    My Lord,

        Your Lordship's obedient Servant,

            D. Haig, Field Marshal,
            Commanding-in-Chief,
            British Armies in France.

LEONAUR

ALSO FROM LEONAUR
AVAILABLE IN SOFTCOVER OR HARDCOVER WITH DUST JACKET

ZULU:1879 *by D.C.F. Moodie & the Leonaur Editors*—The Anglo-Zulu War of 1879 from contemporary sources: First Hand Accounts, Interviews, Dispatches, Official Documents & Newspaper Reports.

THE RED DRAGOON *by W.J. Adams*—With the 7th Dragoon Guards in the Cape of Good Hope against the Boers & the Kaffir tribes during the 'war of the axe' 1843-48'.

THE RECOLLECTIONS OF SKINNER OF SKINNER'S HORSE *by James Skinner*—James Skinner and his 'Yellow Boys' Irregular cavalry in the wars of India between the British, Mahratta, Rajput, Mogul, Sikh & Pindarree Forces.

A CAVALRY OFFICER DURING THE SEPOY REVOLT *by A. R. D. Mackenzie*—Experiences with the 3rd Bengal Light Cavalry, the Guides and Sikh Irregular Cavalry from the outbreak to Delhi and Lucknow.

A NORFOLK SOLDIER IN THE FIRST SIKH WAR *by J W Baldwin*—Experiences of a private of H.M. 9th Regiment of Foot in the battles for the Punjab, India 1845-6.

TOMMY ATKINS' WAR STORIES: 14 FIRST HAND ACCOUNTS—Fourteen first hand accounts from the ranks of the British Army during Queen Victoria's Empire.

THE WATERLOO LETTERS *by H. T. Siborne*—Accounts of the Battle by British Officers for its Foremost Historian.

NEY: GENERAL OF CAVALRY VOLUME 1—1769-1799 *by Antoine Bulos*—The Early Career of a Marshal of the First Empire.

NEY: MARSHAL OF FRANCE VOLUME 2—1799-1805 *by Antoine Bulos*—The Early Career of a Marshal of the First Empire.

AIDE-DE-CAMP TO NAPOLEON *by Philippe-Paul de Ségur*—For anyone interested in the Napoleonic Wars this book, written by one who was intimate with the strategies and machinations of the Emperor, will be essential reading.

TWILIGHT OF EMPIRE *by Sir Thomas Ussher & Sir George Cockburn*—Two accounts of Napoleon's Journeys in Exile to Elba and St. Helena: Narrative of Events by Sir Thomas Ussher & Napoleon's Last Voyage: Extract of a diary by Sir George Cockburn.

PRIVATE WHEELER *by William Wheeler*—The letters of a soldier of the 51st Light Infantry during the Peninsular War & at Waterloo.

www.ingramcontent.com/pod-product-compliance
Lightning Source LLC
Chambersburg PA
CBHW032052080426
42733CB00006B/252